45

42.95
13.50

D0072380

To my parents,
Donald W. Tollefson
and
Juliana M. Tollefson

Contents

Copyright Acknowledgment

Some material in chapters 4 and 6 originally appeared in "Functional Competencies in the U.S. Refugee Program: Theoretical and Practical Problems," by James W. Tollefson, *TESOL Quarterly* 20, (1986), pp. 649–64. Copyright 1986 by the Teachers of English to Speakers of Other Languages. Adapted by permission.

Library of Congress Cataloging-in-Publication Data

Tollefson, James W.
    Alien winds : the reeducation of America's Indochinese refugees /
James W. Tollefson.
      p. cm.
    Bibliography: p.
    Includes index.
    ISBN 0–275–93225–7 (alk. paper)
    1. Refugees—United States—Cultural assimilation. 2. Refugees—
Indochina. 3. Refugees—Education—United States. 4. Indochinese—
United States—Cultural assimilation. 5. Immigrants—United
States—Cultural assimilation. I. Title.
HV640.4.U54T65   1989
362.8′7′089959—dc19   88–31925

Library of Congress Catalog Card Number: 88–31925
ISBN: 0–275–93225–7

First published in 1989

Praeger Publishers, One Madison Avenue, New York, NY 10010
A division of Greenwood Press, Inc.

Printed in the United States of America

∞

The paper used in this book complies with the
Permanent Paper Standard issued by the National
Information Standards Organization (Z39.48–1984).

10 9 8 7 6 5 4 3 2 1

Alien Winds

THE REEDUCATION OF AMERICA'S INDOCHINESE REFUGEES

James W. Tollefson

PRAEGER

New York
Westport, Connecticut
London

Alien Winds

Preface

Wind comes forth from fire: the image of FAMILY. Wind drives over the water: the image of DISPERSION. Wind over lake: the image of INNER TRUTH.

The I Ching, or Book of Changes

On my first night at the Philippine Refugee Processing Center (PRPC), I slept very little. I lay on a wooden platform bed, listening to the noises of the jungle: the croaking of monstrous frogs; the hiss of a million flies, crickets, and mosquitoes; and the lazy lowing of the water buffalo eating leaves off the spindly bushes outside my screen window. Lying there in the heat and humidity, I anxiously awaited my first task—finding Hung Diep, a seventeen-year-old who had left Vietnam alone and whose name had been given to me by Tien, a girl in Seattle who had known him in Vietnam. I carried with me Tien's letter and photo to deliver to Hung.

The next morning, my first in a refugee camp, I found an official at the central office who gave me Hung's billet number. He was in Neighborhood 9 in Phase 2, the new part of camp. That night, I made my way along the broken concrete pathways, across rickety wooden bridges over foul-smelling, five-foot deep drainage ditches. Refugees peering from the doorways of the billets shouted, "Hello, how are you?" as I passed. Unsure how to respond, I waved awkwardly.

Hung was in 914D, which he shared with nine other Vietnamese. Pale and looking worried, he appeared much younger than seventeen. My presence seemed to make him nervous. I slowly explained why I had come, though his reluctance to speak made me unsure how much English he understood. But when I handed him Tien's photo, he smiled slightly and tears filled his eyes. As he read her letter, written in Vietnamese, he leaned forward on the wooden bench, studying this link to his home and to his family. When he had finished, he carefully removed from a plastic case two black-and-white photos. There, standing stiffly, were his parents, his brothers and sisters, and his grandmother, posed in a line before a small store on the outskirts of Saigon, now called Ho Chi Minh City. On the edge of the photo stood Hung, innocent and unsmiling, unaware of the future that would separate him from his family. I learned in later visits that Hung's parents had had enough money for only one of their children to leave on the treacherous boat trip to Malaysia. They had chosen Hung. Now, at PRPC, he was in the middle of his long journey, attending classes while waiting for the next stage, his flight to his new home in Georgia.

As I left Hung's billet that night, just after the lights were turned out in Phase 2, he asked me when I would return. "Tomorrow," I promised, and the next night he was waiting out by the road. For Hung, I was a connection to the United States and, through Tien, back to his home. In the months to come, Hung introduced me to his friends, who in turn led me to others. Their lives would touch me more than I realized that first night in camp. I came to know and to some extent to share in the lives of individual Vietnamese, Laotians, and Cambodians, people connected by a common fate, which was participation in the largest refugee resettlement program in U.S. history.

Acknowledgments

Between 1983 and 1986, I spent approximately 16 months in refugee camps in Southeast Asia, primarily in the main processing center in the Philippines, where I worked in the teacher education unit for the International Catholic Migration Commission. During this period, I attended regional meetings with representatives from other refugee camps and visited the processing center at Phanat Nikkom in Thailand, as well as first-asylum camps throughout the region.

Many staff members in the Philippines provided information, documents, and transcripts of classes. Of special value were materials from classroom teachers, supervisors, and individual refugees. Though they must remain anonymous, I am deeply grateful for their assistance.

Except when otherwise noted, the quotations from refugees are from three sources: transcripts of classes at the PRPC, essays written by refugees in the Philippines, and interviews with individual refugees. In order to protect their privacy, only common names or pseudonyms are used.

Important documents were obtained under the federal Freedom of Information Act (FOIA). While some federal offices, most notably the Office of Refugee Resettlement and the Centers for Disease Control, expeditiously responded to FOIA requests, the Department of State under the Reagan administration did not grant access to the information requested under the Act.

I have presented portions of this work at a number of places during the last several years. These include the Monterey Institute of International Studies in Monterey, California, where Dan Shanahan arranged two public forums; the 1985, 1987, and 1988 Annual Conventions of the Teachers of English to Speakers of Other Languages in New York City, Miami, and Chicago; the Southeast Asian Colloquium of the Northwest Regional Consortium for Southeast Asian Studies; two statewide meetings of the

Washington Association for the Education of Speakers of Other Languages; and the Tacoma, Washington, Community House. These have provided valuable discussion and criticism of my work.

I am grateful to Professor Richard Dunn, Chair of the University of Washington Department of English, who generously granted two years of leave for my research in Southeast Asia as well as travel funds for key meetings.

Three individuals provided important published information that I might not have seen otherwise: Jon Knudsen of the University of Bergen, Norway, Jeff Crisp of the British Refugee Council, and Dennis Clagett of the Geneva office of the International Catholic Migration Commission.

My biggest debt is to the graduate students in my seminar on language policy for Indochinese refugees at the University of Washington during the winter of 1987: April Ahola, Richard Bisbee, Susan Foley, Tammy Guy, Eric Herbel, Art Huddleston, Monica Hughes, Kay Landolt, Muriel Bevilacqua Logan, Mosa Makhobotloane, Julia Menard-Warwick, Cheiron McMahill, Bruce McCutcheon, Noor Ahnis Othman, Robin Preisinger, Mangie Rakale, Pippin Sardo, and Connie So. Their outstanding original research and critical but compassionate reading of each others' work were a model of graduate education.

I would like to acknowledge individuals who critically commented upon drafts of the manuscript: Ron Ward of Remedello, Italy; Art Huddleston of the University of Washington; Linda Nelson Avery, who also contributed immensely to my work in the Philippines; and especially Elsa Auerbach of the University of Massachusetts. Of course, I am solely responsible for the contents of this book.

My deepest appreciation goes to the Filipino teachers and supervisors with whom I lived during my time in the PRPC. They began as hosts and welcomed me to their home; as we lived and worked together, we became friends. Their kindness and generosity inspired this book.

Finally, I would like to thank Jane W. Boone, whose support, encouragement, and endurance made this book possible.

Introduction

The United States might leave Vietnam, but the Vietnam war would now never leave the United States.

Frances Fitzgerald, *Fire in the Lake*[1]

In the basement of Our Lady of Mt. Virgin Catholic Church near downtown Seattle, Diane Clark listens quietly to the volunteer tutors in the refugee English program. Four nights each week, Diane guides her team of volunteers as they help refugees gain the survival skills and language competency they need to live in the United States. In lessons on shopping, the telephone, employment, medical care, housing, and nutrition, the staff patiently works with the several dozen refugees who come by bus and on foot from the surrounding neighborhoods. With the help of their teachers, the refugees struggle to understand the language and culture of their new home. Like hundreds of U.S. citizens in church basements throughout the country, the volunteers and poorly paid staff at Mt. Virgin express their personal commitment to these victims of the Vietnam War and its tragic, continuing aftermath.

Yet for the refugees, these compassionate teachers represent only one side of the story. For in the decaying apartment buildings surrounding Mt. Virgin, the refugees live in poverty and fear, their living-room windows shattered by rocks thrown in the night, their children tormented, jobs all too difficult to find.

The ambivalent U.S. reaction to Southeast Asians must be understood within its social context—a history of contradictory emotions that are rooted in official policy and government orchestration of public opinion. As the best effort of the United States to make up for the suffering it inflicted in the Vietnam War, the refugee program expresses the nation's unresolved ambivalence toward the war itself. The result is a social dilemma with profound economic, political and moral dimensions.

As with similar programs throughout the country, Mt. Virgin does what it can to help the refugees adjust to life in the United States. But the church basement is not the beginning of the effort to prepare these refugees for living in the United States nor even the most important component of that effort. Before Indochinese refugees are permitted to enter the country, they must attend an intensive educational program at official U.S. "processing centers" in Southeast Asia. At these centers, Southeast Asian people learn about America: its language, its people, its values and attitudes, its history, and its culture. For nearly six months, these centers try to undo the cultural bonds holding Southeast Asian communities together and to substitute for them a new set of values, attitudes, and behaviors. The program at these centers is the first and most important step in the traumatic and life-changing process of "becoming American."[2]

THE UNITED STATES REFUGEE EDUCATION PROGRAM

Between 1975 and 1989, the United States accepted for resettlement nearly one million refugees from Vietnam, Cambodia, and Laos. In 1988, twelve years after the Communist victory in Indochina, approximately 3,000 Indochinese per month continued to arrive on U.S. soil, while more than 400,000 others remained in refugee camps in Southeast Asia.[3]

Though resettlement may be the only solution, it is filled with uncertainties and peril, and it is enormously expensive. Its success depends in large part upon the preparation they receive for their new lives. To this end, the U.S. refugee education program was established in Thailand, Indonesia, and the Philippines in late 1980. From modest beginnings, the program grew rapidly, until by 1983 over 17,000 refugees were housed in the Philippine processing center alone. Since the centers opened, 200,000 people have completed the program, with hundreds of thousands of others depending upon these graduates for their economic survival.

From its inception, the educational program faced difficult questions. What should the program teach? What are the main difficulties facing Southeast Asians in the United States? What do the refugees need to know in order to successfully resettle? How can the program ensure that their resettlement will be successful?

As it grappled with these issues, the program came to face even more fundamental questions about life in the United States. How should successful resettlement be defined? Should there be different notions of success for different groups of people? What values do the people of the United States share? Must newcomers adopt these values in order to be welcomed into their new communities?

The official answer to these questions is given in classes at the processing centers. When the U.S. Department of State opened them, it could not have anticipated that it would have to face such important issues, but like the Vietnam War, the refugee program came to have dramatic and unexpected impact. It would also reveal much about the United States and its people and about our view of Vietnamese, Cambodians, and Laotians, whose future, despite all our efforts to forget, remains so intimately tied to our own.[4]

THE AGE OF REFUGEES

It has been said many times that ours is an age of refugees. In every corner of the earth there are people uprooted by war, hunger, disease, and persecution. The nightly news on television becomes a litany of refugees: Biafran, Salvadoran, Palestinian, Haitian, Ugandan, Ethiopian, Guatemalan, Cuban, Sudanese, Cambodian, Laotian, and Vietnamese. By any measure, all these refugee crises have tested the world's willingness to respond to suffering. At the end of World War II, hundreds of thousands of displaced and homeless people were resettled by international agencies in Europe alone. In the 1950s, international relief saved lives in Eastern Europe and Africa. In the 1960s, crises connected with war, famine, and Third World liberation movements led to international relief efforts in which the United Nations played an increasingly important role.

But it was not until the 1970s that refugees entered the center stage of world affairs. The crisis that galvanized the world's awareness and brought the word "refugee" into the public vocabulary involved the Cambodians who appeared on the border with Thailand and the Vietnamese "boat people" who washed ashore throughout Southeast Asia, as far away as Australia. William Shawcross, who has reported on Southeast Asia for nearly two decades, has argued that instant communications and the accessibility of Cambodian refugees, only a four-hour drive from Bangkok, have combined to thrust this particular crisis into the world's living rooms.[5] More deaths have occurred elsewhere, and perhaps greater inhumanity, but the flood of refugees from Southeast Asia was the first refugee crisis to be covered on the nightly news. This was only fitting, since the Vietnam War was also the world's first living-room war. But the refugee crisis in Southeast Asia was also important because it starkly demonstrated that Great Power conflicts and regional wars play a central role in creating and sustaining a refugee problem. So while the world's community may take credit for the survival of many refugees, it also must accept responsibility for their suffering.

In Indochina, refugees have been pawns in the political struggles and strategies of war since the first large refugee movements in 1954. Since the U.S. defeat in 1975, the economic and political impact of decades of war have driven millions of Indochinese to seek a new life elsewhere. It is no surprise that the people of the United States respond to the Indochinese refugees with anger and sorrow, and with a deep frustration that mirrors their feelings about the war itself. While the Indochinese are the first refugees whose suffering has received such massive world attention, they are unique as well in the transition that has awaited them: the U.S. refugee education program.

During a decade of war, Americans and Southeast Asians rarely understood each other. Although they fought and died together, their histories, cultures, dreams, fears, and deepest needs remained mysteries. The refugee program thus far has largely failed to bring about mutual understanding, but it is not too late. For in the processing centers today, Americans continue to teach Vietnamese, Cambodians, and Laotians about the United States, about who we are, as Americans. In order to do this well, the staff members have to try to understand Southeast Asian people: Who are they? What are the values and beliefs that define their cultures? Every day in their work, the staff members in the processing centers, like Clark and the volunteers at Mt. Virgin Church, must face these difficult questions.

It is the purpose of this book to examine the answers to these questions as they are formulated and conveyed to real people in the refugee camps in Southeast Asia. A second purpose is to explore the sources of the answers. To this end, the book examines important assumptions about the process of becoming an American that originated in immigrant education programs in the early part of this century. A third purpose is to explore the aims and structures of the organizations that created and continue to operate the processing centers. And a final purpose is to explore a little the role of the refugee program in our shared memory of Vietnam.

Chapter 1, "Into the Camps," describes the refugees' arrival at the processing centers, their orientation to the program, and their experience in classes. The chapter also summarizes the historical movements of refugees that led to the decision to build the processing centers in late 1980.

Chapter 2, "Survivors," examines the larger picture of refugees in Southeast Asia since the early 1950s, when the United States first became involved in refugee movements in that part of the world. The chapter shows that the refugees since 1975 are the most recent, but not the largest, group of displaced people from the region. The chapter also details the social, psychological, and economic problems refugees suffer during flight and resettlement and the importance of community in healing from the war and its aftermath.

Despite the importance of community in the refugees' resettlement, the overseas program continues a long tradition, which began with the Americanization movement around the turn of the century, of transforming immigrants' communities by changing their individual and cultural identities. Chapter 3, "Becoming American," examines the historical roots of long-held American beliefs about immigration, assimilation, and the American character that are expressed in today's refugee program.

The processing centers pursue the goal of changing the refugees' values, attitudes, and behaviors through a system of reeducation designed to substitute the powerful myths of self-sufficiency and American success for the traditional cultural bonds that provide individual identity and fulfillment for Southeast Asians. Chapter 4, "Counterfeit Universe," examines this system of reeducation as outlined in program documents and presented in classes at the processing centers.

The function of the processing centers is bureaucratic as well as educational: to prepare refugees for membership in the American community and to process them into it. The centers are operated by a complex bureaucracy of private and governmental agencies, which do not necessarily represent the interest of refugees. Chapter 5, "Keepers of the Camps," explores the organization of this bureaucracy, in particular the relationship between private and federal agencies.

The Bureau for Refugee Programs of the Department of State and the private agencies that operate the overseas centers claim that they successfully prepare refugees for resettlement. Chapter 6, "Keeping the Charts," critically examines these claims, as well as evidence suggesting that the primary function of the program is to channel refugees into minimum-wage employment, which guarantees that most Southeast Asian families in the United States will experience long-term economic crisis.

In addition to offering an educational program, the processing centers carefully regulate all aspects of the refugees' lives. Chapter 7, "Humiliation and Danger," describes this system of bureaucratic control, in particular restrictions on individual liberties and exposure to asbestos in classrooms and living accommodations.

Chapter 8, "The Future and the Past," examines the refugee program in our shared memory of Vietnam and lists recommendations for the overseas centers and domestic resettlement programs.

Into the Camps

I am 52 years old. Now is the new life for me. I must start to study
all about to learn English and my experience for the future. I don't
know what I can study for to find the job. I have to try hard work for
to get money and to help my family who still lives in Vietnam.
                                    Loc Pham Huu, cultural orientation class, PRPC

Twenty-eight-year-old Sophal Mea sat in the narrow, straight-backed
wooden chair in Neighborhood 7, Building D, Classroom 4 of the Philippine Refugee Processing Center (PRPC). He had attended class every day
now for over four weeks, six days each week, four and a half hours every
day. Today in his cultural orientation (CO) class, the topic was U.S. ge-
ography. Pointer in hand, his teacher, a Filipina who had taught in an
elementary school in Manila for seven years before taking a higher-paying
job as an English teacher at PRPC, lectured about the main geographical
regions of the North American continent. The assistant teacher (AT), a
Cambodian who spoke English well and so was exempt from the normal
requirement of taking classes, carefully translated each sentence from English into Khmer as the teacher waited until it was her turn again. Most
students focused on the Khmer translation, waiting patiently but without
comprehending when it was the teacher's turn to speak.

Sophal listened to the description of the country which would be his new
home, though it was still 8,000 miles and five months away from this refugee
camp in the Philippines. "This is the northeast section of America," the
teacher said, reading from the bulky curriculum she held in her hands.
"New Hampshire, Vermont, Maine, and Massachusetts are in the northeast." After waiting for the Khmer translation, she continued, "The south-
west region includes Arizona, New Mexico, Texas . . ." *Texas.* Sophal sat

upright with excitement as he recognized the name of his new home. He fixed his gaze on the map behind the teacher, trying somehow to see San Antonio, where he knew he would go soon. Like many students, he wanted to study the map and to ask questions about his state, hoping to ease his deep worry about living in the United States. But it was still nearly an hour until the ten-minute break. And so, as the teacher lectured and the AT translated, Sophal's attention inevitably wandered, until he finally stopped trying to understand. But it did not matter. He would not have learned anything useful about Texas. The teacher had never been to Texas or anywhere else in the United States. And the map on the wall was a map of the Soviet Union.

Nearby, in another building, in a CO class for Vietnamese students, Minh Nguyet Nguyen, 55 years old, listened to the translator. Today's lesson was on the rights and freedoms she would find in the United States. "The law is there to protect and to preserve your freedoms," the teacher said. "The people make the law in America. Many Vietnamese break the law because they do not know how things work. You must remember, in America you will be free, but you must obey the laws."

Today Nguyet was too worried to concentrate on the lesson. Last night her neighbor, Anh Le, had been put in the "monkey house," the jail where refugees were imprisoned. Anh had been arrested for being out after the 9:00 P.M. curfew visiting a friend on the other side of the camp, nearly two miles away. He did not own a watch, and so was late returning, and was arrested as he walked near the Catholic Church. Nguyet knew that sometimes refugees were mistreated while in custody and that there was no food for prisoners. She planned to go there after class, to take Anh some rice and chicken. But she was afraid of the soldiers. She had heard stories of what they did to women who went to the monkey house alone. She hoped one of her friends would accompany her.

"In America, everyone is free," the teacher repeated. "It is not like in your country. In America, the police are your friends. You must tell them if you have a problem. They can help you and protect you, if you trust them." Nguyet did not believe such a place existed. Here the Americans were in charge, but the soldiers could do anything they wanted, and there was no one to protect the refugees. Nguyet believed that it would be no different in the United States. She and her friends would not depend on the police to help them. They would take care of themselves.

In the building next door, in another CO class for Vietnamese students, Tran Hue, 45 years old, was practicing what to say if she ever needed to ask an American landlord to repair a leaking shower. Tran did her best, carefully imitating the sounds she thought she heard her teacher say. "Eye sho lee. Ka u fi i." She repeated it over and over until at last the teacher, satisfied, turned to another student, who did her best too. Tran could see the drawing of the shower the teacher held in his hands, but she could not tell how big it was or where it was kept in American homes. She thought she understood why Americans had them, though in her village in Vietnam nobody had had indoor plumbing. But even after days of practice, Tran, like the other students in the class, did not know the meaning of the strange sounds the teacher made her repeat. And so, though she practiced the sounds over and over—"Eye sho lee. Ka u fi i"—she would never be able to say to an American landlord, "My shower leaks. Can you fix it?"

LEGAL DEFINITION OF "REFUGEE"

Just over one month earlier Sophal, Nguyet, and Tran had arrived in the PRPC. Sophal had come from a refugee camp for Cambodians in Thailand, and Nguyet and Tran from a camp for Vietnamese in Malaysia. They were among the lucky ones to be accepted for resettlement in a third country, rather than repatriated to their ravaged homelands or trapped in refugee camps in the other countries of Southeast Asia.

They were lucky because the United States, Thailand, and the United Nations High Commissioner for Refugees (UNHCR) had declared them to be refugees under the 1951 UN convention regarding refugee status, which defined a refugee as anyone who

owing to a well-founded fear of being persecuted for reasons of race, religion, nationality, membership of a particular social group or political opinion, is outside the country of his nationality and is unable or, owing to such fear, is unwilling to avail himself of the protection of that country.[1]

Since the adoption of the U.S. Refugee Act of 1980, the United States had accepted the UN definition.[2]

The Refugee Act authorized the processing centers in response to two major political pressures. In the late 1970s, supporters of the refugees had argued that the trauma of dislocation and resettlement required special education and adjustment aid. At the same time, refugees arriving after 1975 had had serious difficulties finding employment, and thus had participated in public assistance programs in extraordinarily high numbers. Critics of the resettlement program had argued that the "dumping" of refugees strained state and local resources. The refugee processing centers, along with changes in domestic resettlement efforts, were a response to both criticisms.

To operate the educational program at substantial savings, the Department of State decided to locate the centers in Southeast Asia, where salaries could be one-tenth those paid in the United States. So Sophal, Nguyet, and Tran, like all other refugees accepted for resettlement, prepared for their new lives in the United States of America at specially prepared camps in the Philippines, Thailand, and Indonesia.

But that preparation would take time, for the terrifying memory of their recent past was still fresh in their minds.

THE CAMBODIAN REFUGEE CRISIS: 1975–88

Sophal was one of the nearly 150,000 Cambodians accepted for resettlement by the United States between 1975 and 1986. After the Khmer Rouge victory in 1975, a small number of Cambodians who had worked with the Americans during the war were permitted to resettle: 4,600 in the U.S. fiscal year 1975, immediately after the fall of the pro-U.S. government in Phnom Penh; 1,100 in fiscal 1976; and 300 in fiscal 1977.[3] But in 1979, the number of Cambodians seeking to cross into Thailand increased dramatically, confronting the United States with an important decision: whether to resettle Cambodians in the United States or leave them in crowded camps where they might destabilize the pro-U.S. government of Thailand.

The invasion of Cambodia by the Vietnamese in late 1978, after two years of increasing tension between the countries, led to the fall of Phnom Penh in January 1979. By April, huge numbers of Cambodians were moving across the country just ahead of the advancing Vietnamese forces. As the remnants of the Khmer Rouge waged a losing war against the Vietnamese, a half million Cambodians seeking food and shelter approached the border with Thailand. Millions of others were on the brink of starvation due to war, the collapse of rice production, and the devastation under Khmer Rouge rule prior to the Vietnamese invasion.

The refugees who, like Sophal, actually reached Thailand told horrifying stories of suffering and brutality at the hands of the Khmer Rouge leaders. The number of Cambodians who died from starvation, disease, and murder was extraordinarily high—at least several hundred thousand, perhaps more than one million.[4] But the United States was at first reluctant to resettle Cambodians, fearing that a large resettlement program would encourage people in the interior of the country to move toward the border. Also, the U.S. government had always preferred to focus resources on aiding the politically more important Vietnamese. In fact, it had not been before intense lobbying by the Citizens' Commission on Indochinese Refugees during 1978 that Cambodians were added to the list of Indochinese eligible for admission to the United States under the presidential parole authority, an emergency power used on at least ten separate occasions between 1975 and 1979 to admit large number of refugees from Southeast Asia to the United States.[5]

The number of Cambodians reaching the Thai border during early 1979 created enormous problems for the government of Thailand, which perceived them as a serious threat to Thai stability and security. Thailand initially closed its border, declaring those Cambodians who entered Thailand to be illegal immigrants. Faced with the possibility that several hundred thousand people might attempt to cross into Thailand, the Thai government sought an effective means of attracting world attention to its difficulties. Its strategy was to begin forcible repatriation. In April 1979, thousands of refugees were forced by Thai soldiers to cross treacherous terrain between warring armies, and many died.[6] As the crisis intensified, the United States and other Western countries hesitated to resolve Thailand's difficulties, and so stories of forcible repatriations grew, with one report suggesting that thousands had perished when 40,000 people were pushed down a mountainside across minefields or shot when they attempted to return to Thailand.[7] Still, U.S. policymakers were reluctant to help, because few of the Cambodians had had any direct relationship with the U.S. government or U.S. contractors during the war. It was feared that any decision to begin to resettle the Cambodians on the border might start a rush toward Thailand of over a million more people hoping to become eligible for resettlement.

Despite such fears, press reports during the summer of 1979 led to a groundswell of public support for aid to the Cambodians at the border. Predictions of famine inside the country were especially effective in spreading concern for the future of the Cambodian people. With promises of greatly increased aid and opportunities for resettlement, Thailand agreed at a foreign ministers' meeting of the Association of Southeast Asian Nations (ASEAN) in June and July to move large numbers of Cambodians to holding centers deep within Thailand, away from the fighting between Vietnamese and Khmer Rouge forces near the border. With support from the United States, the United Nations, and other countries, Thailand opened several refugee camps in November 1979, including Khao i Dang near the Thai town of Aranyapratet. Within weeks, Khao i Dang became the largest settlement of Cambodian people in the world outside the Cambodian capital of Phnom Penh.

Still, press reports had begun to predict that millions of people inside Cambodia were threatened with starvation.[8] The U.S. government, along with other governments and international organizations, responded with a major increase in aid. From October 1979 through early 1980, the Carter administration made a series of pledges totaling over $100 million, with an additional $200 million pledged by the international community at a conference in November.[9] The primary goal of U.S. policy, however, was to encourage the Vietnamese, who now controlled Cambodia, to permit refugees in the border area to return to their homes inside the country. But the Vietnamese-backed government in Phnom Penh refused, claiming that many of the border refugees were Khmer Rouge or members of various groups opposed to Vietnam and to the new pro-Vietnamese Heng Samrin government of Cambodia.

Vastly increased aid did not eliminate Thai government concern for its own security. So beginning in January 1980, Thailand refused all new refugees seeking admission to UNHCR holding centers at the border, stabilizing the population at around .16 million. An additional .2 million Cambodians remained in border camps that were not under UNHCR protection; Thailand viewed these camps as temporary shelters for illegal immigrants. As many as .3 million more people remained nearby in Cambodia, hoping to receive relief supplies carried across the "land bridge" from Thailand. Through much of 1980, U.S. officials debated whether to resettle the Cambodians being held in UNHCR camps. Finally, in early 1981, the decision was made to accept 30,000 Cambodian refugees from this group, and processing began in the spring of that year.

But this decision did not end the debate about what to do with the refugees. Thailand remained convinced that the Cambodians, along with refugees from Laos and Vietnam, should not be permitted to stay in Thailand. Many Thai and U.S. officials were concerned that, once some Cambodians were processed for resettlement, there would be no clear criteria for limiting the number who might be considered eligible. At the same time, U.S. labor policy, which favored increased numbers of workers for service industries, farm labor, and other minimum-wage jobs, encouraged a moderate degree of resettlement. Combined with sympathy for the Cambodians in the United States, this meant that a modest resettlement program became feasible.

Although immigration officials looked for ties with family members already in the United States or for a history of employment with American firms in Cambodia during the war, in fact it was impossible to distinguish refugees from economic migrants. Officials feared that any resettlement program for Cambodians would rapidly escalate into general immigration, given the miserable conditions inside Cambodia. As evidence, they cited the several-hundred-thousand Cambodians who were in Thailand or near the border primarily to receive food and other aid supplies that were distributed in the border region. In a worst-case scenario, officials worried that much of the population of Cambodia might seek resettlement in the United States.

As the United States began to resettle Cambodians, officials became concerned that more people would be attracted to the border hoping to be resettled; this came to be called the "pull" factor.[10] Though it was impossible to know how important this factor was, beginning in February 1980, Thailand acted to minimize its effect. The Thai military announced that all newly arriving Cambodians would be incarcerated in border encampments, where they would be provided basic food and shelter but would be prevented from being interviewed by potential resettlement countries. Only Cambodians registered in UNHCR camps prior to early 1980 would be eligible for the U.S. resettlement program.

Despite the decision in 1980 to increase admissions to the United States, the number of Cambodians handled by the U.S. resettlement program was never enough to solve the problem of the Cambodians trapped in the border area. The largest number of Cambodians in any single year during the entire resettlement program, 27,100, were resettled during fiscal 1981. The number dropped to slightly more than 20,000 in 1982 and to only 13,000 in 1983. Between 1975 and 1988, fewer than 150,000 Khmer were resettled in the United States.[11] In 1988, nearly .25 million Cambodians remained in the border region under the jurisdiction of the UN Border Relief Operation (UNBRO), which provides food and water, basic medical aid, and shelter. Because they are not classified as refugees under UNHCR protection, these Cambodians have no opportunity for resettlement.[12] Another 30,000 "residual" refugees remained in UNHCR camps in early 1988. Many had been rejected for resettlement, while others still held onto the slim hope that they would someday be able to leave the Thai refugee camps for the PRPC and then the United States.

Thai policy in 1989 continued to be aimed at discouraging Cambodians from attempting to cross into Thailand. This policy is based upon the assumption that refugees move to the border for a variety of reasons other than fear of persecution, which is the only reason that justifies refugee status. In a sense, the Thais are correct in this assumption. For instance, many of the refugees in 1979 were Khmer Rouge soldiers and their families fleeing Vietnamese forces. Many of those Cambodians who were in the worst condition at the border were supporters of the Khmer Rouge, which had been responsible for such widespread suffering within the country prior to the Vietnamese invasion. Other refugees at the border were former urban residents seeking escape from the peasant life that the Khmer Rouge had forced them to lead since 1975. This group, which comprised a large portion of the original population at Khao i Dang, was not motivated primarily by fear of persecution, since that had been greatest under the Khmer Rouge and had ended with the Khmer Rouge defeat at the hands of the Vietnamese. Former urban residents were most likely to have relatives in other countries, and so many of them hoped to find a way to be resettled with their relatives. Many other Cambodians came to the border to trade. In fact, the movement of huge amounts of food and other aid into Cambodia was made possible, to some degree, by the many traders who worked the border region.[13] Other people at the border came to join one or other of the groups comprising the Khmer Serei, the Free Khmer, who planned to fight the Vietnamese in the hope that one day they could install a system like that under Sihanouk or Lon Nol. This group was opposed to the Khmer Rouge and to the Heng Samrin government, and hoped to receive weapons and other aid from the United States and other anticommunist governments.

Because people come to the border for these reasons, the Thai government continues to view the situation as only a pseudorefugee problem, with a small minority of Cambodians actually in danger of persecution if they return to their homes inside Cambodia.[14] Clearly, Thailand has struggled to pick up the pieces of U.S. policy in Indochina in a situation the Thais did not create. But Vietnam and the Heng Samrin government have refused to cooperate in arranging for repatriation of Cambodians to the interior of the country, claiming with some justification that these Cambodians are opponents of the government who might join resistance groups operating in the interior. Thus it remains impossible for the Thais to effect any long-term solution to the border situation. With well over .25 million Cambodians still in the border region, those, like Sophal, who have been accepted for resettlement must be counted among the most fortunate of all the displaced Cambodians.

VIETNAMESE BOAT PEOPLE

The number of Vietnamese who, like Nguyet and Tran, have been accepted for admission to the United States since 1975 is over .5 million. Unlike the Cambodian refugees, during the war many of the Vietnamese had professional or personal connections with U.S. companies, government agencies, or the military. In addition, the U.S. involvement in the war increased public awareness of Vietnamese refugees, and so political pressure to admit them to the United States has been much greater than for Cambodians.

Approximately 125,000 Vietnamese were admitted immediately after the Communist victory in 1975. After that initial emergency admission, the number of Vietnamese admissions to the United States dropped sharply, to 3,200 in fiscal 1976 and only 1,900 in fiscal 1977.[15] As the number of "boat people" landing throughout Southeast Asia began to increase in 1977 and 1978, the United States was slow to develop any strategy to deal with the growing crisis. Resettlement was based at first upon a series of ad hoc parole decisions, beginning in 1976, that made it possible for Vietnamese to be admitted to the United States. During 1976, about 100 Indochinese refugees, mostly Vietnamese, were resettled each month. During 1977, larger admissions were authorized, with approval granted in August for 7,000 Vietnamese to be admitted. Yet no clear resettlement policy was formulated, even though in late 1977 about 2,000 refugees per month were arriving in various countries in Southeast Asia. For many months, U.S. government officials did not recognize the significance of the fact that the number of Vietnamese landing in asylum countries throughout Southeast Asia was getting larger. As a result, each new State Department request for additional admissions was presented as a solution to the refugee problem.[16] Yet to many observers in Southeast Asia, the American resettlement program was inadequate to handle the growing number of refugees from Vietnam.

In late 1977, State Department officers and the International Rescue Committee finally responded to the problem by organizing a lobbying effort designed to build domestic support for an enlarged resettlement program.

In November and December 1977, the Citizens' Commission on Indo-chinese Refugees was formed, with representatives of religious groups, organized labor, former government officials, and business.[17] The commission was extraordinarily effective in its efforts, which led to approval in March 1978 of an additional 25,000 admissions.

The commission's work was aided by reports that authorities in Malaysia, Thailand, and elsewhere were refusing to permit refugees' vessels to land on their shores. Thailand announced in November 1978 that damaged vessels would be repaired, but that no boat would be permitted to land. Malaysian authorities began to patrol the coastline, towing approaching vessels out to sea, where some inevitably sank. Despite these dangers, the number of people who arrived by boat leaped dramatically in late 1978: 2,829 in August, 8,558 in September, 12,504 in October, and 21,505 in November.[18] By the end of the year, it had become clear that a startling crisis had developed, overwhelming what only a few months earlier had seemed to many Americans to be a generous resettlement program, capable of solving the refugee problem.

Refugees who reached shore in late 1978 found themselves in miserable facilities. On the Malaysian island of Pulau Bidong, over 40,000 Vietnamese were held in a quarter of a square mile, with open latrines, no water other than what was brought from the mainland, and makeshift shelters offering little shade or relief from the crowding. Among the worst refugee camps in Southeast Asia, Pulau Bidong represented the failure of the international community to provide humane living conditions for the growing number of people in need.

With the outbreak of war between Vietnam and China in February 1979, ethnic Chinese began to leave Vietnam in greater numbers than ever before. In April, 26,602 refugees from Vietnam arrived in countries of asylum; in May, 51,139, and in June 56,941.[19] Yet, during May, only 8,500 Vietnamese left Malaysia, Thailand, and other first-asylum countries for the United States. At that rate, the resettlement program clearly could not offer relief to first-asylum countries in Southeast Asia.

As a result the governments of the first-asylum countries became increasingly desperate. Malaysia intercepted a majority of the refugees' boats during mid–1979, towing them back out to sea. Thailand, Indonesia, and the Philippines used naval vessels to block harbors and to stop the boats from entering their waters. Finding no place to land, some refugees continued southward as far as Australia. As the number of refugees increased, so did the number of pirates who preyed on them. Reports mushroomed of robbery, rape, kidnapping, and murder of refugees.[20]

During the spring of 1979 the world gradually came to realize that tens of thousands of boat people were finding no safe haven, that thousands had died as a result of their wanderings through the region, and that even those who reached refugee camps were being held in squalid conditions. It had become clear that the United States and the first-asylum countries in Southeast Asia were unable to resolve the crisis on their own. Therefore, in July 1979, an international conference was called in Geneva to deal with the human crisis.

The Geneva conference was attended by representatives of 65 countries. Despite the great differences among the refugee policies of the countries in attendance, the conference resulted in pledges of $160 million in resettlement aid and an increase in the total number of resettlement positions worldwide from 125,000 to 260,000. The participants also reiterated their commitment to the principle of asylum and agreed to cooperate in rescuing refugees at sea. The United States promised to use naval vessels to search for refugees. Vietnam, which had played an active role in encouraging and facilitating the flow of refugees from its shores, agreed to "make every effort to stop illegal departures."[21] The great irony of the conference was that the United Nations, with the support of the United States and other resettlement countries, was put in the place of making a successful effort to pressure Vietnam to reduce refugee movements by restricting the right of people to leave, even though they might face persecution if they remained. It also was at this conference that the Philippines agreed to provide a site on the Bataan Peninsula for a refugee processing center. The site of unspeakable suffering and death in World War II, this land would now offer relief and hope to hundreds of thousands of homeless people.

With Vietnam beginning to discourage refugees' departures, the number of boat people arriving in Southeast Asia decreased in July 1979, for the first time in a year and a half. The arrivals dropped from a high of over 56,000 in June to 17,839 in July, 9,734 in August, 9,533 in September, 2,854 in October, 2,209 in November, and 2,745 in December.[22] Meanwhile, governments and relief agencies had time to improve conditions in the refugee camps and to begin planning for the processing center in the Philippines. The U.S. resettlement program could finally begin to make a dent in the backlog of people in first-asylum camps. From 44,500 Vietnamese resettled during fiscal 1979, the number jumped to 95,000 in 1980, then 86,000 in 1981, 44,000 in 1982, and over 20,000 in each year from 1983 to 1986.[23] The reduced numbers in the mid–1980s reflected fewer new arrivals, as well as the U.S. effort to encourage emigration through the Orderly Departure Program (ODP), a system for facilitating legal exit from Vietnam. Though the desperate, overwhelming numbers have diminished, the Vietnamese refugees have continued to arrive by boat in asylum countries into 1988. During the first nine months of 1988, over 15,000 Vietnamese arrived seeking asylum.

Like the Cambodians, the emigrants from Vietnam left their country for a variety of reasons. The government of Vietnam had adopted a policy of forcing out large numbers of Chinese, approximately 250,000 of whom crossed into China, where they were accepted for permanent resettlement.[24]

Tens of thousands of other Chinese left by boat and were resettled in the United States and elsewhere. Other refugees left Vietnam after being released from prisons, where some had been held for as long as seven or eight years.[25] Vietnamese who had supported the former government of South Vietnam or who had aided the U.S. war effort had difficulties finding employment or educational opportunities in Vietnam after 1975. For them, leaving their home provided the only chance for greater opportunities. Families with children of American fathers also have had special reason to leave. The estimated 8,000 "Amerasian" children, called "bui doi" (dust of life) in Vietnam, are unwelcome in Vietnamese society, and their families suffer as a result.[26] Therefore some mothers of Amerasian children have abandoned their offspring, while others have left to be resettled by the United States.[27]

Though many Vietnamese leave their country for economic reasons, it is impossible to determine when unemployment or other economic difficulties are acts of repression and when they are due simply to the harsh realities of the Vietnamese economy. There is no doubt that some Vietnamese have left to escape general economic problems, brought about in part by U.S. efforts to isolate Vietnam and create economic chaos that might destabilize the government. Yet under U.S. regulations, economic hardship does not qualify individuals for refugee status. As a result, the United States has increasingly viewed Vietnamese, as well as other Indochinese, as economic migrants rather than refugees. H. Eugene Douglas, U.S. Coordinator for Refugee Affairs, argued in 1986,

It has become increasingly clear over the past several years that the exodus from Indochina, while smaller than in earlier years, contains larger numbers of individuals who cannot make compelling claims of persecution as laid out in the Refugee Act, but are departing their countries of origin for pressing economic, family reunification, or other reasons.[28]

In 1986 and 1987, U.S. policy reflected a consensus in the government that large numbers of refugees leave Vietnam primarily for economic or family reasons. The number of boat people arriving in asylum countries increased dramatically in 1988. The greatest increase occurred in Hong Kong, which experienced an eightfold rise in the number of arrivals over 1987. The irony is that, because U.S. policy prohibits economic aid to Vietnam, the United States contributes to the economic conditions that lead to these departures.

More generally, the distinction between economic and political refugees is applied arbitrarily. When refugee immigration quotas are high and officials wish to score ideological points against the Communist governments of Indochina, they claim that people are fleeing political repression and therefore qualify for refugee status. But when refugee resettlement quotas for Southeast Asia are reduced, as they have been in the late 1980s, then officials claim that the departures are motivated by a desire to improve economic conditions; insisting on this distinction permits officials to be arbitrarily selective in admitting Southeast Asians to the United States.

In order to gain control over departures from Vietnam, the United States since 1980 has encouraged Vietnamese to apply through the ODP. Although the United States and Vietnam do not have formal diplomatic relations, the two countries have worked together through this program to resettle over 50,000 Vietnamese in the United States between late 1979 and 1987. The program has involved enormous difficulties, however, including a significant decrease in the number of completed cases since 1984.[29] Also, from 1986 until late 1987, U.S. staff members were not allowed to interview new applicants for the ODP because of Vietnamese dissatisfaction with the backlog of approved cases that the U.S. had not finished processing.

Nevertheless, individuals with ODP applications completed prior to 1986 have been permitted to leave Vietnam. Also, ODPs continue to operate between Vietnam and other countries, including France. Since 1984, the total number of immigrants leaving Vietnam through all ODPs has been greater than the number of boat people. In 1985, for instance, there were 22,258 boat arrivals in first-asylum countries and 24,940 orderly departures.[30] Although this represents a major decrease since the crisis days of 1979 and 1980, between 2,000 and 3,000 Vietnamese continue to arrive by boat each month in Malaysia, the Philippines, and other countries, and as many as 500,000 Vietnamese still in Vietnam may wish to leave through the ODP.

REFUGEES FROM LAOS

Although the Cambodian and Vietnamese refugees have received the greatest public attention, refugees from Laos have also been resettled in the United States, and many continue to be held in first-asylum camps in Thailand. Laotian refugees have moved into Thailand for a number of reasons. Of special importance to the United States during the Vietnam War were the Hmong highland people, who played a major role in the CIA's secret war in Laos. After the United States ended its involvement in the war, the Hmong were left without a source of supplies, though they attempted to continue their resistance to the Pathet Lao. As a result, thousands of Hmong died in the fighting and in their flight to Thailand. Some lowland Lao, as well as smaller highland groups such as the Mien, also opposed the Pathet Lao and were driven into Thailand. Individuals who were released or who escaped from prison camps have fled to Thailand. The government of Laos has admitted holding as many as 10,000–15,000 people under much harsher conditions than in similar camps in Vietnam.[31] For these people, escape to the overcrowded refugee camps of northern Thailand meant a major improvement in their living conditions.

Since 1976 there has been heated debate about the motivation of people for leaving Laos. UNHCR representatives have argued that many people depart because of economic difficulties. During 1976–78, the United States generally argued that this was not the case and that people from Laos were just as likely to suffer persecution as those in other countries in the region.[32] More recently, however, the United States has insisted that many Laotians do not fit the UN definition of a refugee. For instance, a U.S. Senate subcommittee staff report in 1984 stated that "UNHCR officers should thoroughly and strictly review all new arrivals. If they did so, most observers believe only a few refugees would be accepted."[33]

In Laos, as elsewhere in the region, the distinction between economic migrants and refugees is difficult to make. One of the major reasons for the severe economic conditions experienced by the Hmong has been an attempt by the government to create agricultural cooperatives in lowland areas as a way to gain control of the remaining Hmong population and to integrate them into the country's administrative structure. Many Hmong, unaccustomed to life in the lowlands, have succumbed to disease and have had difficulty growing lowland crops. Clearly it is impossible to separate the economic hardships of the remaining Hmong in Laos from their historical opposition to the government.

Still, the view that many Laotians are economic migrants has spread steadily. With U.S. support, Thailand began in June 1985 to screen new arrivals from Laos to determine whether they were refugees or economic migrants. During the first year of screening, June 1985 to June 1986, 1,900 individuals (mainly ethnic Lao) were accepted as refugees, while 1,000 cases were rejected and 1,000 put on hold.[34] Those who were rejected were placed in temporary holding camps near the border, as Thailand and Laos bickered over procedures for their repatriation. Thailand's policy of discouraging refugees from Laos has also been implemented in pushbacks of Laotians attempting to enter Thailand. At crossing points in northeast Thailand, Thai police routinely force Laotians to return to Laos, with some deaths reported from shootings by Lao border guards.[35] More than other refugees in the region, Laotians are subject to forcible return, to mistreatment by local officials, and to serious doubt among U.S. and other resettlement officials about their claim to refugee status.

Laotians who are fortunate enough to pass through the Thai screening procedure find themselves in overcrowded camps with severe health, sanitation, and safety problems. At the camp for ethnic Lao at Na Pho in northeast Thailand, nearly 30,000 people were being held in mid–1986 in an area designed for half that number. No educational programs existed, so that boredom and a range of psychological problems were widespread. At the Hmong camp at Ban Vinai, over 40,000 Hmong have lived for nearly a decade in makeshift shelters, with poor educational and training programs and no prospect for large-scale resettlement or repatriation.

Since 1978, the United States has generally been reluctant to view resettlement as a solution to the problem of Laotian refugees. As a result, U.S. resettlement of Laotians has been much smaller than for Vietnamese. From fiscal 1975 through fiscal 1986, slightly more than 100,000 ethnic Lao and 60,000 highlanders were resettled in the United States.[36] During 1986 and 1987, the situation improved somewhat, as the rate of approval of Laotians by U.S. immigration officials increased. During that period, Laotians constituted more than half of the 17,000 refugees approved by U.S. officials in Thailand. Yet these cases were drawn from a group that was predetermined to be of special interest to the United States. Therefore it is likely that future processing will result in fewer approvals and that many Laotians remaining in refugee camps in Thailand will never have the opportunity to be considered for resettlement in the United States.[37] As Thailand increases its pressure on Laotians, including greater use of forcible pushbacks and stricter screening procedures, Laotian refugees will find themselves in increasingly difficult circumstances, with greater numbers having no possibility of local integration in Thailand or resettlement in the United States.

ARRIVING AT THE PHILIPPINE REFUGEE PROCESSING CENTER

Sophal, his mother, and his two children had come on a flight from Thailand along with 73 other Cambodians from the Khao i Dang holding center on the Thai-Cambodian border. They were lucky to leave Khao i Dang, a dangerous, overcrowded camp where security is inadequate and armed bandits and gangs often assault, rob, rape, and kidnap refugees. After lengthy interviews with U.S. immigration officials in Thailand, Sophal and his family had been accepted for resettlement because they had family members already in the United States and he had been able to prove that he had not been a soldier of the Khmer Rouge in Cambodia. After three and a half years in refugee camps, his stay in the Philippines was the final stage of his long journey to the United States.

Tran had arrived in the Philippines only two days after Sophal. She had come from Malaysia, where she had spent 13 months in Pulau Bidong before receiving approval for resettlement. Her son, who had been in the South Vietnamese military, had left Saigon in April 1975, making his way to a U.S. naval vessel and eventually to the United States. It had taken Tran nearly 10 years before she and her husband had been able to leave Vietnam. But her husband had died on the boat trip to Malaysia, leaving her alone to face the hardships of refugee camps and the journey to the United States to be reunited with her son. Nguyet had arrived with Tran, after nearly three years in Pulau Bidong. Nguyet was alone, frightened, and unable to speak English. She had the name of her cousin's friend in

Chicago, though she would live in Los Angeles, where a church group was her sponsor. She knew nobody in California.

After the confusion and tension of Khao i Dang and Pulau Bidong, the orderly bureaucracy that greeted Sophal, Nguyet, and Tran upon their arrival at PRPC had been reassuring. The Reception, Processing, Deprocessing Group (Reprodeg) had inspected their belongings, confirmed their identities in a simple interview, examined their papers, and channeled them through a brief medical examination to make sure they were not ill after their long trip. Due to persistent malaria at PRPC, they were given chloroquine tablets, an antimalaria drug. Next, their billet assignments were handed them on a simple form, and they had signed for their household items: cooking gas, pots, a large spoon, and bamboo sleeping mats. Finally, exhausted after the ordeal of their journey and arrival, they walked through the red glow of the spectacular South China Sea sunset to Phase 2, the newer section of the camp, 4 kilometers from the Reprodeg building.

Sophal and his family were assigned to Section 8, officially called Neighborhood 8, one of ten in the camp. On the way, they had passed through Neighborhood 7, one of the Vietnamese billet areas, where Tran and Nguyet were assigned. Like most refugees, they were relieved to learn that ethnic groups were housed separately. Tired and resigned, they began their new lives at PRPC, joining the 17,000 other refugees from Cambodia, Vietnam, and Laos and nearly 1,000 Filipino and American staff members who populated this small city on a ridge overlooking the sea.

On their second morning in camp, Sophal, Nguyet and Tran were interviewed by Joint Voluntary Agency (JVA) officers, who gathered information about their family members in the United States in order to begin sponsorship processing. Having a sponsor was essential, and both Tran and Sophal were lucky to have letters proving that they had relatives in the United States. After the JVA interview, they went to the office of the Intergovernmental Committee for Migration (ICM) for chest x-rays, blood tests for syphilis, immunizations, and a quick examination for other venereal diseases, physical defects or disabilities, and obvious mental conditions. Like many refugees, Tran was found to have tuberculosis. Because no one was permitted to leave for the United States with TB, she knew that she would probably remain at PRPC longer than most others. But it was still better than Pulau Bidong, and she decided she could spend her time usefully, attending English classes, learning about America, preparing herself for living in the land she had dreamed about, and feared, for so long.

Before beginning classes, Tran, Nguyet, and Sophal spent their first two weeks in the camp going through Phase 1 of the Adaptation Process for Displaced Persons, the plan for gradually reducing the trauma and dependence that are characteristic of inmates of first-asylum camps. Mostly this had meant endless waiting in lines, repetitious interviews, cursory physical examinations, and orientation meetings. They had learned that they, like all adults, would have to work two hours each day in addition to their English and cultural-orientation classes as part of the work credit system. Unless they completed this requirement, they would not be permitted to leave PRPC for the United States. Because Sophal could speak some English, he was assigned to the registration office, where the staff of the International Catholic Migration Commission (ICMC) did the paper work for the 9,000 refugees enrolled in its classes. Nguyet and Tran, who spoke no English and could not read Vietnamese, were assigned to a cleanup crew, which meant they spent 12 hours each week under a Filipino overseer cutting grass with a bolo knife and clearing the brush that constantly encroached on the living areas of refugees and staff. Like other refugees, they understood the hierarchy of camp: Americans were in charge of the camp, while Filipinos exercised much of the day-to-day control over the refugees.

After their two weeks of orientation and the difficult English placement test, Sophal, Nguyet, and Tran had been assigned to their English classes. Nguyet and Tran entered Level A classes, for refugees with no English and no literacy skills in their first language. Sophal went to Level D for those who could speak some English and read simple sentences and signs. (There was only one level above Sophal's, for refugees who could speak and read English rather well.) All three were also assigned to cultural orientation classes, where they studied American culture and how to adapt to a society a world apart from their own. Finally they were placed in preemployment training (PET) classes, intended to prepare them for minimum-wage employment.[38] In their PET classes, they would be taught to work as janitors, dishwashers, and laundry workers in the United States.

Refugees assigned to the other processing center, at Phanat Nikhom in Thailand, find fewer than 4,000 refugees in classes. Until 1986, a third processing center operated on the island of Galang in Indonesia. Even smaller than the other two, Galang held from a few hundred to as many as three thousand refugees, until it was closed in late 1986. Other sites, at Ban Vinai and Nong Khai in Thailand and in Hong Kong, have also offered educational programs for refugees going to the United States. Though these camps continue to house refugees, the educational programs were closed in 1982, and the few refugees accepted for resettlement from these locations are sent to the Philippines for their classes.

Since 1980, the Phanat Nikhom educational program has been run by the Consortium, a cooperative program of the Experiment in International Living of Brattleboro, Vermont; the Save the Children Federation; and World Education. The educational program in the Philippines is operated by the International Catholic Migration Commission, with its head office in Geneva. As the number of refugees admitted to the United States continues to drop, it is increasingly likely that the Phanat Nikhom center eventually will be closed as well. Until then, some Cambodians will attend classes at Phanat Nikhom, while most will go to the Philippines. At both sites, refugees are required to spend about six months completing the intensive educational program.

Sophal planned to study hard and to make his six months in class as productive as possible in order to prepare himself for his new life in the United States. With his 61-year-old mother and his two children, 28-year-old Sophal would have to support four people. He knew he would have to work hard, and that he would need help.

With three grandchildren under 12 years of age, Tran would rely on her son and daughter-in-law already in the United States. She did not plan to look for a job, but instead would care for her grandchildren while her son and daughter-in-law worked. She dreamed that life in the United States would be just like in Vietnam, before refugee camps.

Nguyet did not know what would happen to her. She would arrive in Los Angeles knowing no one. Though her sponsor would meet her, she did not know where she would live, shop, or work. She was afraid that she would never be able to talk to anyone.

The stories of Sophal, Nguyet, and Tran, like those of hundreds of thousands of other refugees, is a chronicle of misery, inhumanity, and trauma, as well as of cataclysmic changes in the social and political organization of Indochina.[39] But it is also a story of the struggle by the world community to fulfill its responsibility to help people who cannot help themselves and whose suffering is a result of the actions of the world's governments. Thus the refugees of Southeast Asia are witness both to the awesome power of individuals and nations to inflict suffering upon their fellow human beings, and to the world's effort to respond with compassion and generosity. As refugees, their lives are in the hands of the world. As participants in the U.S. resettlement program, their future is in the hands of the program staff, and ultimately the American people.

Survivors

How teach again ... what has been taught correctly and incorrectly, learned a thousand times, throughout the millenniums of mankind's prudent folly? How render back into light-world language the speech-defying pronouncements of the dark? ... How communicate to people who insist on the exclusive evidence of their senses the message of the all-generating void?

Joseph Campbell, *The Hero with a Thousand Faces*[1]

I can still remember the hot smell of war. It made me cry "Daddy, Mommy" in the din and disorder.

Le Thi, refugee from Vietnam, in an essay written in the Philippines

Sophal, Nguyet, and Tran are only the most recent refugees from Southeast Asia. The migration of displaced people in that part of the world did not begin in 1975, but rather has been a part of the misery of war for a generation. Indeed, though the processing centers opened as recently as 1980, the United States has been intimately involved with Southeast Asian refugees for an entire generation. From its inception, this involvement has meant that the fate of the refugees is inseparable from the political and military conflicts in the region.

INDOCHINESE REFUGEE RESETTLEMENT IN THE 1950s

The connection between the United States and the Indochinese refugees began in the mid–1950s, with the resettlement in South Vietnam of large numbers of people from the north. Under the terms of the Geneva agreement, which divided the country into North Vietnam, under President Ho Chi Minh, and South Vietnam, under Prime Minister Ngo Dinh Diem, people were permitted to resettle in either place with guaranteed international protection. Between August 1954 and mid–1955, approximately .9 million people moved from north to south, while about .1 million people, mainly soldiers of the Vietminh forces, went to the north. In this huge movement of refugees, 20 years before the Communist victory in South Vietnam, the United States played a central role by encouraging, funding, and carrying out the refugee resettlement program. It was the beginning of the heavy U.S. involvement in the politcal and ideological battle for control of Vietnam.

After the Geneva agreement, the United States sought to ensure that South Vietnam would be ruled by a pro-U.S. government. The refugees from the North offered an opportunity to build the political base for such a government. Most of these refugees were Catholics—between 600,000 and 790,000.[2] Many had been members of militias that had fought the Vietminh. By the time Ho Chi Minh returned to Hanoi in October 1954, after eight years in the jungles and mountains of Vietnam as leader of the Vietminh revolutionary forces, these militia members and their families had disbanded and headed south. Other refugees followed from the northern Catholic dioceses of Phat Diem and Bui Chu. Led by their bishops and priests, they moved toward traditional Chinese Catholic enclaves and new refugee settlements established by the government in the south.[3] In less than two years, over 60 percent of all Northern Catholics moved south, while 99.5 percent of all non–Catholics stayed in the North.[4] Some of these refugees had been collaborators, war profiteers, officials, and professionals with anti-Vietminh views; about 90,000 were fishermen and their families;[5] others were artisans, shopkeepers, and business people who feared that their livelihood was threatened by the new government. Peasants made up the largest group. Approximately 700,000 peasants and small farmers abandoned their land for new lives in the South. Indeed, their migration southward significantly reduced pressures on land and food in the overpopulated North.

The United States played a key role in this first Vietnamese refugee resettlement program. The northern refugees were transported to the South by U.S. and French aircraft and naval vessels. Much of the organizational work for the program was carried out by Col. Edward G. Lansdale, the famous CIA agent who had just finished helping to defeat the leftist Huk rebellion in the Philippines. Lansdale had come to Vietnam to set up the Saigon Military Mission, a covert group of soldiers and intelligence agents who organized sabotage against the Vietminh. Though there is disagreement about the importance of Lansdale's role in the refugee program, it is clear that he was a central figure not only in organizing transport, but also in encouraging Northern Catholics to flee to the South, in part by spreading frightening stories about what would happen to Catholics who remained.[6] In the South, U.S. Marine Col. Victor J. Croizat, the first marine assigned to the U.S. Military Assistance Advisory Group (MAAG) in Saigon, was reportedly responsible for establishing refugee centers that were built and supported by massive amounts of U.S. aid.[7]

Though precise figures on U.S. funding of the refugee program are impossible to obtain, historians and analysts agree that the funding was substantial. One widely respected estimate is that in 1955, $55 million, including $44 million for naval transport, went to refugee resettlement, out of total U.S. aid to South Vietnam of $320 million, and that, in 1956, $37 million was applied to permanent resettlement in the South, out of total U.S. aid of $196 million.[8] This aid was used to reclaim several hundred thousand acres of fertile land that had been uncultivated during the years of the war and to construct some 300 new villages in the South, most of which became permanent Catholic enclaves. The government of South Vietnam claimed that .5 million refugees eventually resided in these new settlements.[9]

But U.S. aid was not the only reason for the success of the resettlement program in creating permanent new communities. During the war against the Vietminh, the Catholic community had remained tightly knit, with its leadership intact. As a result, its leaders were able to take major responsibility for the program. Indeed, the effectiveness of local priests and other Catholic leaders is widely considered to be one of the most remarkable yet least analyzed features of the entire resettlement effort.[10] The program also benefited from the availability of huge tracts of land that had been abandoned during the fighting. Much of this land was near the border between North and South Vietnam. Diem took the opportunity to resettle many refugees in these sparsely populated areas as a buffer against the Communist forces in the north.[11]

Diem, a Catholic, was able to benefit politically from the presence of the northern refugees in other ways as well. Diem saw the refugees as a major source of political support in his struggle to consolidate his authority against rival Buddhist leaders. In September 1954, he called on the Catholic refugees to demonstrate publicly their support for him in his effort to win control over the army. Though the demonstrations were brutally dispersed by police, they showed that Diem could count on the Northern refugees in his continuing political battles in Saigon.[12]

From the moment of their arrival in the south in 1954 and 1955, the Northern refugees played a central role in the ongoing conflict between Catholics and Buddhists. They supported the string of pro-U.S. governments in the south and cooperated with the U.S. war effort throughout the 1960s and 1970s. Accordingly, they comprised a major portion of the Vietnamese who fled after the Communist victory in 1975. After 1975, many of the Vietnamese refugees arriving in the United States were members of their families.

It was during the 1950s that U.S. voluntary agencies began their crucial role in Indochinese refugee resettlement. Among the most important were Catholic Relief Services, Operation Brotherhood, CARE, the Church World Service (CWS), the Mennonite Central Committee, the Protestant Evangelical Church, the American Red Cross, and the International Rescue Committee.[13] Throughout the war, most of these agencies continued their work in Vietnam, and they handled important aspects of the resettlement of Indochinese refugees in the 1970s and 1980s.

Although the refugee resettlement program in the mid–1950s involved the movement of Vietnamese people from one part of their country to the other, and was therefore different from refugee movements after 1975, the program nevertheless established important patterns that persisted during later resettlement efforts. First, individuals became refugees for a complex set of reasons. Ho Chi Minh's government encouraged massive departures in order to rid itself of former opponents and to free hundreds of thousands of acres of land for redistribution among peasant farmers in the heavily populated north. Officials of the U.S. and Diem governments encouraged the refugees to leave in order to build a strong pro–Diem, pro–U.S. political base within the population of the south. The closely knit Catholic community and its strong leadership benefitted politically and economically by supporting Diem and the U.S.

Second, the movement of refugees from the north to the south established a pattern of heavy involvement by U.S. military and intelligence agencies in refugee affairs in the region. Because the refugees supported Diem, they were an important resource in the political battles among competing South Vietnamese leaders. Therefore U.S. military and intelligence officers saw the refugee program as part of the larger effort to defeat the Vietminh in the struggle for control of the country. Throughout the next three decades, the refugees would continue to be used for their strategic value by all sides in the conflict.

Third, the refugee program in the mid–1950s established a pattern of heavy, though reluctant, involvement by voluntary agencies in political and military affairs. Because the refugee program was a component in the effort to build a pro–U.S. government in the South, agencies that aided refugees found themselves to be tools of U.S. and South Vietnamese policy. These agencies inevitably came to be used for U.S. strategic interests in Indochina and for the interests of a particular political group, Diem and his supporters, in the internal politics of the country. In later periods as well, voluntary agencies involved in refugee relief would be unable to avoid entanglements in the strategic struggles in the region.[14]

REFUGEES DURING THE U.S. WAR IN VIETNAM

Refugee movements in Vietnam did not end with the last Northerners to arrive in the South in mid–1955. In fact, this was only the beginning, for as the war escalated, the number of refugees increased steadily. Eventually, the problems associated with massive dislocation and resettlement overwhelmed the efforts of the governments of Vietnam and the United States to provide relief.

As the war spread in the 1960s, it had a devastating effect upon the civilian population in the South, creating huge numbers of refugees and swelling the cities with hundreds of thousands of displaced people. By early 1965, it was estimated that there were .5 million refugees in South Vietnam, with another 1 million expected within the year.[15] But with the arrival of large numbers of U.S. troops and a shift in military strategy, a far more dramatic increase in the number of refugees took place. This new strategy was to destroy villages and force the population into refugee camps and cities in order to eliminate the rural base for the Communist guerrillas.

Huge bombing campaigns leveled villages, while free-fire zones forced civilians to flee to miserable camps near U.S. and South Vietnamese military posts. In one site alone near the demilitarized zone, 17,000 refugees were housed in barracks, with no possibility of cultivating land or finding employment.[16] By the middle of 1966, the refugee population had grown beyond anything ever imagined, as millions of people crowded into camps and many square miles of tin shacks in the cities. In areas of especially heavy bombing, refugees became one of the largest groups in the general population. For instance, in Quang Nam Province in 1966, one-quarter of the population consisted of refugees.[17]

As refugees moved to the cities seeking housing and employment, the population of Saigon exploded, from around .5 million to about 3 million by 1966. It was estimated that .2 million juvenile refugees roamed the streets of Saigon.[18] As the population continued to grow, competition for employment and housing became more intense with refugees finding work as laborers, cycle drivers, and sellers of stolen goods. Many became prostitutes. Before the war, about 15 percent of the population had lived in cities, but by 1971, nearly 50 percent of the people in South Vietnam lived in and around the sprawling urban areas. By 1971, there were 5 million refugees in the south, out of a total population of 17 million. A nation of villages and peasant farmers had become, by 1971, a nation of squalid cities, military bases, and refugee camps.[19]

But the U.S. bombing and free-fire zones were not the only cause of the explosion of the refugee population. Attacks by northern forces also drove thousands of people into refugee camps and southern cities. The Tet offensive in 1968 had an especially important impact on the number of displaced people. By one estimate, the Tet offensive increased the number of refugees in the south by 40 percent.[20] In response, U.S. and South Vietnamese officials announced Operation Hearts Together, a program to resettle families displaced by fighting, but the growing numbers of homeless people quickly overwhelmed the effort. Later, as North Vietnamese forces made military gains, the number of refugees in the northern provinces of South Vietnam increased dramatically.

Like the Tet offensive, the North Vietnamese spring offensive of 1972 drove several hundred thousand more people from their homes. When North Vietnamese forces captured Quangtri City, the first provincial capital taken during the offensive, 80 percent of Hue's population, which already included .3 million refugees, moved south to Da Nang. In July, when South Vietnamese forces fought their way back into Quangtri, the civilians who had remained during the occupation by soldiers from the North then joined the exodus south to Hue. By October, several hundred thousand people who had fled Quangtri province found themselves permanently settled in refugee camps at Da Nang.[21]

Conditions in these camps were appalling. People lived in shelters that would normally be used for pigs and chickens. District leaders often stole meager food supplies. Malnutrition was widespread, and the death rate among infants and young children skyrocketed. Malnourished, in shock at the loss of their homes, and unable to envision a future for their families, many people did little more than sit all day long, staring blankly ahead in the universal expression of human misery.[22] In 1975, when the order was given to evacuate Hue and abandon it to the North, these refugees were joined by 1 million more people, driven by the memories of the slaughter of civilians during the Tet offensive and the devastating fighting of the 1972 spring offensive.

Even the end of the war brought more refugees. The evacuation in 1975 was a desperate, violent struggle. In only two days, April 29 and 30, Option IV, the largest helicopter evacuation on record, carried some 6,000 Vietnamese, along with 1,000 Americans, from Saigon to U.S. aircraft carriers waiting offshore. The carriers and amphibious ships were overwhelmed by the tens of thousands of Vietnamese who fled by sea on naval vessels, barges, and private craft. Helicopters had to be pushed off flight decks into the sea in order to make room for more people. Others reached Thailand by boat, the first of the many thousands of such journeys that continue today. By the end of 1975, nearly 130,000 Vietnamese had fled, finding their way to refugee camps and, eventually, to the United States. They were South Vietnamese soldiers, government officials, business owners, employees of the U.S. government and U.S. companies—professionals, middle- and upper-class leaders of the defeated South. They were the last of the wartime refugees in Vietnam.

By the time the war ended, it had devastated Vietnamese society. By one estimate, the total number of refugees between 1965 and 1973 in South Vietnam alone was over 10 million.[23] But numbers alone do not convey the effects of such a massive displacement of people. Almost overnight, Vietnam became an urban nation. With the destruction of village life and the system of agriculture on which it had depended, the Vietnamese people lost the foundation of traditional Vietnamese society. By leaving their land, the millions of Vietnamese who moved from their villages to the cities lost everything: places of worship of their ancestors, homes for their families, their source of food production, and the essential social and political order of the villages. The destruction of village life meant more than a change in life-style; it meant the loss of personal identity. In her classic analysis of Vietnamese society, Frances Fitzgerald described what this meant for individual Vietnamese.

To leave the land and the family forever was therefore to lose their place in the universe and to suffer a permanent, collective death. In one Saigon newspaper story, a young [South Vietnamese] ARVN officer described returning to his home village after many years to find his family gone and the site of his father's house a patch of thorns revealing no trace of human habitation. He felt, he said, "like someone who has lost his soul."[24]

REFUGEES DURING THE WAR IN LAOS

Like the war in Vietnam, the war in Laos created many homeless people, primarily because of U.S. bombing. Begun by Thai mercenary pilots recruited by the CIA in the early 1960s, the bombing campaign became a U.S. operation in June 1964. At first, only a few missions were flown each week, but soon the bombing escalated, with drastic increases in 1968 and again in 1969. In 1967, an average of 120 bombing raids were flown each day, but later over 700 raids a day sometimes took place, and the average for all of 1969 was nearly 400 per day.[25] The total bomb tonnage dropped on Laos by 1973 was a staggering 2,092,900 tons, approximately the total dropped by U.S. forces in all of World War II in Europe and the Pacific. This was two-thirds of a ton of bombs for every man, woman, and child in Laos.

The U.S. bombing destroyed village life in vast areas of Laos. Over one-third of the 9,400 villages in Laos were Pathet Lao during the mid–1960s. By 1973, virtually all of these villages had been destroyed by bombing. Especially hard hit was the Plain of Jars, a high plateau east of Luang Prabang. On the Plain of Jars, destruction of village life was nearly complete. In 1960, the area had supported 150,000 people, but by the early 1970s, fewer than 9,000 people were left, and not a single village remained.[26] Refugees reported continuous terror: "There wasn't a night when we went to sleep that we thought we'd live to see the morning."[27] To escape the bombing, those who remained often lived underground during the day, rarely seeing the sun. The area, which had supported rich forests and grasslands, was bombed so totally that it came to resemble a barren, crater-filled desert landscape.[28]

Refugees fleeing the bombing often died from disease and exhaustion while trying to escape. U.S. aid officials estimated that 10 percent of all people involved in evacuation marches died in this way; on some of the more difficult journeys, as many as 20 percent of the people perished.[29] Such journeys were all too common, as one-fourth of the population of the country was displaced at some point during the bombing.[30]

But refugee movements did not stop with the bombing halt in 1973. The Hmong and other highland groups who fought for the CIA found themselves under constant attack by the Pathet Lao forces. When the Pathet Lao gained control of the government in 1975, most of the Hmong population fled to Thailand, along with other groups such as the Mien. Ethnic Lao who had supported the U.S. side during the war were forced to leave as well. In the decade following the end of the war, over .3 million people— 10 percent of the total population of Laos—crossed jungle borders or swam the Mekong river to camps in Thailand. Ban Vinai, the Hmong camp in northern Thailand, became one of the largest refugee camps in Southeast Asia, holding over 40,000 refugees as late as 1987.

REFUGEES DURING THE WAR IN CAMBODIA

Though refugees from Vietnam and Laos suffered from the terrors of war, from the dangers of flight, and from the misery of refugee camps, no group in Southeast Asia suffered more than the people of Cambodia. During the war itself, after the Khmer Rouge gained control of the country in 1975, and then later while fleeing from fighting between Vietnamese and Khmer Rouge forces, the Cambodian people experienced some of the worst conditions and most extreme brutality in the history of Southeast Asia.

Misery came late to Cambodia. Because the war was not waged heavily in Cambodia during the 1960s, the country was spared much of the dislocation of people that took place during that time in Vietnam and Laos. In fact, many of the refugees in Cambodia in the late 1960s were Vietnamese, who often came into conflict with Cambodians due to the traditional hostilities between them. In May 1970, the presence of South Vietnamese forces in Cambodia inflamed this hostility, leading to an evacuation of between 50,000 and 80,000 Vietnamese to South Vietnam. Even after the evacuation, some 70,000 Vietnamese remained in refugee camps in Cambodia, though the South Vietnamese government officially declared that Vietnamese in Cambodia were not in danger.[31]

By 1971, however, Khmer Rouge attacks made life precarious in many regions of the country. Late in that year, attacks outside Phnom Penh led to a tremendous increase in the number of people fleeing to the capital. But even this increase was minor compared to the explosion in numbers of refugees created by the combination of heavy U.S. bombing, which began in 1973, and the two-year-long Khmer Rouge offensive that ultimately led to the capture of Phnom Penh.

During seven months of constant U.S. bombing late in 1973, over .5 million Cambodians entered the capital, doubling its population. U.S. planes dropped 50 percent more tonnage within Cambodia than was dropped on Japan during World War II. The devastation of the countryside led to the collapse of rice production, with the total land in cultivation dropping from 6 million to slightly more than 1 million acres.[32] As a result, output dropped from over 2,100 tons during 1971–72 to only 762 tons during 1973–74.[33] As farming, fishing, and road travel became unsafe, hundreds of thousands of peasant farmers had no place to go except the capital. For the first time, beggars appeared on the streets of Phnom Penh. Refugees stripped bark for firewood from the shade trees lining the boulevards, and shantytowns sprang up throughout the city.[34] By late 1973, traditional Cambodian life had come to an end.

Food shortages began in the refugee camps of the capital, and rapidly escalated to malnutrition and starvation. Khmer Rouge forces made road travel to Phnom Penh extremely dangerous, so that food could be brought only by air or, with increasing risk, up the Mekong River. By 1974, all land routes were blocked, and ultimately an airlift was the only way to bring supplies to the city. But the airlift proved to be inadequate, so with food supplies low and the capital cut off from the countryside, life for refugees soon became unbearable. Rice riots were commonplace, while government soldiers set up roadblocks where they stole refugees' food and belongings and bought young girls for army brothels.[35]

Many Cambodians became almost totally dependent for food on outside aid. Catholic Relief Services and World Vision tried to handle the crisis, but the U.S. government refused to provide adequate aid for the starving refugees. Total U.S. government aid was minuscule: between July 1972 and July 1973, $1.2 million was for refugee assistance, out of a total U.S. aid package of $244.1 million.[36] As a result, the private agencies were unable to meet the pressing needs of the city.[37]

By the time the war ended with Khmer Rouge victory in April 1975, Phnom Penh was a city of refugees, many near starvation. Statistics on the total number of refugees are uncertain. The Cambodian government estimated that 2 million people were refugees, out of a total population of 7 million.[38] Others place the figure as high as half the population.[39] Regardless of the exact figure, the country had been devastated by war, malnutrition, and starvation. The people desperately needed peace, security to reconstruct their traditional agricultural economy, and a chance to rebuild their personal lives. When the Khmer Rouge soldiers entered Phnom Penh, many people hoped that they would have the chance to do all these things. Instead, they were about to begin almost four years of rule by the mysterious and deadly Angka, the Khmer Rouge leadership, that would lead to the deaths of hundreds of thousands more people and eventually to invasion by Vietnam and exodus of the survivors to Thailand.

RESPONSIBILITY FOR REFUGEES

Clearly, since the early 1950s, Southeast Asian refugees have been victims of regional and world conflicts. The U.S. involvement in Vietnam was not the start of war in the region, nor was it the first cause of refugee movements, but its actions led to the largest refugee movements in recent Indochina history. Without a doubt, the governments of Indochina have also contributed to the suffering, dislocation, and death of hundreds of thousands of people. Vietnam deliberately forced as many as a quarter million ethnic Chinese to flee to China to escape a series of increasingly repressive measures, and it drove hundreds of thousands of others to risk the dangerous journey by boat to Malaysia, Thailand, the Philippines, or elsewhere in the region. Laos destroyed the remnants of the CIA-supported army, killing thousands and driving others across the border into Thailand. The Khmer Rouge government in Cambodia was guilty of atrocities that the international community recognizes as among the most brutal since World War II. The world's television viewers will not soon forget the scenes of the survivors of Khmer Rouge rule moving in starving bands toward the Thai border. But for Americans, it is important to understand the paradoxical responsibility of the United States both for creating refugees and for providing aid to them. The United States has been linked, for a generation, to Indochinese refugees. Though many Americans would like to forget, or to say that the U.S. responsibility has been fulfilled, the historical record requires that the United States accept both aspects of its responsibilities in Indochina. Because it has resettled nearly 1 million Indochinese, this responsibility continues.

FLIGHT AND RESETTLEMENT DURING THE 1980s

Though the international community, including the United States, has provided asylum and relief to many refugees, the experience of flight, camp life, and resettlement is intensely emotional, terrifying, and traumatic. Most importantly, virtually all refugees undergo a serious crisis of identity as a result of the trauma of flight and the extreme physical and emotional dislocation of resettlement.

The central unifying experience of Indochinese refugees is the feeling of having been involuntarily uprooted, often violently and with little or no preparation, and then placed in a strange and frightening new world under the control of incomprehensible individuals from strange cultures. Like soldiers in the military, refugees have little control over most of the important details of life: choice of food and its preparation, housing, the daily schedule of activities, freedom of movement, and freedom to leave. Thus those newly arrived in refugee camps are frantic to gather information for their survival.[40] Rumors abound, as refugees struggle to anticipate and prepare themselves for their unknown and frightening futures.

But along with all the tension and uncertainty, refugee camps are heavy with boredom. While the trauma of flight is still deep, and uncertainty about the future grows daily, there is little to do but wait. As one mother with three children said, "I hope that when I will be in the U.S., I will feel less sad than now, because I will be very busy." Many refugees can do little except worry about family members left behind.

For many refugees, life in the first-asylum camps is life in a war zone. In an essay written in his cultural orientation class in the Philippines, a Vietnamese man described his arrival on the Malaysian island of Pulau Bidong. "From the distance, I saw many soldiers with guns. They made us fear when our boat came to the wharf. One by one we sat on the wharf like prisoners. A soldier said 'don't move, don't talk if you don't want to be killed.' "

Camps along the Cambodian border with Thailand are occasionally shelled or attacked. The holding centers are filled with terror, daily threats of death by murder or starvation, and loss of virtually every aspect of the traditional Cambodian social system. Before reaching the refugee camps, many saw members of their families tortured, mutilated, and killed. For them, the violence of the border camps is a continuation of years of struggle to survive.

For refugees from Vietnam and Laos, on the other hand, violence and fear of death may be limited to the period of flight from their homelands, though in some cases this lasts weeks or even months. Many Vietnamese hold memories of terrifying hardships on their journeys by boat across the South China Sea. Thang Nhan, a young Vietnamese man in an English class in the Philippines, described his worst memory of what he saw during his journey from Vietnam. "My boat trip began on June 1, 1981, with twenty-nine men and one woman. . . . By June 21, nine people had died and when the bodies were thrown into the sea, they were ravenously eaten by the fish." In recent years, pirates have attacked between one-third and one-half of all boats arriving in Malaysia and Thailand, often raping, kidnapping, and murdering refugees.[41] Even refugees who escaped these attacks without physical injury remain psychologically scarred. In a touching effort to express herself in English, one survivor described the effect of such an attack upon her feelings about humanity.

I beheld the actions of pirates on the Gulf of Thailand, when the men had teared the clothes off body of teen girls and oppress their violation before all of people in the boat. The pirates don't a human being. They enjoyed joking while women feel anxious, pitiable and then they caught three girls to bring [to] their boat while [their mothers] crying and [asking] pardon for loss of child. But pirates didn't have conscience and break into laugh with many person very afraid by bestial[ity] between person by person.

Nearly two years after a pirate attack, another teen-aged girl still remembered vividly their "wild animal faces." Untold numbers of vessels have been sunk, with thousands of lives lost. Starvation and death by dehydration often decimate the bands of refugees' in the boats, with the survivors arriving near death in first-asylum countries. Reports of refugees surviving by eating dead comrades are widespread.[42]

Even before experiencing such terror, many refugees spent long periods imprisoned at home, often ill, at hard labor, and near starvation, isolated for years from family, friends, and normal life. Huynh Nguyen, a former officer in the army of South Vietnam, spent six years in a prison camp. "We ate rice with salt, sometimes we had meat or fish but only 50 grams. . . . We didn't have enough protein and vitamins, but we worked equal two or three man. . . . If I didn't have my family feed me, I think I die." After being released, Huynh, like many former prisoners, was unable to find employment. He tried six times to leave by boat before he successfully reached Malaysia. Another former prisoner said of himself that he survived by "becoming a robot, a hungry and thin robot."

Many refugees, after arriving in countries of asylum, find themselves stuck for years in prison-like conditions with no hope of resettlement. In late 1986, almost one-third of all Vietnamese in refugee camps in Southeast Asia had spent more than three years in the camps, nearly forgotten by the outside world.[43] In the best of circumstances, refugees suffer the petty humiliations of prisoners everywhere: loss of belongings, mandatory haircuts, curfews and confinement to barracks after hours, verbal and physical abuse at the hands of guards, fear of speaking out, and lack of any semblance of due process. As one middle-aged Vietnamese man said of his confinement in the Lantau Island closed camp in Hong Kong, "It is beyond my imagination, really, that we have to flee a Communist country to be detained later in what you call a concentration or closed camp. . . . People in the camp are really detainees. We are treated as criminals."[44] For many, this feeling of betrayal can be expected to remain with them for years to come.

Virtually all refugees, regardless of their circumstances of flight, live through extreme, life-threatening experiences. They try to cope with long-term dislocation and disorientation in refugee camps, and then, if they are fortunate, they try to adjust to new societies and cultures in countries of resettlement. Like soldiers, refugees must develop ways to cope with violence, fear, and extreme inner disorganization. Because their struggles are so similar to those of soldiers, it is not surprising that the coping mechanisms of refugees and U.S. Vietnam veterans are also remarkably similar.

U.S. soldiers in Vietnam used two strategies for coping with the war: many *numbed* themselves, either psychologically or, in some cases, through drugs and alcohol, while others *denied* the psychotic reality around them.[45] This psychic numbing, so essential to survival in extreme circumstances, is found among concentration camp victims, soldiers, and refugees. It is not a numbing of the will to action, for that can lead to death; instead, it is a focusing of resources for the struggle at hand. Will, intelligence, and physical action and response are all directed toward survival. Terrence Des Pres describes this process among World War II concentration camp survivors. "The function of intelligence is not to judge one's chances . . . but to make the most of each day's opportunity for getting through that day, . . . a question of surviving today without thinking too much about tomorrow."[46] Among the soldiers, this focusing of resources normally occurred after one or two heavy engagements in combat. The resulting change involved a transformation of personality, a psychic realignment to the reality of combat. Many veterans report that they became like the walking dead, their normal range of emotions having been blunted, replaced by the overwhelming imperative to remain alive through it all.[47]

When they first arrive in the camps, many refugees exhibit the same kinds of numbing and denial.[48] Their former lives have been destroyed, and their survival depends upon their ability to cope with the dangers and near total disorientation that have characterized their flight and continue in many of the camps themselves. The assault upon their psychic and physical survival requires a drastic sharpening of focus and directing of resources, as well as an ability to refuse to be overcome by the death and terror surrounding them.

Refugees learn that they should trust no one. In many border camps, guards attack individuals, raping women and stealing refugees' meager belongings. Armed gangs often invade camps at night, as the guards retreat to safety rather than risk their lives to defend the refugees. In some camps, competing groups of armed refugees battle for control of trade, territory, or people. Like soldiers in a guerrilla war, refugees in many first-asylum camps live every day with violence, fear, and the possibility of death. Refugees themselves recognize the numbing that results from the terror. One Vietnamese man described people he met in the Pulau Bidong camp in Malaysia. "Many people lived there for a long time. . . . They told me that they were afraid to be a person. They became more and more withdrawn. No smiling."

Even camps without such immediate threats to physical safety create enormous stresses that lead to withdrawal. Refugees have little control over their lives in the camps, and no control over their futures. In fact, until they are accepted for resettlement, refugees have no future beyond camp life and no past to which they can return. As more and more refugees find themselves turned down by every resettlement country, the first-asylum camps gradually fill with people who have no hope at all of leaving. Tension, violence against other refugees, and depression increase as the camp becomes, for many, a prison. Thus the need grows to deny the awful reality of their own circumstances or to numb themselves against its pain. Yet to survive, refugees must clearly understand their situation and accurately determine what they must do. The result may be a numbed, emotionless, yet precise and accurate assessment of their reality. As Thue Lam wrote of her life in the Philippine processing center, "I'm just a Vietnamese refugee whose past was a time of great hardship and difficult decisions, whose present is crowded by emotional distress and anxiety, whose future is full of uncertainties." Those fortunate survivors who are accepted for resettlement escape these conditions, but they quickly discover, like the U.S. soldiers who survived to return home, that their new life in the United States is just as bewildering as the life they left behind. The journey to the United States is a new and equally devastating shock, the beginning of a different struggle for survival.

REFUGEES IN THE UNITED STATES

Like U.S. Vietnam veterans in the 1970s, the refugees suffer from their association with the Vietnam war, which came to embody deep divisions within U.S. society. While some critics point to the war as evidence of the injustice and moral depravity of the United States, others believe it represents weakness, collapse of national will, and a historical failure requiring revenge. Both the veterans and the refugees have sometimes been held responsible for the war and all that it represents.

This reaction by the community compounds the guilt that many refugees feel. Robert Jay Lifton, who has studied survivors of cataclysmic events such as Hiroshima and Nazi concentration camps as well as Vietnam, discovered that survivors feel a powerful bond with those who died and a sense of guilt for having lived. Survivors may also feel as if they have been contaminated by contact with evil.[49] One survivor of a particularly vicious pirate attack said that afterwards those on the boat felt despair because "the death spirit" had "come to the boat." The women who were raped or whose daughters were kidnapped by the pirates feel they have been tainted forever, while the men feel deeply guilty for having been powerless to stop the attacks. The burden of guilt often seriously disrupts family life long after the events have passed. Many refugees wonder why they survived while others died. They may feel responsible for the deaths of others, as if their survival were made possible by those deaths, and so they may come to believe that they, too, should have perished.

Some refugees say that they envy those who, through death, have been freed from the terrible loneliness and struggle of daily life. Tran wrote about her father, who died after six years in a reeducation camp,

I'm very sad to come to Philippines without my pitiful Dad. I hope he's resting somewhere in the sky, not to be involved in the struggle for life here any longer.

Truly I say that I haven't any plans for the future. What do I want to do? What can I do?

Both in refugee camps and in the United States, the suicide rate among Indochinese is higher than among the U.S. population generally. Some refugees die mysteriously, without explanation, in the middle of the night. This phenomenon, called sudden unexpected death syndrome (SUDS), has been linked with the death of more than 80 refugees in the United States since 1975. Among Hmong adult men, SUDS accounts for as high a percentage of death as the four leading causes of natural death combined for American men of the same age group.[50] Thu Le observed in his Philippine cultural orientation class: "All refugee have got a general sadness, to my mind."

Though research on the psychological adjustment of refugees has been less extensive than research on that of veterans, it is clear that many symptoms of posttraumatic stress disorder appear among Indochinese refugees as well.[51] Hyperalertness and extreme startle reactions at sudden noises, fear of the sounds of airplanes, recurrent dreams, and flashbacks have been documented.[52] Researchers and the refugee communities have become increasingly concerned about high rates of depression and more severe forms of psychotic behavior, paranoia, uncharacteristic aggression and hostility, unexpressed grief, failure to maintain good nutrition, and drug abuse among refugees.[53] The feeling of being "vitiated by an evil presence" is experienced by Cambodian survivors as well as Vietnamese boat refugees.[54]

The refugees' first contact with Americans often is with sponsors who try very hard to understand, but cannot comprehend the refugees' experiences or their cultures. Sponsors buy hotdogs at baseball games for newly arrived refugees, or try to teach them how to cook hamburgers, when most refugees want to find an Asian store where they can buy familiar foods. Because of their past experiences with governments and their complete lack of familiarity with their new home, most refugees see the resettlement agencies as hostile bureaucracies. As a result, their behavior may be aggressive and, from the perspective of the agencies, inappropriate, which compounds the refugees' difficulties in interacting with these first Americans.[55]

Many refugees, especially older ones, stay inside their homes for weeks at a time, afraid to go out, unsure what will happen, and unable to speak English. Even those who have the energy and the courage to try to familiarize themselves with their new city or town inevitably feel isolated, lonely, and depressed. The loss of old patterns of living combines with uncertainty about what kinds of behavior are acceptable in the new environment, so many respond by restless searching for something to do. Others develop an unrealistic hope that they will be able to reconstruct their past lives.

I'm very sad because I have no friend with the same age to talk to, to play with. . . . In Saigon, when the holidays come, my friends and I have often so many parties, picnics. And we are very happy. Now I don't know how my friends are, alive or dead. (cries) I miss them. I hope that I will have many new friends as lovely as my old friends.[56]

For those with families, family life may be disrupted in many ways. Often, some family members remain in Indochina. Nguyet described the feeling of loss that came from leaving her daughter behind in Vietnam. "When I have spare time, I like to find a quiet place where I can imagine about my daughter. Then I shed tears." Even families that remain largely intact undergo great stress. In most families, the children usually learn English much more quickly than their parents. As a result, they take on the major responsibility for translation and for contact between the family and U.S. institutions. The children also may adopt U.S. values and patterns of behavior that the parents find offensive: lack of respect for teachers and elderly people, loss of the home religion. So while the children gain great power through their ability to speak English and their familiarity with U.S. society, the adults deeply resent their own loss of authority and the dramatic changes they see taking place within their family.

This change of family organization is part of a larger breakdown in traditional culture, particularly among refugees from rural areas who find themselves living in large U.S. cities. Traditional culture cannot operate as it did in rural Asian villages. In most cases, people have come to the United States without their extended families, so that the support and security of extended family life cannot be reconstituted. Yet many refugees live in areas with a high population of other refugees, so that community pressure in the form of gossip and censure may be exerted on anyone who tries to live outside traditional patterns. Religious belief and organization, an essential part of both individual and group identity in Southeast Asia, also weakens or collapses altogether, particularly among the young. Older adults may try to take measures to reinstitute religious practices, and this often further alienates young people. Overall, the painful paradox is that community structures try to exert traditional authority without being able to provide traditional security.[57]

In traditional Southeast Asian society, women were passed from their fathers to their husbands; widows either remarried or lived with their sons' families. Yet many refugees are women without husbands. Among adult Cambodians in the United States, as many as two-thirds are women; many are widows with children. This puts great pressure on families, as men pay attention to unattached women and married women develop resentments. Males also feel they have lost prestige. They are often unemployed and unable to learn English as quickly as their children, who as a result may have to support them. Their wives may find employment, yet the traditional male role does not permit the husband to care for the children while the wife works. Women have formed support groups and economic cooperatives to market their crafts, deepening the conflict between traditional economic roles and the realities of life in America. Abuse of women and children has grown, becoming a serious problem for the first time in these communities.

Children suffer in other ways as well. As families become inoperative, children become despondent, resentful, unable to feel emotional attachments to others. They may be further isolated by their difficulties in school, due to their inadequate English proficiency and the deep distrust many American students feel for them. Even when there are other refugees at the school, they may feel pressured not to speak their own language, and this effectively isolates them within themselves, as they are unable to communicate with a voice which is truly their own.[58] Children or adolescents facing isolation at school and their child-as-parent role at home may eventually become the "symptom bearers" for the dysfunctional family.[59] Some children, unable to tolerate the pressures of a family whose structure is disintegrating, turn to other children for support. The result in many urban areas is an increasing number of youth gangs, especially among Vietnamese males, and resulting high rates of crime.

The widespread collapse of traditional social structures and economic roles, especially family life and religious practices, results in an extraordinary rate of depression among refugees. One study, by Elizabeth Hiok-Boon Lin, a physician who specializes in health services for refugee communities, found that over 52 percent of Vietnamese refugees were depressed.[60] Although this number is shockingly high, what is even more surprising is that 98 percent of these individuals were diagnosed only after they reported to clinics to complain of physical symptoms such as stomach pain, headaches, and backaches. This is in contrast to Americans, who typically report psychological symptoms such as feeling sad, tired, or unmotivated. The difference is that in Southeast Asian cultures, people do not communicate psychological and social distress directly. In counseling, Southeast Asians often do not feel comfortable talking about their emotional problems. Because they expect physicians and other health care specialists to be expert, they may think that counselors' questions are a sign of incompetence, and therefore mistrust any advice or suggestions for further diagnosis and treatment.

As a result, some health care specialists have begun to recognize that the deep and long-lasting problems within refugees' communities require fundamentally different approaches to mental health from those used with Americans. Innovative approaches include use of traditional healers operating within the refugees' own spiritual and cultural belief systems. Though many refugees benefit from such practices and achieve a reasonable sense of identity and belonging in the United States, long-term psychological and emotional problems are widespread within all Southeast Asian communities.

Because the United States is an adopted home, few Indochinese refugees have deep, personal, or immediate understanding of the culture, the people, or the language around them. Therefore refugees recovering from the trauma and alienation of resettlement face enormous difficulties in satisfying their overpowering human need to find a place where they can belong. For the refugees, the war and its aftermath have meant a permanent loss of home. The danger now is that it may mean a permanent loss of hope as well, for many continue to feel like people who have lost their souls.

In an essay written in the Philippines, Nguyet described her sense of loss. "I have lived sadly and lonely during the period of time in the Malaysian camp and in the PRPC. I very heartbroken because my first daughter is still in Vietnam. I miss my daughter day by day. Now I just meet her in my dream." Nguyet's essay captures the fundamental experience of being a refugee: loss of family, of home, of belonging—of community.

The key to the recovery of a sense of belonging is the reconstruction of community. Indeed, it is no exaggeration to say that human life itself requires community to survive. A true community is more than a group of people with common interests; it is a living organism that seeks to include, that elicits personal commitment from individual members, that seeks to extend itself through consensus, and that provides a safe place, a home.[61]

If Southeast Asians are to truly recover from the trauma of flight and resettlement, they must be able to reconstitute community. The centrality of community to successful resettlement can be seen by the intensity with which refugees express their fear that it is lost forever. Ngo Thi Bich Le, a Vietnamese refugee in Australia, expressed the fear of many that they would live out their lives isolated and alone, never feeling that they belonged. In her essay, written in an English class, she imagined the future of a Vietnamese man who had left his entire family behind in Vietnam.

Day by day he felt he was getting older and time didn't wait for him. During this time his parents died but he didn't know. . . .

Then one day he knew he was going to die and he wrote a letter to send to his parents. . . . He said, "Oh mama and papa, I'm very tired of waiting. I'm very sad, it's the sadness of homesickness. I would like to say to you I love you very, very much. . . . I'll never forget your faces in my life, also I can't wait for you because I'm becoming an old man. Do you understand me? I'll die lonely. Don't give me your tears, but your heart. When I die you won't be here and no one will stand next to me, not even a friend. All of you are far away from me. Oh papa and mama it's raining and I'm crying again. Before I die I wish to have wings and fly back to our home, then I can see you again and my lovely country.

"Mama hold me in your arms again and sing a song just as when I was a little boy; please don't leave me because I need to be in your heart. Oh, my lovely country I'll live down in another country but I can't forget you, the place where I was born and grew up. I would like to say so much to you but . . . oh, my heart will stop working. Mama and papa, my country, my friends please wait for me. . . . I'll come back.''

At last that man died calmly, nobody knew him, there were no tears for him, but he was relieved.[62]

While refugees struggle to reconstruct community, they have not been left totally on their own. Largely unknown to the general public, the federal government operates the overseas education program, an intensive effort designed to prepare refugees for their new lives in the United States. The program recognizes the complexity of the difficulties facing the Southeast Asian refugees. It recognizes that they bring with them traditional patterns of life, assumptions about right and wrong and the nature of human reality, and values and attitudes that differ markedly from those of most Americans. The program attempts to prepare refugees for successful resettlement and adaptation *by changing them*—their patterns of living, their beliefs about what is acceptable and unacceptable behavior, and the social structures in which they operate. Most importantly, the program sets out to change the refugees' values and attitudes toward themselves, their social systems, and the United States. In short, it attempts to change their identity. But in doing so, it undermines their sense of community.

How is this attempt carried out? What are its effects? Does it help the refugees become better adjusted, more able to handle the challenge of a new life in a new culture? How does the program fit into the larger historical process of U.S. involvement in Southeast Asia? The answer to these questions is to be found in the U.S. processing centers in Southeast Asia.

But these centers are not the first attempt to give immigrants to the United States a new identity. In fact, they are part of a tradition that presumes that living successfully in the United States requires "becoming American." That tradition provides the assumptions and principles upon which the current refugee program was founded, and therefore the successes and failures of that tradition are the context in which the current program must be judged.

_____ *3*

Becoming American

These proponents of education who sought to uphold freedom by in-
doctrinating norms of belief in religion, politics, and economics eventually became known as Americanizers. They applied their remedy for
diversity, Americanization education, to nearly all areas of life. Their
quest for doctrinal orthodoxy led them to seek for uniformity in . . .
personal appearance, language, and personal habits. . . . Americanization
education in the interest of liberty thus became, paradoxically, an im-
perious demand for individual conformity to societal norms.

> Robert A. Carlson, *The Quest for Conformity*[1]

I also want to send them a message: When you come to America, I
expect you to behave, to dress like the people around you.

> PET Supervisor, Refugee Processing Center[2]

American ideology professes that the nation expresses its commitment to
community by welcoming oppressed peoples from around the world. The
civic myth of immigrants building America by contributing the best of their
many cultures offers a powerful vision of a country learning from diversity.
This metaphor of America as a "salad bowl," in which different cultures
retain their individuality while combining in a greater whole that protects
diversity, is a vision of true community.

Yet this compelling vision of America-as-community has not been the
basis for most immigrant education programs. Instead, the programs often
further exclusivity and suppress differences by teaching newcomers that
they must adopt "American" attitudes, values, and behaviors if they wish
to fully enter the national life. This approach began with the effort at the
turn of the century to educate European immigrants for successful living
in the United States, and it continues in today's overseas refugee program.

Both programs serve as gatekeepers for the national community by admitting only those who successfully complete a reeducation program designed to change behaviors, values, and attitudes—to help immigrants "become American."

CHANGING PATTERNS OF IMMIGRATION IN THE NINETEENTH CENTURY

Migration of oppressed people has always been at the core of U.S. history and identity. The Statue of Liberty, perhaps the country's most powerful national symbol, welcomes the "huddled masses yearning to breathe free." In 1783, George Washington claimed that the United States would receive the oppressed of all nations.[3] The early colonists encouraged migration in order to open new territories, expand trade, and develop local industries. Though the voyage from Europe was long and arduous, more than a million people made the journey during the period of English colonial rule (1607–1776).[4] After independence, the number of immigrants steadily increased, reaching nearly 3 million during the decade between 1850 and 1860.[5] Although immigration dropped during the period of the Civil War, it recovered quickly to reach over .3 million in 1866 and over .7 million by 1882.

Until the 1880s, the vast majority of the immigrants had been from northern and western Europe. In 1869, for example, over 300,000 arrived from northern and western Europe and only about 5,000 from southern and eastern Europe. In the mid–1880s, however, increasing numbers arrived from southern and eastern Europe. In less than a decade, the traditional pattern of migration almost exclusively from the United Kingdom, Germany, and the Scandinavian countries shifted to equal numbers from Italy, Russia, and the Slavic regions. In 1887, 353,000 immigrants arrived from northern and western Europe and 129,000 from southern and eastern Europe; by 1892, 300,000 from the traditional sources were nearly equalled by 270,000 from southern and eastern countries.[6] The proportion of these new groups rose from less than 10 percent in the early 1880s to over 75 percent by 1907. By 1920, fully one-third of the population consisted of immigrants, children of immigrants, and children with one immigrant parent.[7]

This rapid shift in the source of immigrants brought to the surface long-held concern about the effects of ethnic diversity on the nation's unity and identity. As early as the 1750s, Benjamin Franklin had warned that increasing numbers of German settlers threatened the Anglo character and cohesion of Pennsylvania.[8] Yet the need for settlers to carry out the westward expansion required massive immigration, and so the new country developed a powerful ideology of immigration. The idea of the United States as the asylum for the world was linked to the demand that newcomers leave behind the inferior ways of the Old World, adopting instead the principles and practices of the New World. There was little room within this ideology for ethnic enclaves that would threaten the unity and stability of the new nation.

This ideology of immigration had always included a powerful discourse of immigration and Americanization. "Ethnic diversity" was to be avoided, and instead "Constitution," "Protestantism," "nation," "race," and the "American language" became central symbols in the public debate.[9] The early and mid-nineteenth century saw protracted battles about the use of languages other than English in U.S. public schools, especially in cities such as St. Louis, where Germans constituted a quarter of the population, and in the industrial cities of the Midwest. In Chicago German-language instruction began in 1865, while in Milwaukee more than half the students in city schools studied German.[10] Yet the pressure to "become American" was so great that supporters of German-language instruction felt obliged to argue that it would encourage German families to send their children to public schools rather than to ethnic German private schools.[11] Like most immigrant enclaves, these German communities publicly acknowledged their commitment to shake off the old ways and adopt the new.

In the latter third of the nineteenth century, the growth in the population of immigrants from southern and eastern Europe led to a major escalation in public debate and concern about the effects of immigration on U.S. society. The reason for this escalation was that the new immigrants were perceived as being significantly different from the old ones—and inferior. Unlike immigrants from Great Britain, they did not speak English or come from countries having long democratic traditions. Unlike the skilled immigrants from Germany and Scandinavia, they were generally peasant farmers, often without formal education, Catholic rather than Protestant. They were perceived as having come from inferior cultural backgrounds, with little to contribute to the still-evolving American culture. Writing in 1888, the English historian James Bryce conveyed the concern that many Americans had for the new immigrants.

These immigrants . . . come from a lower stratum of civilization . . . and, since they speak foreign tongues, are less quickly amenable to American influences. . . . There seems to be some danger that if they continue to come in large numbers they may retain their own low standard of decency and comfort, and menace the continuance among the working class generally of that far higher standard which has hitherto prevailed in all but a few spots in the country.[12]

Such public concern about the new immigrants was expressed in a growing belief during the first century of the country's existence that there was an increasingly unified, well defined American character, distinctly not European, but better. Though most Americans would have had difficulty describing this new national character, they were sure that the new immigrants were a threat *because they were different*. They spoke strange languages, wore different clothing, and had different customs from the earlier immigrants. They were Italians, Poles, Greeks, Czechs, Ukrainians, Armenians, Slovaks, and eastern European Jews. The tremendous public concern about the effects of these immigrants showed that the assumed underlying American identity included patterns of language, custom and dress, religion, and standard of living. It was not that the "old stock" of Americans required conformity in all these aspects, at least not in the 1880s. Rather, they feared anyone who was too different. Because the new immigrants were seen as threatening their standard of living and their culture, they believed that something had to be done to protect the nation's wealth and emerging identity. Too much diversity was perceived to be the problem. And so the solution was to do something about difference.

The response to the new immigrants was the Americanization movement, which began in the 1880s and continued until severe restrictions on immigration were instituted in the early 1920s. This was the first nationwide attempt to enlist the educational system in a coordinated effort to prepare immigrants for living in the United States by changing their behavior, their values, and their attitudes. It was the precursor of the U.S. refugee program and the source of many contemporary assumptions about the role of education in limiting the impact of immigration on the national identity. Whereas earlier immigrants were generally thought to be capable of making important contributions to the economy *and* to the evolving national character, these new immigrants were seen as threatening that character, and so they had to change who they were in order to reduce their threat to the nation. In striking similarity, today's refugee program emphasizes the differences between Indochinese refugees and past immigrants and claims that, as a result of these differences, special programs to prepare refugees for American life must focus on changing their behavior, their values, and their attitudes.

THE AMERICANIZATION MOVEMENT

The Americanization movement was not initially a highly coordinated and centralized effort. Instead, it began as a series of distinct and localized responses to the widespread feeling of being menaced by the new immigrants.[13] Local school boards, churches and church schools, city councils and state legislatures, and private industries began programs to teach immigrants the English language, as well as a variety of subjects designed to "Americanize" them: patriotic songs and stories, ways of borrowing money, voting and election procedures, workplace rules, even the American way to brush one's teeth and make one's bed. One program taught immigrants to prepare "American vegetables instead of the inevitable cabbage."[14] By 1918, a National Americanization Day Committee survey of agencies and groups involved in Americanization education included 1,100 chambers of commerce; 2,350 trade organizations; 48 state councils of defense; 295 national, "racial," patriotic, immigrant, and philanthropic societies; 50 national religious societies; 1,070 newspapers; 5,270 superintendents of schools; and 269 railroads.[15]

As the federal government and big business became involved, these programs became increasingly well coordinated and their content increasingly standardized. Three related developments contributed to the centralization of the Americanization movement. One was the fear among industrial leaders that the new immigrants would be "radicalized" and might contribute to the fledgling labor union movement or to leftist political organizations. To a large degree, the Americanization movement became an attempt by chambers of commerce and other business-oriented organizations to channel immigrants away from organized labor. To this end, labor organizations were gradually excluded from participation in Americanization classes.[16] Later, the revolution in Russia added to the fear of foreign elements and drove the Americanization movement further to the political right. Frances Kellor, the leading propagandist of the movement and the founder of the Americanization Day Committee, convinced many business leaders that plant harmony and increased production and profitability resulted from "100 percent Americanism" among employees.[17] Articles in trade magazines also gave advice to managers on how to Americanize employees. In factories, harsh lectures were given to employees who did not speak English. Gradually, the gauge of an employee's degree of Americanization became use of English on the job.

But the Americanization movement was not only the political response of business and industry to the growing socialist and labor-union movements. It was a response as well to a second development: increased awareness of conflict in Europe and the threat of war. In the last half of the nineteenth century, the debate about the relationship between ethnicity and nationhood had been intense on both sides of the Atlantic. Ethnic communities in Europe had begun to clamor for recognition of their national rights, a process that culminated in the breakup of the Austro-Hungarian Empire and the formation of the ethnic states of the post-war period. The assumption that ethnicity was a legitimate basis for claims to nationhood meant that ethnic diversity was to be feared as a potential cause of national disintegration. It was widely feared that ethnic communities would have split loyalties between their old countries and the United States. In the event of war, they could not be trusted.

With the outbreak of World War I, ethnic communities in general and German communities in particular were subjected to intense pressure to prove they were fully Americanized. One lasting result was that the public schools were given major responsibility for weakening ethnic loyalties and ensuring that children became fully Americanized. Schools began to give grades not only for classwork but also for "citizenship." Just as workers' use of English became the measure of their Americanization, so childrens' classroom behavior became a measure of their level of citizenship and their dedication to the U.S. national community.[18] By the early 1920s, it was widely assumed that the educational system should play a significant role in weakening ethnic loyalty and in Americanizing immigrants. This assumption is at the heart of today's refugee education program.

The third development contributing to the Americanization movement in education was the modern language movement of the 1880s. Until the mid-nineteenth century, formal language study was valued primarily as a mental discipline. Language courses—often Latin or classical Greek—emphasized logic and rhetoric. The increase in school and college enrollment, the rise of elective courses, and the popular notion that the purpose of education is to produce practical professionals rather than to preserve high culture, shifted the emphasis in language study toward the practical value of modern languages.[19] Organizations dedicated to the formal and practical study of modern languages were formed in the 1870s and 1880s. The most important of these, the Modern Language Association, established in 1883, today is the largest professional association of language educators.

This new concern for formal study of modern languages led to an important distinction in American attitudes towards language study. Studying the languages of immigrants and ethnic communities came to be seen as a way to preserve ethnic diversity, and thus was dangerous and had to be discouraged. The central task of educational programs for immigrants, therefore, was to teach English as the key to developing loyalty to the United States. On the other hand, studying foreign languages as subjects in school came to be seen as a means of developing a practical skill that was useful for national development and that would not threaten national integration.[20] This distinction became the enduring basis for efforts to restrict the study of immigrants' languages while expanding the teaching of foreign languages to native English speakers.

The Americanization movement thus is one source of today's ambivalent attitude toward language study. Programs that teach immigrants' languages ("bilingual education") are viewed as compensatory programs designed to remedy social problems or as radical efforts to preserve ethnic diversity, while foreign language education is associated with academic pursuits and higher education. Immigrants' languages and bilingual education are seen as concerns of local communities and therefore as sources of national divisiveness, while foreign languages represent global concerns, national security, and international trade.[21]

But the Americanization movement was not simply a language teaching program. Rather, teaching English was part of a broad effort to develop in immigrants a truly American character. Indeed, one of the most important effects of the Americanization movement is that it formalized the belief that there is a unified American character and a fully developed national community, with one language. The most explicit statement of this belief was the important 42-volume report issued in 1911 by the U.S. Immigration Commission, headed by Senator William Dillingham.[22]

THE DILLINGHAM COMMISSION

The Dillingham Commission report, published after more than three years of hearings and meetings, concluded that the American tradition did not permit foreign enclaves and that cultural assimilation of new immigrants was the key to national unity and to material wealth. The report emphasized that immigration policy should ensure rapid assimilation of new immigrants. It recommended that groups that do not easily assimilate, such as single men who intend to return to their homelands, should be barred from entering the United States, while immigrants with young children who would attend the public schools should be welcomed because they assimilate more quickly. The report argued that immigration policy should become increasingly exclusive and that educational programs for immigrants should play a central role in limiting and reducing cultural and linguistic differences within the national community. The Dillingham Commission report was the culminating expression of the view of the relationship between immigration and national identity that had evolved from 1880 to 1910. Official policy would thereafter reflect a belief that the American character was fully formed and intact, and that future immigration should be regulated so that the cohesiveness of the community was not threatened.

To this end, the Dillingham Commission made several recommendations. It supported continued restriction of immigrants from Asia under the Chinese Exclusion Act of 1882, on the grounds that Asian immigrants had shown, by their continued distinctiveness, that they did not intend to become Americans. The commission recommended adoption of a literacy test as a prerequisite to entry, on the grounds that literate immigrants would more quickly assimilate. This recommendation was enacted by Congress over President Wilson's veto in 1917. The commission also supported immigration quotas by race, which were enacted in the 1920s.

But the most striking indication of the importance that the commission gave to assimilation was its excitement over research conducted by Franz Boas of Columbia University. At the request of the commission, Boas had studied whether children of immigrants exhibited the physical characteristics of their parents. On the basis of preliminary findings, he claimed that major changes in physical appearance took place in the first generation of immigrants' offspring. This meant, he believed, that social and cultural assimilation led to physical assimilation as well. The commission excitedly suggested that this was a "discovery . . . that is fundamental in importance . . . [with] children born not more than a few years after the arrival of the immigrant parents in America developing in such a way that they differ in [physical] type essentially from their foreign-born parents." The commission suggested that America alone was uniquely capable of bringing about such rapid and complete changes in immigrant communities. "Even racial physical characteristics do not survive under the new social and climatic environment of America." The commission chose to end its 21-page conclusion by praising this line of research: "The investigation has awakened the liveliest interest in scientific circles here and abroad, and as the subject is of great importance the commission expresses strongly the hope that . . . the work may be continued."[23]

The Dillingham Commission, for its time, was not crudely racist or isolationist in its views; indeed, it was considered a moderate and highly respected group. It consisted of three U.S. senators, three representatives, and three members appointed by the president.[24] Its emphasis on social, cultural, and physical assimilation reflected the popular notion of the time that assimilation was a natural and desirable process reflecting the unique power of U.S. democracy. In 1901, the sociologist Sarah Simons, for instance, had distinguished American "democratic" assimilation from repressive European "aristocratic" assimilation, such as the tsars' Russification programs.[25] Like most Americans, Simons believed that assimilation involved the creation of a new and improved American character: free, democratic, rational, hard working, and self-sufficient. Assimilation meant the loss of undesirable Old World qualities of character: hierarchy and privilege, laziness, lack of self-reliance, and dependency. The members of the Dillingham Commission believed in the natural power of the American democracy to bring about assimilation, but they feared that the huge numbers of "different" immigrants from southern and eastern Europe might overwhelm the population of old immigrants and "native-born" Americans, thereby changing the American character for the worse. The commission was not the first group to view cultural difference as a source of disunity, disintegration, and national weakness, but its report was a landmark because it ensured that official U.S. policy would resist diversity and encourage rapid cultural and linguistic assimilation. By its recommendations, the commission made sure that the country's dominant institutions did not take any chances.

The Dillingham Commission report also enshrined important changes in the educational system that had begun to be made in the 1880s. The commission praised the work of civic, religious, and educational institutions that promoted assimilation by teaching immigrants "the duties and privileges of American citizenship and civilization."[26] In particular, the commission saw a close connection between teaching English and developing desirable American traits of character and citizenship. "Teaching the English language . . . is a primary feature in most of this work."[27] Speaking English symbolized belief in the "democratic" values immigrants were expected to adopt and a commitment to "becoming American." Learning English became a rite of passage for acceptance into the American community. Literacy tests to screen prospective immigrants conveyed the fundamental importance the nation placed upon language. After 1911, failure to learn English would be un-American.

The content of Americanization classes was not, however, limited to language and citizenship lessons. Many programs were designed to teach vocational skills as well, reflecting the role of the movement in serving the needs of burgeoning U.S. industry. But the spread of vocational training for immigrants meant that many immigrant children had little opportunity for a well-rounded education. Often, foreign-born children were automatically placed in vocational classes, a kind of tracking that ensured that the immigrants would be at the bottom rung of a two-tiered educational system. In many school districts today, English as a second language (ESL) classes play a similar role in tracking refugee children into a subordinate curriculum.[28]

Many schools encouraged immigrant students to earn high school diplomas while working long hours at factories, often for a substandard salary. At one school in Beverly, Massachusetts, for example, students spent 25 weeks of the 50-week term working 50-hour weeks in the Union Shoe Company, the largest employer in town. The students were paid about one-fourth the salary of other workers, and half their salary was withheld to pay for the company's expenses in cooperating with the local high school. The students had to spend four years in this program to qualify for regular employment in the company. Thus the company was given four years of work at exceptionally low wages under the guise of an educational program.[29]

As the movement spread in the 1890s, many factories throughout the country established their own Americanization classes, requiring foreign-born workers to attend during their lunch breaks and after work. As the factories played an increasingly important role in determining program content, many Americanization classes taught immigrants to serve the interests of their employers. Perhaps the most important example of the role of industry in determining the content of Americanization classes is the work of Peter Roberts for the YMCA.

PETER ROBERTS AND THE CONTENT OF AMERICANIZATION CLASSES

Roberts was an educator who developed what came to be called the Roberts Method of Teaching English. As an employee of the YMCA, which played a major role in developing Americanization courses, Roberts became a renowned leader in industrial education, and his method is still recognized as one of the most important in the early history of formal ESL teaching in the United States. Many large corporations, such as U.S. Steel and International Harvester, hired Roberts and the YMCA to set up English programs tailor-made for their companies.

Roberts divided his lessons into three series: domestic lessons, which focused on household matters such as cooking and cleaning; industrial lessons, which focused on searching for a job and on-the-job behavior, including safety; and commercial lessons, which focused on shopping, buying stamps and train tickets, banking, and other activities.[30] His stated goal was to build lessons on the daily experience of immigrants in order to best meet their practical language needs. For instance, the first lesson of the domestic series focused on waking up. In class, Roberts acted out the sentences, dressing and undressing himself as he spoke the lines:

> I awake from sleep. . . .
> I look for my watch. . . .
> It is six o'clock.
> I must get up. . . .
> I put on my pants. . . .
> I wash myself.
> I comb my hair.
> I put on my collar and necktie.
> I put on my vest and coat.[31]

Lessons typically proceeded in this fashion, with the language being connected to explicit, observable behavior. Other lessons in the domestic series were based on similar common, everyday experiences: getting wood to light the fire, lighting the fire, preparing breakfast, using table utensils, eating breakfast, washing oneself, and welcoming a visitor.

To be sure, Roberts's purpose was not only to teach English, but also to teach proper American behavior. The industrial series, for example, included lessons on shining one's shoes, the message being that shined shoes are essential in the American workplace. Many lessons gave practical advice on unfamiliar topics. In one dialogue, students heard about the legal steps involved in purchasing property and building a house.

A. In transferring the property, what was necessary?

B. I secured a lawyer to look up the title in order to see that the property had no encumbrances.

A. What then was necessary?

B. When the deed was delivered to me, I took it to the Court House to have it properly registered.

A. What is the process of registering a deed?

B. You take it to the clerk in the office of Register of Deeds, leave it with him for a week or ten days and then call for it again. . . .

A. How do you proceed in the matter of building a house?

B. I first find out what kind of house I need, then ask some contractor to bid upon the plans.[32]

In such lessons, students learned the importance of following legal and bureaucratic procedures. They also learned that, in the modern economy, individuals depend upon the marketplace to satisfy their needs. Unlike the Old World, Americans do not build their own houses with the help of friends; they hire a contractor.

Today, ESL teachers accept as common practice the attempt to base lessons on their perception of students' daily lives, but in the early twentieth century, Roberts's approach was revolutionary. Earlier language education had emphasized academic study of grammar rules and literary texts. Lessons focusing on the daily life and language of poor immigrants reflected a new respect for the practical value of learning everyday spoken English. The goal, according to Roberts, was to meet the everyday needs of immigrants.[33]

In practice, however, many of Roberts's lessons were designed to meet the needs of employers, particularly when the lessons were developed for specific companies. The program for U.S. Steel, for instance, taught immigrants to obey company rules. A typical lesson included the following sentences for practice:

I go to the Mill to start work. . . .
I go to the clock. . . .
The clock shows the time I start to work.
I see a sign on the clock house.
It reads "I must know the safety rules."
I think of the little rule book.
It was given at the Employment Office.
I must read the rule book.[34]

Roberts also taught employees to obey supervisors, to purchase goods at company stores, and to buy on credit. His lessons did not attempt to teach critical thinking, but rather were intended to teach immigrants the proper behavior on the job. As companies came to be the dominant source of funding for Americanization classes, proper behavior often came to be identified with company rules. As a result, many factory officials and industrial leaders praised the Roberts Method for its positive effect on workers' productivity and plant operations.[35]

Nowhere were company interests more clearly expressed than in lessons about safety and job supervisors. Lessons about safety only partly expressed a concern for the welfare of workers. They were also designed to absolve companies of responsibility for industrial accidents. For instance, the widely used federal citizenship textbook, developed by the Bureau of Naturalization and based upon Roberts's approach, included the following lesson entitled "Careless James."

James worked on a machine in the factory. This machine had a small circular saw. A safeguard was over the saw. One day this safeguard was broken. A part fell off. James knew it. He did not tell the overseer. He thought he would be careful. . . .

James was careful for two days. Then . . . he slipped and fell across the small saw.

It cut into his clothes . . . James was cut. He was not badly hurt . . . but James was badly frightened.

"I'm glad my hand did not touch that saw," he said. "I am to blame for the accident. I did not report the broken guard. The rules say I should. The company was not to blame. I was careless."[36]

Though the stated aim of the lesson was to teach English, the implied message was that workers' carelessness was the main reason for industrial injuries. The implied message would have been quite different if James's injury had been due to company neglect in maintaining its equipment.

The federal citizenship textbook also taught workers to respect and obey the plant supervisor. In the following lesson, titled "The Foreman," the plant was depicted as one link in a production line that must not be disrupted.

The foreman comes into the room. He says "Good morning, boys."

"Good morning Mr. Smith," they answer.

He stops to look at the work. He knows how to do the work himself. He knows good work. He knows poor work. The factory must turn out only good work.

He says to George, "Let me show you how to do this. You are not doing it right."

George does not get cross. He watches the foreman. He sees how the foreman does it. Now he tries again. This time the work is right. . . .

The foreman goes down the room. He knows the good workers. He knows the poor ones. He is willing to help the workers. He can not keep careless people. There is much to be done in a factory. This work goes to the next room. The foreman must send only good work. It must be ready in time.

Be good natured with everybody in the factory. Keep busy. It does not pay to get cross.[37]

The foreman was like a father, with the power to see into the workers' souls to know whether they were "good" workers or "bad." The foreman had the ability to guide workers, to teach them what they needed to know, and he had the authority to pass judgment on them if they failed to meet his standards. In this lesson, the workers learned that they must do what the foreman says, for to do otherwise "does not pay." The foreman's name indicated that he was not an immigrant.

Such lessons were designed to encourage workers to comply with company policy and line of command. Union organizers had no place in company programs or in classes using the federal textbook. In this way, Americanization classes supported the interests of the private industries that funded and organized them.

But the stated aim of Americanization classes was not to serve the interests of industry. Rather, it was to teach immigrants to meet the demands of citizenship. Students were taught to work hard, comply with government and company policies, and adopt proper American behavior because that was what good citizens did. Materials used in teacher training programs emphasized the importance of teachers' attitudes in inspiring immigrants' allegiance to this "practical citizenship." For instance, widely used teacher training materials prepared for Colorado schools included the following admonition:

No simple rule can be set whereby proper attitudes can be inculcated. The first concern of the teacher should be that he, himself, has the right attitude. Then he may turn to the task of inspiring others with the sentiments that are a part of him. . . . when he approaches the subject of patriotism and the duties of the patriot, he should put renewed vigor into his presentation. . . . The immigrant is very impressionable.[38]

Students were taught that hard work was their civic duty. They "should be led to feel that the duties of the worthy citizen in times of peace are as definite as his duties in times of war. The citizen who idly disregards his duties in time of peace is a slacker."[39]

Most supporters of the Americanization movement were proud that the Dillingham Commission had praised their "practical efforts calculated to promote the well-being and advancement of the immigrant."[40] They sincerely believed that they worked on behalf of the immigrants themselves and genuinely expected the immigrants to reap many benefits. For instance, teaching English was expected to reduce mental retardation in immigrant families[41] and to significantly reduce injuries on the job.[42] Immigrants would be happier, and social problems such as crime and alcoholism would be eliminated, if the immigrants cast aside the old ways to become American. Proper character formation among immigrants was expected to solve social problems and ensure the economic success of immigrants as well as of American society in general.

EDUCATION AND SOCIAL JUSTICE

The Americanization movement also sought to aid established institutions and native-born Americans by reducing the chance that immigrants would change power relationships in American society. The movement did not attempt to relieve the misery of immigrants by bringing about social justice, but instead it tried to manipulate their psychic well-being. Rather than confront sources of inequality that ensured that Mr. Smith, the foreman, had complete control over his immigrant employees, the Americanization movement taught workers to willingly accept their position and to appreciate the importance of their work in the expanding industrial machine. Thus the movement taught immigrants to seek an accommodation with the existing social and economic order. The historian Jackson Lears summarizes this view of education at that time: "If only the proper educational balance could be struck, immigrants could be assimilated, angry workers calmed, and an incipient leisure class returned to productive life."[43] Nowhere was this belief in the power of education more clearly expressed than in the work of Jane Addams and Ellen Gates Starr, who pioneered immigrant education at Hull House in Chicago.

Addams and Starr were deeply concerned about the growing alienation of labor. Involved in the Chicago Arts and Crafts Society, founded in 1897, they sought to revitalize art through the transformation of work. In an essay "Art and Labor," published in 1895, Starr argued for "the freeing of the art power of the whole nation and race by enabling them to work in gladness and not in woe."[44] In her well known *Twenty Years at Hull House*, Addams wrote moving accounts of the crushing tedium of factory work and the social problems among immigrants that resulted from it.[45]

Neither Starr nor Addams, however, supported restructuring U.S. industry and labor. Nor did they support what they considered to be radical attacks against industrialism. Instead, they favored what Lears has called the "therapeutic approach" to education: The social and psychological problems of laborers are best solved through education, which helps them to change their attitudes toward their work. Addams argued that, by recognizing the historic national importance of their jobs, workers would see themselves as key links in the development of U.S. industry.

If a child goes into a sewing factory with a knowledge of the work she is doing in relation to the finished product, if she is informed concerning the material she is manipulating and the processes to which it is subjected; if she understands the design she is elaborating in its historic relation to art and decoration, her daily life is lifted from drudgery to one of self-conscious activity, and her pleasure and intelligence is registered in her product.[46]

Addams and Starr believed deeply that education could end the misery they saw in immigrants' communities in Chicago. But their belief in the power of education to change personal experience led them to reject the progressive goals of economic reform and social justice. The immigrants' tremendous social problems were not due to the nature of their work nor to the industrial system that required cheap manual labor. Their problems were in their heads. And so the solution to their problems was to change their way of thinking.

Education designed to change immigrants' attitude towards their work required nothing of industry other than support for classes in Americanization. By and large, these classes furthered immigrants' accommodation to modern industrial capitalism by building into the American ideology of education the assumption that the immigrants' massive social problems—poverty, unemployment, malnutrition, and poor health—resulted from their cultures, their languages, and their personal qualities of character. Children were retarded because their parents did not speak English, and so the industrial cities of the East and Midwest were absolved of responsibility for the health and nutrition of immigrant families. Workers were injured on the job because they did not speak English, and so factory owners were absolved of responsibility for creating safe working environments. The issue was not social justice, but whether immigrants accepted their lot in life. It was the role of education to teach them that acceptance. Americanization teachers were exhorted that the student

should be taught the dignity of labor, for it is in the ranks of labor that he is probably best adapted to serve society. It should be explained to him that "equality" discards all thought of inferior and superior occupations. Our national security depends on the contentment of our citizenry. If the least incentive toward contentment can be given in the classroom, the opportunity to give it should not be passed by.[47]

The national security rested upon immigrants' acceptance of their role in the industrialization of America. This acceptance depended upon education, which effectively taught immigrants to accept their menial jobs without complaint. So Addams claimed, "A man who makes, year after year, but one small wheel in a modern watch factory, may, if his education has properly prepared him, have a fuller life than did the old watchmaker who made a watch from beginning to end."[48]

NEW VALUES

It would be an oversimplification to see the Americanization movement merely as a deliberate attempt to indoctrinate a docile workforce. Sincere efforts, such as those of Addams and Starr, to aid immigrants in their search for personal accommodation with industrial society contributed to the formation of new values and beliefs that helped to shape twentieth-century culture. These new values and beliefs were expressed in and transmitted through the Americanization movement. Gradually, they came to compete with traditional culture in the immigrant communities, and eventually they inspired allegiance among immigrants and native-born Americans alike.

The new values and beliefs evolved from the enormous changes in American culture taking place at the turn of the century. As the remnants of the nineteenth-century moral order, based upon religious authority in agrarian societies, gave way to twentieth-century urban industrial agnosticism, Americans struggled to sustain an individual sense of purpose and morality. The modern morality that emerged from this turmoil was both highly individualistic and bureaucratic. Its most central component, taught in all Americanization classes, was a new perception of time.[49]

The colloquial phrase "to be on time" did not appear until the 1870s. The concern with "being on time" that the phrase expressed was an outgrowth of the demands of industrial capitalism in the second half of the nineteenth century. Factories and bureaucracies operated with rigid time schedules that demanded disciplined personal schedules. To satisfy the requirements of work, Americans became increasingly sensitive to the movement of the clock. With the spread of the time clock after 1890, workers learned that their wages depended upon personal commitment to precision timing. The assembly line demanded that natural processes, such as going to the bathroom, be regulated according to the clock. Although immigrant workers often resisted, with the spread of modern industrial factories, the triumph of the time clock, and of clock time, was assured.

Factories that ran "like clockwork" increased production, and thus the ability of individuals to conform to the demands of the clock ensured industrial growth and material progress. But being "on time" required discipline, and so meant even more than increased material well-being; it meant moral progress as well. The basis for this equation of material and moral progress was the emerging conception of the disciplined, self-sufficient, autonomous individual.

The end of the nineteenth century brought the end of the traditional sources of morality: religion, royalty, and clan. But social order was threatened by the spreading market economy and its principle that material progress was a natural result of competition among individuals seeking to improve their own material conditions. Without external forms of moral authority, individual amorality seemed to be all that was left. Therefore a powerful ethic of self-control evolved, which historians have called the Victorian superego.[50] External forms of control, symbolized by the time clock, were extended into the individual's inner life. The autonomous individual became the ideal, in control of time, emotion, thought, and passion. The esteem accorded to the new industrial leaders, the "self-made men" who built the giant industrial companies of the early twentieth century, represented the triumph of this ideal in the popular culture. Anyone could "make it," it was claimed, if they had the inner drive, the determination, and the dedication that comes from total self-control.

This optimistic belief that material success was intimately connected to moral principles of self-control required a denial of the contradictions of modern industrial society. The belief in progress, in harmony resulting from unbridled competition, and in social justice as an inevitable outgrowth of industrial development could be sustained only by denying the obvious:

that millions of wretchedly poor people were working themselves literally to death without enjoying the benefits of material progress, that industrial development required masses of laborers working at minimal wage, and that social justice was no natural result of economic growth. Moreover the ideal of the autonomous individual could be sustained only by denying the awesome dehumanizing power of the urban marketplace, the industrial factory, and the modern bureaucracy. Major life decisions—what occupation to take up; how many children to have; whether to stay with one's family or move alone to a distant city to find work—became increasingly dependent upon circumstances largely beyond the control of individuals. Immigrants who in the old country had had the skills to supply virtually all of their basic needs, including shelter, food, and clothing, found themselves in an urban marketplace in which they were dependent upon those who paid their meager salaries. And so individual independence and self-sufficiency were increasingly undermined, precisely as the myth of the self-sufficient individual came to dominate modern secular morality. The denial of the brutalities of modern industrial society through blind faith in the power of individuals to triumph over the misery of poverty is at the core of twentieth-century success ideology.

Historians have long recognized the tendency of Victorian moralists to equate material and spiritual progress. This underlying belief persists in our contemporary notion of "self-sufficiency," which evolved from turn-of-the-century success ideology and continues as the moral foundation for modern capitalism. The modern ideal is the self-sufficient individual who needs no government handout, no extended family or clan, the "self-made" person who succeeds through relentless hard work and the ability to produce what the public needs. To be sure, the ideal is more visionary than real, yet the power of the ideal is such that the shared anger of the culture is directed at anyone who is perceived as having violated it: "welfare cheats"; those who succeed through bribes, payoffs, or family connections; and anyone who benefits from the un-American principle that "it's who you know, not what you know that matters." With the triumph of individual success ideology, loyalty to America came to mean loyalty to the ideal of the autonomous individual. This loyalty is at the foundation of the contemporary moral principle of self-sufficiency.

Modern concern with time focuses on efficiency: "time is money," don't "waste" time, be careful how you "spend" time. Preindustrial societies simply passed time, but out of time passed together came the historical connections that are the basis for community. The triumph of individual success ideology required the destruction of ties of blood, kin, and history, the bonds of community. But immigrants from southern and eastern Europe had brought with them their ties of historical community, which threatened industrial capitalism by competing with the emerging ideal of the autonomous individual. By seeking to replace ethnic loyalties with loyalty to

American ideals (which increasingly meant the ideal of the autonomous, self-sufficient individual), the Americanization movement in education sought to undermine traditional communities. The emphasis on learning English in the schools and using it on the job was at the core of this process.

While speaking English was the symbol of becoming American, immigrants' native languages were the glue of their traditional communities. English may have been an efficient tool for commerce and business, but Italian, Czech, and Polish represented the blood connections of history, so many immigrants resisted the Americanization movement. Some believed that speaking English led to a loss of tradition and faith, and so they sought to protect their religions by preserving their native languages. Some Catholics, for instance, opposed English-language schools on the grounds that children who learned English became alienated from Catholicism.[51] But the pressures to speak English were enormous, and so also were the pressures to trade a morality based upon historical community for the new morality of individual self-sufficiency.

The morality of self-sufficiency did not offer simply a banal optimism founded on denial of industrial reality. In its insistence that material and moral success were inseparable, the ideology of self-sufficiency was brutally unforgiving. To immigrants who failed to succeed materially, it could turn only the harsh face of indifference. If individual hard work, conducted in English, led naturally to material well being, then material suffering had to be due to a failure to adopt the language and the new American morality of self-sufficiency. Anyone languishing in the impoverished ethnic enclaves of the East and Midwest must be guilty of refusing to become American. In other words, cultural assimilation was more than a practical advantage; it was a moral imperative as well. The punishment for those who failed to assimilate was material and immediate: They were condemned to the ghettos of America's industrial cities.

The Americanization movement was not the only way in which the new morality of individual self-sufficiency was spread through immigrant communities, nor was it the only basis for the accommodation with modern industrial capitalism that ethnic communities had achieved by around 1920. But for our purposes, the Americanization movement was of profound importance for two reasons. First, it defined a new role for the educational system: to teach immigrants to "become American." The specific meaning of "becoming American" would change through the decades, and the system of immigrant education would have to adapt to these changes. But this essential function of immigrant education would remain unchanged. Second, the Americanization movement enshrined as the central components in the curriculum of immigrant education programs the fundamental cultural principle of bureaucratic-industrial time and the enduring moral principle of individual self-sufficiency. Since 1920, educators of immigrants to the United States have assumed, largely unconsciously, that their task is to transmit these principles of the dominant culture.

CHANGING CONCEPTIONS OF "BECOMING AMERICAN"

Continuing the tradition begun by the Americanization movement, today's Indochinese refugee program furthers the enduring belief that refugees' ability to solve their social, psychological, physical, and economic problems is directly related to their degree of cultural assimilation. That is, the program assumes that refugees' resettlement difficulties are a result of their cultural differences from "Americans." The program assumes that they must change who they are if they are to overcome their difficulties in the United States. The task set for the educational system is to bring about this change in individual and group identity. As in the Americanization movement, the central feature in this process of assimilation is the moral imperative of self-sufficiency.

But it would be oversimplifying to suggest that the refugee program merely repeats the aims and practices of the Americanization movement, as changes in U.S. society since 1920 have resulted in important changes in the conception of what it means to be an American. While the Americanization movement stressed good citizenship (voting, George Washington and Abraham Lincoln, national holidays, and picnicking on the 4th of July), the refugee program stresses the need to be a good consumer. Immigrants in Americanization classes proved their patriotism by reciting the Pledge of Allegiance; Indochinese refugees prove their patriotism by reading want ads, buying at volume discounts, knowing about unit pricing and the advantages of supermarkets, and paying their rent on time. While the Americanization movement emphasized traditional citizenship as the price of joining the community, the refugee program emphasizes *functional citizenship*, the ability to become a consumer in the consumer economy.

Mary McGroarty, a scholar who has studied the history of immigrant education, has traced this change in ESL textbooks for immigrants during this century. McGroarty found that texts published just after the end of World War I promoted civic responsibility as a major goal of assimilation.[52] Dialogues included lessons such as "What is the State? The people are the State." Students were taught to make American sandwiches and pies and to adopt patriotic symbols such as the flag. In contrast, current ESL texts rarely include such explicit lessons in civic responsibility, but focus instead on the ethos of the consumer society. Rather than didactic patriotism, texts teach economic patriotism—the importance of proper market behavior and of accepting the principle of starting at the bottom on the employment ladder. Yet the lessons are often oversimplified, reflecting a distorted vision of immigrants' living conditions. For instance, the following dialogue from a survival English text fails to capture the difficulties many refugees experience in obtaining credit:

A. How can I get a loan?

B. Why do you want the money?

A. To buy a car.

B. How much money do you need?

A. $2,000.00

B. Please fill out this application.

A. When do I get the money?

B. Next week.[53]

While the change in focus in ESL texts since the early twentieth century reflects the shift from an industrial to a consumer society, it also reveals a consistent underlying assumption. In both periods, immigrant education expresses the concerns of the society at large. What is taught in classes for immigrants is what the culture considers to be the essential values, attitudes, and behaviors of full-fledged members of the American community. Good Americans in 1920 spoke English and flew the flag on July 4th. Good Americans in 1989 speak English and shop at garage sales. Most importantly, in both periods, good immigrants assimilate into the minimum-wage workplace by accepting their subservient position, along with the myth that they will prosper through hard work and perseverance. Nowhere is this perspective more explicit than in a text written by the director of the curriculum department of the International Catholic Migration Commission in the Philippines and used in the camp. After a recipe list of properly subservient workplace behavior ("Get along with everybody."), the text warns, "If you are a bad worker, the company can fire you. Then it might be hard for you to get another job."[54]

Immigrant education programs are not only a light illuminating for immigrants the myths of American society; they are also a mirror of the society, reflecting the society's own vision of itself. The mirrors provided by the Americanization movement of the turn of the century and the refugee program of today reflect the persistent belief that American society has little or nothing to learn from immigrants' cultures. Instead, both programs assume that the immigrants' primary civic responsibility is to transform themselves by adopting that society's dominant values, attitudes, and behaviors. According to the ideology of self-sufficiency, the payoff for assimilating is material well-being, while the penalty is isolation, poverty, and a wide range of continuing social and psychological problems.

SUFFERING AND RESPONSIBILITY

Despite educational programs, immigrants and refugees suffer persistent and serious problems. In order to sustain the underlying principles of success ideology, both the Americanization program and the refugee program deny the contradictions that these serious problems imply. The Americanization movement did this by blaming immigrants for "failing" to assimilate. To an American population convinced that cultural diversity was unpatriotic and that immigrants from southern and eastern Europe were inferior, the continued presence of ethnic communities and the arrival of new immigrants elicited ever more hysterical responses. Czech-Americans were stoned for wearing their native dress when seeing their sons off to join the U.S. Army. The National Education Association recommended in 1919 that anyone who could not read and write English should be legally bound to attend Americanization classes. The postal service sought to restrict the foreign-language press. Even native-born American citizens who spoke languages other than English became targets of Americanization fanatics.[55]

Finally, however, the national frenzy could no longer be sustained, particularly in the "back to normalcy" period of the Harding administration. The result was a new consensus among supporters of Americanization that the movement had been unable to guarantee the ideological purity of the country. In 1921, a *Saturday Evening Post* editorial argued that harsher action was required if American identity was to be preserved. "In spite of the evidence on every side, sentimentalists still picture Uncle Sam as a clever chef who can take a handful of foreign scraps, a sprig of Americanism and a clove of democracy, and skillfully blend the mess into something fine and desirable." The *Post* pessimistically proclaimed that foreigners "will always be Americanski—near-Americans, with un-American ideas and ideals."[56] President Calvin Coolidge took up the call, demanding, "America must be kept American." The result was the restrictive National Origins Act of 1924, which limited immigration to 164,000 people per year until 1929 and only 150,000 per year after that. These quotas limited immigration to numbers that the educational system could adequately handle and permitted Americanization classes to focus on the vast numbers of immigrants and children of immigrants already in the country. As a result, the Americanization movement became more fully integrated into the existing educational system. But its fundamental assumptions remained. Industrial productivity, national security, and the immigrants' own well-being required an educational program designed to teach immigrants to adopt "American" values, attitudes, and behavior. The future of America depended on it.

Continuing this tradition, today's refugee program assumes that there is a unified American culture and character; that the refugees' cultures and characters are the source of their social, psychological, and economic problems; and that the purpose of the program therefore is reeducation: to teach the refugees to give up their old ways of thinking, believing, and behaving.

The belief that culture is the source of the refugees' problems is combined in the educational program with modern success ideology, which teaches that hard work and individual self-sufficiency will inevitably lead to material well-being and personal happiness. Thus the refugees are taught to accept their subordinate position in the economic system while they assimilate culturally and thereby work their way up the socioeconomic ladder. In this way, the program promotes the nineteenth-century myth that cultural assimilation and hard work will bring about both individual well-being and the American "city on the hill," the culmination of the nation's inherent virtue and its special place in human history.

State Department analyses of the refugees' resettlement problems sound strikingly similar to justifications for Americanization courses: While past immigrants were able to assimilate with ease, today's Indochinese refugees are often from peasant backgrounds; they may have little or no formal education; and they may be unable to read or write in any language.[57] The logical conclusion of this belief is that the refugees' problems will be reduced when their differences are reduced as well, and that refugees who complete the program but remain impoverished are responsible through their refusal to assimilate, an argument explicitly made in various official publications.[58]

The overseas education program plays a key role in attempting to transmit these beliefs to the refugees. The core of the refugee program is the complex, highly organized curriculum used in the overseas classes. Like materials in the Americanization movement, this curriculum expresses and transmits the myths of American success ideology. But while Americanization classes were often taught at workplaces, where their content was controlled by industry, the refugee program operates at overseas processing centers, where the State Department and its contracting agencies "simulate" the American workplace. Teachers pretend to be job supervisors; classroom rules become workplace rules; and class activities imitate assembly-line production.

The picture of the American workplace presented in these classes is one in which workers have duties but no rights; supervisors have authority without limit; and the company has no responsibility other than to make a profit. At one refugee center, the program even adopts a company name: the Pre-Employment Training Corporation (PETCO). This simulated corporation reproduces and transmits American success ideology while teaching refugees to deny their cultural heritage and to accept their subordinate position in U.S. society. Like the mythic vision of innocent America that sustained the war in Vietnam, the vision of life in the United States depicted in the processing centers is characterized by distortion and deception. As we shall see, it is a counterfeit universe.

Counterfeit Universe

Teacher: Today we are going to practice weighing beans. Okay, Vinh, put one pound of beans in the bag. . . . Good. That's good. . . . Wait! What do you say when you're finished?

Vinh: I forget.

Teacher: Class? What do you say to your supervisor when you are finished with the job?

Class: Is this right?

Teacher: Good. And what do you say when you make a mistake?

Class: I am sorry. I won't do it again.

Teacher: Good. That's right. Now, sit down, Vinh.

Preemployment class at PRPC

Vietnam veterans are by no means the only ones asking, "Where does Vietnam end and America—the America one used to believe in—begin?" . . . If the counterfeit universe is not to remain *everything*, one must explore its manifestations everywhere.

Robert Jay Lifton, *Home from the War*[1]

Before Vang Nhia stepped into his preemployment training class at the Galang Processing Center, he made sure he punched his time card in the automatic clock just outside the classroom. Every day upon arriving for class, Vang and his friends searched for their names next to the slots in the rusty metal rack to the left of the classroom door. Then they pulled out the long cards, dropped them in the hole below the clock until the machine banged the time, and replaced them in a second rack to the right. On the door frame, the program officer had posted 17 "company rules," including: "No horseplay. Work quickly and accurately—don't waste time and materials. If you don't understand, ask. Your mistakes are expensive and cause delays in work." Rule Number 17 read, "Any violation of these rules will require disciplinary action."

Once inside, Vang discovered that rows of old manual sewing machines had been placed along two walls. His teacher stood at the front of the room at a table labeled "foreman's desk." Today would be another American workplace "simulation." This time, it was the "sewing assembly room."

The teacher began the simulation by reviewing safety rules. "Check over your machine before you begin to work. Keep your fingers away from the needle. Report any problems you may have with your machine. Remember, in America, time is money." Today, the assignment was to produce seat covers that would be used later in another simulation, the airplane walk-through. Some students worked on half-scale drawings used as patterns by the cutters, while others completed work order forms and laid out the material for cutting. Vang's job was quality control—examining finished pieces for flaws.

As the class worked, the teacher supervised. "Hey! Be careful!" she shouted. "If you drop those scissors again, guy, you'll go to work at the seamstress station. Got it?"[2] She filled out a violation form for a student who had handed a pair of scissors blade-first to a coworker. She criticized everyone, keeping detailed notes so she could go over their mistakes when the simulation was over. She noted that one student "dropped the scissors without apologizing."[3] "Work faster. You're making the other stations wait!" she shouted at Vang. "In America, you must work fast or the company will lose money and fire you." Vang hurried, examining the seat cover quickly before handing it to the packer.

On his small farm in Laos, Vang had worked long hours, but he had enjoyed his work. Now, as the "foreman" shouted at the "workers," he worried that he would be unhappy in an American assembly plant. There seemed to be no chance to talk to other workers, and he felt embarrassed by the constant criticisms. Vang reminded himself of the lesson from the previous day, when the teacher listed the keys to success in America: willingness to learn, ability to follow orders, and dependability.[4] She had assured them that if they learned these qualities, they would become self-sufficient. In America, Vang knew, being self-sufficient is what matters.

THE COMPETENCY-BASED CURRICULUM

When the refugee education program began in 1980, the first question for the U.S. officials in charge was, "What shall we teach?" Though the curriculum began simply as an effort to list the content of courses, it eventually required the U.S. staff members to articulate what they believed to be the path to success in the United States. As it grew over the early years of the program, the curriculum came to depict the official program vision of life in America, including its key values and fundamental beliefs. Also, in order to determine what Southeast Asians needed to learn before resettlement, the officials had to articulate their conception of the cultural values, the fundamental beliefs, and the resettlement needs of people from Southeast Asia. Within three years after the program began, the curriculum had evolved into a fascinating statement by the U.S. Department of State of its vision of the peoples, cultures, social systems, and political values of the United States and Indochina.

The curriculum of the refugee program uses a "competency-based approach" for all components at all centers. In recent years, competency-based education (CBE) has come to be the most widely supported approach among federal education agencies.

Perhaps the best general definition of CBE is one developed from a survey of its leading supporters. "Competency-based adult education is a performance-based process leading to demonstrated mastery of basic life skills necessary for the individual to function proficiently in society."[5] This definition was adapted by the Center for Applied Linguistics in its promotion of competency-based ESL: "A competency-based curriculum is a performance-outline of language tasks that lead to a demonstrated mastery of the language associated with specific skills that are necessary for individuals to function proficiently in the society in which they live."[6] In CBE, the assumption is that successful functioning in society is best defined in behavioral terms. The emphasis is on what learners must *do* rather than on what they must *know*, on life skills required for situations in which students will find themselves. The lessons focus on specific tasks, such as balancing a checkbook, shopping within a budget, and filling out applications for employment. Language skills are also defined in concrete behavioral terms. For instance, the refugees must master competencies such as "making apologies," "asking for clarification," "verifying understanding," and "responding appropriately to supervisors' instructions." In CBE, students are told specifically what tasks they are expected to learn, and competency-based tests measure their ability to complete these tasks. Assessment, in other words, is based upon the ability to demonstrate prespecified behaviors directly related to essential concrete life skills.[7] Differences among programs primarily involve decisions about what skills are presumed to be essential.

Competency-based curricula have been adopted in response to demands for teacher accountability and better measures of students' progress. These demands have increasingly defined education as a social contract, in which teachers must be evaluated in terms of their ability to achieve learning goals specified in the curriculum. This means that teachers are held accountable for their teaching through quantifiable evidence of students' learning. In response to this movement, many local, state, and national educational agencies now mandate the competency-based approach. The city of Boston, for example, developed the competency-based Adult Literacy Initiative, while the state of California developed a standardized competency-based curriculum and testing program called the California Adult Student Assessment System. At the federal level, the competency-based Adult Performance Level (APL) project developed for the Office of Education by the University of Texas became the basis for federally funded adult basic education in the late 1970s and was used as a major resource for development of the program in the refugee processing centers. In domestic refugee programs, the competency-based Mainstream English Language Training (MELT) project has been adopted as the standard curriculum, testing, and placement package for all programs funded by the Office of Refugee Resettlement (ORR). In late 1986, ORR regulations made participation in a Refugee Education and Employment Program (REEP) an eligibility requirement for Refugee Cash and Medical Assistance; all REEP programs are required to use the competency-based MELT package. Thus the decision to adopt the competency-based approach for English language, cultural orientation, and preemployment classes in the refugee processing centers reflects a broad movement in U.S. education toward CBE.

CBE supporters widely praise the competency-based approach, in adult education generally and in ESL specifically. In 1975, Terrell H. Bell, the United States Commissioner of Education, called the competency-based APL project "a very useful project that the education community has to examine with great seriousness and deliberation."[8] Because CBE seems to offer clear-cut measures of learning and of teaching effectiveness, Virginia Knauer declared that it represents a major breakthrough in adult education. "For the first time, we have defined the specific areas in which adults need education and the precise skills required to make use of information... [and] a method of assessing an individual's skills in coping with his environment."[9] The Center for Applied Linguistics (CAL) asserted that "the incorporation of insights from competency-based instruction into the ESL curriculum is perhaps the most important breakthrough in adult ESL."[10] In a classic article about competency-based ESL, Charles A. Findley and Lynn A. Nathan promoted it as a "successful model for the delivery of educational services that allows for responsible and accountable teaching."[11]

Another important claim made by proponents is that CBE has no inherent social, economic, or political bias because it is "student-centered." The basis for this claim is the concept of "needs analysis." Needs analysis in CBE means that the sole basis for deciding which competencies students must acquire should be educators' assessment of learners' concrete employment and survival needs. CBE supporters argue that needs analysis is particularly appropriate for adults because "adults generally don't study subjects which someday may be useful; rather they study subjects that have relevance to their present situations."[12] Like other CBE programs, the refugee program claims that class content is determined by analysis of refugees' resettlement and survival needs.

Critics of CBE, however, question many of these claims, in particular whether CBE is really a new approach, free from the biases of educational planners and the inequalities of society. In response to the uncritical acceptance of CBE among federal education officials, William S. Griffith and Ronald M. Cervero, two respected specialists in adult education, traced the historical precedents of CBE in U.S. schools as far back as the mid-nineteenth century. In 1861, for example, Herbert Spencer had identified five major areas of life that he believed should serve as the basis for curriculum development in schools: self-preservation, securing the necessities of life, raising and disciplining children, maintaining social and political relations, and gratifying tastes and feelings.[13] These categories provided the basis for a curriculum of life competencies much like the APL project over a century later. In the 1920s, Franklin Bobbitt had argued that the correct basis for establishing objectives in educational curricula was the normal activities of adult life, including recreation and health, religious life, raising children, and vocational activities.[14] With its emphasis on teaching immigrants specific skills for industrial employment, the Americanization movement had also used a practical, competency-based approach. After surveying the history of CBE, Griffith and Cervero concluded that "the concept of building a curriculum on an analysis of the requirements of adult living is embedded in a tradition at least a century old." They suggested that, despite the claims of its promoters, CBE is merely "an old idea with a new name."[15]

The similarity between today's competency-based programs and earlier immigrant education has led CBE critics to question whether it is truly free from the social and economic inequalities that plague traditional education. Some critics have observed that the competency-based approach has been used historically in programs that prepare immigrants and minorities for menial, unskilled labor, and that the content of such programs often serves the interests of employers rather than of students.[16] At issue is the role of CBE in individual skills development, social mobility, and allocation of political and economic power.

Clearly, education plays a significant role in offering opportunity for— or limiting—social and economic advancement. By preparing students to carry out specific tasks in society, schools function as one of the main agents for maintaining economic and political divisions or for changing them.[17] Paul Willis, for example, argues that one of the main functions of education is to maintain—to "reproduce"—social and economic inequality in order to preserve dominant economic interests. "Education [is] not about equality, but inequality. . . . Education's main purpose . . . could be achieved only by preparing most kids for an unequal future, and by insuring their personal underdevelopment."[18]

At present, the role of education in this process is one of the major debates among educators, pitting traditional forces that wish to preserve existing educational policy against those who condemn it for sustaining economic, social, and political inequality. As the major system supported by traditional "back-to-basics" educators, the competency-based approach is at the center of this debate. In order to understand the kinds of social and economic opportunities the competency-based refugee education program offers to Southeast Asians, we must examine the actual content of the program. But first, it is important to understand the process by which program content is determined. How, in other words, do program officials determine refugees' resettlement and survival "needs?"

DETERMINING REFUGEES' NEEDS

Planners in the newly established refugee program in late 1980 had to ask themselves the fundamental question that confronts all developers of a competency-based, employment-oriented curriculum: What must Indochinese refugees be able to do in order to "function proficiently" in U.S. society?[19] By providing consultants and curriculum development teams from the Refugee Resource Center in Manila, the CAL played a key role in the effort to specify program objectives for this purpose.

The first step in defining the content of the refugee program—writing the curriculum—was to set a program-wide criterion for decisions about refugees' needs. The criterion established by CAL staff was that competencies must be "considered essential for the survival of Indochinese refugees newly arrived in the United States."[20] Beginning in early 1981, at meetings in Manila, Bangkok, Singapore, and Washington, D.C., CAL staff members, U.S. State Department officers, and representatives of the processing centers met to decide which competencies meet this criterion. Since then, at separate annual meetings considering the ESL, cultural-orientation, and preemployment components, these representatives prepare updated competency lists for use in all centers.

How are these lists developed? The procedure for developing the list of ESL competencies in June, July, and August 1981 was described by the Center for Applied Linguistics as follows:

Consensus was used as much as possible to determine which language items would be included. In many cases, consensus either could not be reached or was not truly possible, given that there is often more than one common and appropriate choice of language for any survival situation. The product of these meetings was a Standardized ESL Curriculum Guide which was to be used as the basis for curriculum development in all sites.[21]

The same procedure has been used for deciding the content of the cultural orientation and preemployment components. In other words, program content is based upon the opinions of a group of individuals about what might be necessary for resettled refugees. No resettled refugees are present at these meetings, and no refugees are asked to review the decisions made by the committee. Few of the people present at these meetings have any experience in the cultures and languages of Southeast Asia, other than what they may have gained in a few months working in the refugee camps. At the preemployment meeting in Singapore in 1985, for example, only one official present had ever been to Indochina, and only that one spoke a language of one of the refugee groups.

Program development in the individual processing centers follows a similar procedure. Using the master content list developed at the regional meetings, the staffs at the different sites decide what will be included in the separate ESL, cultural orientation, and preemployment classes. In most cases the regional list is adopted, with some competencies deleted, others added, and a few rewritten. In addition, the site staff members determine appropriate teaching methods, prepare classroom materials, and list daily activities for all components.

Yet curricular decisions are not made in complete isolation; staff members use a variety of sources. Though it is claimed that the curricula represent the refugees' needs, the sources focus on *employers'* needs: a survey of employers' reactions to Indochinese refugees as employees[22] and a handbook for training industrial workers that emphasizes employers' needs.[23] Indeed, the State Department journal *Passage* summarizes the general principle for determining refugees' needs as follows: "Instruction must be directed toward meeting refugees' employment needs. Such needs are best determined by an employer needs assessment."[24]

At no stage in this process can the staff members work from a validated list of the competencies *known* to be required for adult living in the United States, because no such list exists. The essential problem is that there can never be a fixed list of competencies for "adult living," for "survival," for "functioning proficiently," or for "successful resettlement." As a result, different groups of curriculum developers make up different lists of competencies that they "consider" to be "essential for the survival of Indochinese refugees." Margaret Ammons, in her encyclopedia of educational research published in the late 1960s, pointed out that the validity of competency lists developed in this manner depends entirely upon the judgment of the individuals who prepare the list. With such a procedure there is no scientific basis for selecting competencies or for evaluating the competency lists. As Ammons observed, this method of determining program content relies solely upon the consensus of some group or groups.[25]

Because there is no basis for making curricular decisions other than the beliefs of staff members at the processing centers about which competencies refugees must acquire, program content is revised repeatedly as staff members change. The cultural orientation curriculum at Bataan, for instance, underwent three complete revisions between 1982 and 1985, each revision using a different set of competencies, a different format, and different materials. In such circumstances, confusion often results. At the Philippine center during 1985, ESL teachers had to shuffle pages from three different curricula in order to keep the students busy for the entire 20 weeks of the program.

But confusion is not the only risk in establishing program content solely on the basis of the opinions of current staff members. The greater danger is that the program that results from this process will reflect the values and attitudes of the curricular staff members rather than the educational needs of refugees. Indeed, a nontheoretical approach to curriculum development—one that relies primarily upon the opinions of individuals—inevitably leads to a central role for values in the curriculum. In the *Second Handbook of Research in Teaching*, J. MacDonald and D. Clark describe the importance of values in this kind of curricular decision making.

Curriculum development is a continuous process of making human value judgments about what to include and exclude, what to aim for and avoid, and how to go about it—difficult judgments, even when aided by technical and scientific data and processes.[26]

Because competency-based education in the refugee program is not based upon scientific data and processes, value judgments by staff members play the central role in program content. However, because the values that result from this process are usually implicit rather than explicit, few curricular staff members, state department officers, or CAL consultants directly address the role of their own values and attitudes in the content of the program.

But this is not to say that the central role of values and attitudes goes completely unnoticed, for one of the major aims of the program is to change refugees' values and attitudes. For instance, Loring Waggoner, Deputy Coordinator for Refugee Programs at the U.S. embassy in Manila in 1984, stated that the refugees "have to understand that there is a philosophy of employment embodied in the language, and I think that's the basic reason that the pre-employment curriculum came about."[27] Presumably, Waggoner meant to suggest that anyone speaking American English must adopt a certain "philosophy of employment," which the program calls "self-sufficiency." Though no scientific analysis has ever proposed such a notion, Waggoner's comments reflect a widespread belief that refugees must learn more than the American language; they must also *become Americanized.*

This belief in the importance of changing refugees' values is expressed explicitly in several program documents. The introduction to the regional preemployment curriculum informs teachers that "values of the American workplace should be taught. . . . Every effort should be made to help students internalize the values discussed and to practice the behavior which demonstrates that they are understood."[28] A publicity brochure prepared for the Philippine center declares that the educational program is "geared towards attitudinal change and designed to develop and enhance certain basic attitudes such as social awareness and social responsibility."[29] Similarly, the former deputy project director of the PRPC, in an article published in the State Department journal *Passage*, argued that changing the refugees' values and attitudes should be the central aim of the cultural orientation curriculum.[30]

In CBE, such statements are exceptions, as the values and attitudes contained in competency-based programs are usually implicit rather than explicit. Because these implicit values and attitudes are determined by the individuals involved in curriculum development, it is important to keep in mind the confusion, uncertainty, personal conflicts, and bureaucratic wrangling that go into preparation of an educational program. Curriculum development and revision in the processing centers often is chaotic and piecemeal, despite the apparent orderliness of the process as it is usually described.[31]

Despite these problems, administrators in the processing centers expect instructors to follow the curriculum closely and to proceed at a standard pace through the lessons. Moreover, the curriculum is exceptionally detailed, including explicit lists of objectives, materials, and suggestions for activities. This unusual level of detail results in part from the wide variation in teachers' experience. Some have taught as long as 20 years, while others have had no previous classroom experience at all. Moreover, the number of teaching hours (as many as 26 per week, plus 12 additional hours each week in required training sessions and meetings) means that teachers have little time to prepare the necessary lessons for their students. As a result, the curriculum must include many details that, in other settings, would be left to the daily lesson planning of individual instructors.

THE CONTENT OF CLASSES

What is the result of this process of curriculum development? What do refugees study in the State Department education program? One way to answer these questions is to list the competencies. In the ESL component, for example, language competencies are divided into 17 topic areas: banking, clarification language, community services, directions, finding a job, on the job, health, housing, literacy, money, personal information, post office, shopping, social language, telephone, time, and transportation. Within each topic area, different competencies are listed for each of the five levels of students' language proficiency. For instance, the list for the lowest proficiency level for the topic "on the job' is as follows (the language to be practiced is listed in parentheses):

1. Follow simple one-step oral instructions to begin and perform a task which is demonstrated, including simple classroom instructions. (Put these away.)

2. Ask if a task was done correctly. (Is this right?)

3. Ask simple clarification questions about routine job tasks and instructions. (Please repeat. or Do this?)

4. Acknowledge understanding of instructions. (OK. All right. Yes.)

5. Respond to direct questions about work progress and completion of tasks. (Are you finished? No.)

6. Ask supervisor/co-worker for help. (Can you help me?)

7. Respond to oral warnings/basic commands about safety (Watch out!)

8. Read common warnings/safety signs at the work site. (DANGER)

9. Give simple excuses for lateness or absence in person. (I was sick yesterday.)[32]

Such basic lists of ESL competencies cover about 25 pages, although the total ESL curriculum is over 700 pages long, including lesson plans, materials, and detailed suggestions for teaching these competencies. Preemployment and cultural orientation curricula are of similar length.

Although lists of competencies provide important information about program content, of greater significance are the assumptions about refugees, resettlement, and life in the United States expressed in the lessons. These assumptions, discussed in detail among staff members at program development meetings, form the basis for decisions about which competencies should be included in—and excluded from—the program. Moreover, by examining the assumptions behind the program, we can better understand the social and economic opportunities that the program offers, as well as denies, to refugees from Southeast Asia.

Analysis of the ESL, cultural-orientation, and preemployment components suggests that 13 major assumptions about refugees, resettlement, and America underlie the educational program. Taken together, these assumptions constitute a vision of the peoples and cultures of Southeast Asia, as well as of the society awaiting them in the United States. As we shall see, these assumptions are remarkably similar to those implicit in the Americanization movement.

Assumption 1: Indochinese Must Be Taught to Work Hard

In other words, Indochinese people lack the American work ethic. In the view of the program, refugees' use of welfare results not from their inability to find employment, but rather from their own system of beliefs and their expectations about federal assistance. Officials claim that refugees feel the United States has a responsibility to care for them until they are able to care for themselves; that the United States owes them payment because they fought on its side in the war; and that the United States is a kind of Asian extended family to which they can turn when they are in need. The basic argument is that Indochinese cultures lead to "welfare dependency," and that, therefore, if the goal of low welfare rates is to be achieved, the refugees' cultures must be undermined.

These views are outlined in an article in the State Department journal *Passage* by Christopher Blass, of the cultural orientation program at Phanat Nikhom in Thailand.[33] Arguing that the role of a host in Southeast Asia entails responsibility for financially assisting a guest "who experienced some great misfortune," Blass speculates that the refugees see the United States as a "host" and welfare as the fulfillment of the host's obligations. He suggests further that the refugees view public assistance as repayment for fighting on the side of the United States during the war: "Some refugees . . . might think of welfare as something that is owed to them for what they did for the U.S."[34] (This argument implies that the war was a U.S. endeavor fought with the assistance of Indochinese, though the official program view is that the war was an effort by the people of Indochina to fight Communism, with the Americans there to assist.) Blass argues that refugees must be actively discouraged from seeking public assistance. Without evidence for his claims, he depends upon a second common assumption.

Assumption 2: The Refugees Have a Dependency Syndrome and So Must Be Taught to Be Self-Sufficient

Officials claim that a "dependency syndrome" is caused by the refugees' cultural norms and by the free benefits they enjoy in camps.

In some [refugee camps], conditions were, and still are, harsh. In other places, however, shelter, food, clothing, medical care, schooling, and even jobs may be made available to refugees now looking ahead to resettlement in the U.S. By providing for so many of the refugees' basic needs, the camp inadvertently may be creating dependence.[35]

Interestingly, this argument by Blass implies that harsher conditions in camps should help to lower welfare rates in the United States by reducing the refugees' dependency syndrome.

The curriculum includes many lessons designed to overcome this assumed dependency syndrome, as well as the refugees' alleged culturally determined expectation of public assistance and reluctance to work. Lessons in cultural orientation classes contrast Americans' work ethic with refugees' welfare dependency. One lesson depicts a group of hard-working Americans in a factory who receive their paychecks only to "find that some money has been withheld from them. . . . When they go home, they see the refugees next door watching TV. . . . They suspect that the refugees are receiving welfare money because they never go to work." Near the end of the lesson, the Americans are asked "how they feel about the government taking money from their paychecks and giving it to the refugees."[36] American supervisors in the processing centers tell host-country teachers that Americans have "negative attitudes" about refugees and believe refugees are a burden on the United States.[37]

Perhaps the most striking expression of the belief that refugees must be taught to work in order to overcome their dependency syndrome is a lesson called the Free Money Game, developed at the Galang processing center and heavily publicized by State Department officials.[38] In the game, students are divided into two groups, a Blue Team, which is employed and receives a paycheck, and a Pink Team, which receives public assistance payments. Both teams must pay for housing, food, transportation, education, and other necessities with the money they receive from their salaries or welfare payments. The students are told that the purpose of the game is to practice handling U.S. currency, while the real aim stated in the curriculum is to discourage use of welfare.

This takes place through systematic differences in the treatment the two teams receive throughout the game. Blue Team members (those who receive a paycheck) are addressed by name, while Pink Team members are addressed by a number, which they must wear around their necks. Blue Team members sit on chairs, while Pink Team members must sit on the floor. Teachers who hand out paychecks and welfare checks treat Pink players rudely, while they treat Blue players courteously and respectfully. Only Blue players are permitted to sponsor relatives still in Southeast Asia; Pink players are forbidden to apply for relatives' resettlement. The Blue players are treated generously by beneficent employers, who grant a raise and a Christmas bonus during the game, while Pink players receive abrupt and hostile treatment from teachers acting as welfare officers. The game's designer, who later became the director of the cultural orientation program in the Philippines, claims that it expresses the reality of welfare and employment in the United States.[39]

Many other lessons assume that refugees must be taught to work hard and to be self-sufficient. In the preemployment program, refugees discuss the story of "Duc's family," which suffers because Duc does not like his job or want his wife to work.[40] The story teaches that Duc must give up his goal of supporting his family alone and instead permit his wife to work, even if they work different shifts and cannot spend much time together as a family. The lesson teaches that such sacrifices will pay off in the long run because "self-sufficiency is highly regarded in American society, . . . upward mobility is possible by hard work and perseverance . . . and . . . men and women have equal access to employment opportunities."[41] Repeatedly, refugees are told that "your supervisor will always like to see you work hard and work well. If you're a good worker you have a better chance of keeping your job or of moving up to a higher level."[42]

In such lessons, refugees are encouraged to measure their success in America in terms of their jobs. One lesson in the preemployment program teaches that "in the U.S., people's status in society is based on their job. Unemployment causes psychological and family problems."[43] In ESL classes, refugees practice dialogues in which they immediately accept minimum-wage night jobs without benefits.[44] In several lessons, refugees are presented an idealized vision of American employers. For instance, the preemployment curriculum describes employment conditions refugees can expect to find in America: sick leave from three to twelve days each year; an average of twelve paid holidays each year; two weeks' paid vacation each year; free employee medical insurance, with family members covered for an additional "small amount per month."[45] Though the program teaches refugees to accept minimum-wage jobs, it depicts benefits enjoyed by few minimum-wage employees.[46]

Assumption 3: The Refugees Must Be Taught Democracy

In their classes, the refugees learn that self-sufficiency is more than an economic necessity; it is also the central moral principle of American democracy. The cultural orientation curriculum emphasizes that "in the United States, the *government is the people*. . . . A central concept of American philosophy is the belief in individual freedom. Government is expected to do for people only those things they cannot do for themselves."[47]

Refugees are taught that democracy begins in the American workplace. One lesson proclaims that "three important attitudes pervade the American workplace: egalitarianism in relationships; cooperation for efficiency; and harmony in on-the-job relationships."[48] They are taught that the key to harmony in on-the-job relationships is to "focus on careful listening (taking directions) and on confirming orders (asking for clarification) when needed."[49] Coworkers and supervisors are depicted as friends and helpers. One lesson in preemployment classes assures refugees that many of their coworkers will be descendants of recent immigrants who "are sympathetic towards people who are trying to learn English [and] impressed by multilinguals."[50] Above all, refugees are taught that the fundamental civic duty is to stay off welfare. "Self-sufficiency" is a "basic value with its roots in America's historical development."[51] In the vision of America depicted in the refugee program, harmony in the workplace depends upon obedience; work is self-sufficiency; and self-sufficiency is freedom.

Assumption 4: The Refugees Are Likely to Break U.S. Laws

The emphasis on teaching democracy to refugees is based in part upon the fear that they will violate U.S. laws and democratic principles. In several lessons, refugees are depicted as criminals, but nowhere are they depicted as victims of crime. One lesson warns that "many refugees run afoul of laws and ordinances on property rights, community living, alcohol use, graft and bribery among other transgressions."[52] Other "unacceptable and/ or illegal behavior" listed in the curriculum: "urinating in public, spitting in public, bare-bottom babies, unclothed children, breastfeeding in public, people of the same sex (especially men) holding hands in public, blowing the nose without tissue, coining, and burping or belching in public."[53]

No lessons prepare the refugees for the frightening experience of being victims of crime, despite the fact that many violent crimes and property crimes are directed against individual refugees. For instance, a study of the law enforcement needs of Southeast Asian refugees reported that 64 percent of the refugees surveyed in Orange County, California, considered crime in the streets to be a major problem and that 58 percent felt that better police protection was needed.[54] Though news reports throughout the United States document significant crime against Indochinese refugees,[55] the educational program assumes that the greater need is to reduce the refugees' crime rates.

Assumption 5: The Refugees Discriminate against Americans

Of the topics on law and democracy, the largest amount of time is spent on lessons that focus on the refugees' racial prejudices. Activities require them to "examine the stereotypes they have developed" and to "confront their racial or ethnic biases."[56] Cultural orientation lessons encourage Southeast Asians to be as tolerant as Americans are.[57] In the program for secondary-school-age children, Preparation for American Secondary Schools (PASS), a course on Indochinese culture is designed to "help lessen the . . . ethnic prejudices and misperceptions among the refugee groups."[58] Though refugees are often victims of discrimination, no lessons prepare them for the discrimination that they will experience.[59]

The program also teaches refugees to be skeptical of government remedies for discrimination. One lesson, apparently designed to discourage support for affirmative action programs, includes a brief history of affirmative action:

For many years good employment was available only to whites. In trying to undo the wrongs of past discrimination, some new problems have been created. The working majority (white males) speak of reverse discrimination because of a law called Affirmative Action. This law requires that firms with government contracts show that their employees represent a cross-section of the local community. For example, if a town is 1/3 black and 1/3 white and 1/3 Asian, a company's employees should roughly reflect this ratio. If a company has 99 employees, 33 should be black, 33 Hispanic [sic], and 33 white. This law also mandates that the ratio be apparent at all levels: 1/3 of management should be black, 1/3 Hispanic etc. Additionally, women are to be represented at all levels within the hierarchy.[60]

The directions to the teacher included in this lesson require that "the teacher explains that there is a law in the U.S. that requires most large businesses to hire particular percentages of different racial groups." Then the teacher asks the students to consider a situation in which a marginally qualified Asian woman is given a job rather than a superbly qualified white man because "the president of the company has been told by the U.S. government he needs more women and minorities in management." The discussion questions for this situation include, "Is it fair to everyone? Are there better ways of doing what the law tries to do? How would you improve the law?"

In addition to its inaccurate summary of the legal requirements of affirmative action regulations, this lesson implies that all white males oppose affirmative action, that its main effects are unfair, that the law needs to be changed, and that refugees should not take advantage of it. Indeed, this lesson, entitled "The Multi-Ethnic/Racial Society II," depicts white males as the victims of discrimination and Asian females as the source of injustice.

Assumption 6: The Refugees Must Accept a Subservient Position in American Society

As the solution to the refugees' prejudices, as well as to their dependency syndrome, they are taught a highly restricted range of English-language competencies. The preemployment program does not encourage refugees to produce supervisors' language; they are to listen to it, understand it, and respond appropriately to it in their role as "workers."[61] In ESL classes, they are taught how to ask for permission, but not how to give orders; how to apologize, but not how to disagree; how to comply, but not how to complain; and how to ask about American customs, but not how to explain their own.

The emphasis on the language of subservient social roles determines teaching methods as well as class content. For role-playing activities in preemployment classes, the curriculum encourages the teachers to retain a strict hierarchy of authority.

If [a] student makes a mistake, do not ask the rest of the class if it is correct. Instead, the teacher, in a firm voice, says 'NO! That is Wrong!' . . . The teacher is promoting some kind of . . . apology from the student, such as "I am sorry, I do not understand."[62]

In other lessons, the refugees practice dialogues in which they accept any salary and working hours offered to them.

Is $4.00 an hour OK?

Yes.

When can your start?

Tomorrow.

Can you work nights?

Yes.[63]

They learn to ask whether they have performed a task correctly and to "respond appropriately to supervisor's comments about quality of work" by practicing "I'm sorry. I won't do it again."[64] They learn how to "respond appropriately to written communication from a school (e.g., permission forms)," but not how to complain when their children's English-language education is inadequate.[65] In lesson after lesson, they learn to ask permission: "Can I smoke here? Can I use the phone?" "Is it all right to wear my shoes in the house?" "Is this right?"[66]

Subservience is taught in housing lessons as well. In a lesson on landlord-tenant relations, students are required to memorize their responsibilities as tenants: pay rent on time; keep housing clean; report damage to the landlord; observe limits on the number of occupants; give notice before moving; ask permission before making repairs; respect the rights of neighbors; and abide by the terms of the lease. Yet the lesson lists only the following responsibilities of the landlord: provide for general maintenance and enforce the terms of the lease.[67] The lesson does not include information about tenants' rights, nor does it teach the refugees what to do when landlords violate housing, safety, or health regulations. Instead, it teaches that tenants must "abide by" the lease, while landlords have the right to enforce it.

Assumption 7: The Refugees Must Give Up Their Cultural Traditions

The goal of Americanizing Indochinese reaches further than teaching English and employment skills or subservient social rules. It implies changes at the very core of the individual.[68] In this way, the curriculum repeats the assumption of the Americanization movement that immigrants must undergo personal, social, and cultural transformations in order to successfully resettle in the United States.

In some lessons, successful resettlement is defined as losing one's cultural heritage. For instance, one lesson includes a discussion of the fact that "many Americans have no idea of their ethnic origins."[69] This lesson then moves to a discussion of "what the students can learn . . . from the experiences of other ethnic and racial groups in the U.S. as it might apply to them," the clear implication being that assimilation has benefited these groups. Other lessons emphasize that Americans ("except perhaps the Native Americans")

have ancestral roots outside the United States, and that these past immigrants survived because they were willing to become Americanized.[70] In
another lesson, refugees are shown pictures of Americans, whom the teacher
explains are descendents of "refugees and immigrants [who] set down roots
. . . after fleeing . . . great hardship." The lesson teaches that they sacrificed
their traditional identities to become Americans and that today's Indochinese
refugees must do the same.[71]

One of the main objectives of the cultural orientation classes is to provide
the refugees with "strategies for overcoming resistance to adapt to the new
circumstances."[72] The cultural orientation curriculum states, "Lessons
should develop a positive ATTITUDE toward becoming involved in America."[73] In order to accomplish these important changes in attitude, the program offers advice for becoming Americanized. One of the most common
suggestions is that refugees form friendships with Americans.[74] More importantly, the curriculum includes lessons promoting potentially traumatic
changes in Indochinese family life. Perhaps the most striking examples are
the lessons designed to teach refugees the value of birth control and the
need to adopt different attitudes toward women.

In several lessons exploring family life, major attention is given to the
size of Southeast Asian families. These lessons assume that Americans value
small families while Asians value large ones. (The curriculum does not
examine the economic reasons for differences in family size.) The lessons
explicitly aim to reduce the size of Southeast Asian families by "promot[ing]
the attitude that it is reasonable for couples to consciously determine the
number of children they wish to have and the timing of having them."[75]

Classes on family life also promote a change in refugees' attitudes toward
women. The curriculum assumes that most refugees believe the man should
work at a job while the woman stays at home "tending the children."[76]
The lessons are designed to convince the refugees that women should work
at jobs outside the home. For instance, one lesson explains that "upward
mobility for a family is normally faster when there is more than one paycheck in the household," while another lesson "foster[s] the attitudes that:
it may be necessary and also advantageous that women work outside the
home; there can be a sense of fulfillment that can occur for women whether
married or single, when they *do* work."[77]

Employment and income data suggest it is indeed necessary for many
Indochinese women to work in the United States. This is because as many
as a third of all refugee families are headed by women and a majority of
working Southeast Asian women make a crucial contribution to family
income.[78] The lessons in the processing centers are not, however, designed
simply to inform the refugees that women may need to work due to economic necessity; rather, the goal is to change their attitudes toward women
and toward the traditional family structure before the refugees are admitted
to the United States.

The lessons emphasize a variety of other cultural changes. Children in the PASS program are required to wear American clothing, while adults are taught to dress like Americans in order to be able to obtain and hold jobs. In an interview in the State Department publication *Passage*, "Philip" Van Bui, one of two former refugees employed at the Galang Processing Center in Indonesia, explained why he wore rubber "flip-flops" on Galang rather than fancier Western shoes.

I want to fit in, because then [the refugees] will tell me the story of their lives. . . . I also want to send them a message: When you come to America, I expect you to behave, to dress like the people around you. . . . If you behave differently, you are not easy to approach, you cannot adapt quickly.[79]

The refugees are also encouraged to adopt America's "crucial stress on time."[80] To this end, they punch time clocks before entering classrooms, they do many timed activities in class, and they are repeatedly told the importance of working quickly on the job. In cultural orientation classes, the refugees are taught that they will offend Americans if they wear Asian clothing, eat "strong smelling" food, share food from a single plate, "squat" or sit cross-legged on a chair, or speak their own language to Asian-Americans.[81] Other lessons develop the "attitude that . . . the purchasing and use of second-hand items is appropriate."[82] Throughout such lessons, the quest for conformity is justified with the ideology of self-sufficiency: If the refugees want to succeed, they must give up their old ways and adopt new ones.

In some lessons, the program makes a limited effort to recognize the value of Southeast Asian cultural traditions in providing a sense of identity and community among newly resettled refugees. For instance, cultural orientation lessons state that American families have a wide range of different forms, so that the Indochinese extended family can expect to "retain much of its Indochinese character."[83] This lesson encourages the refugees to value their families and to depend upon them during the stress of resettlement. Such lessons do not, however, confront the severe economic pressures that lead to fragmented families, spouse and child abuse, and other serious problems. Moreover, the lessons, designed by Americans with little knowledge of Southeast Asia, analyze Indochinese cultural traditions within an American context. Thus the extended family is called a "support system"[84] and ethnicity is equated with "life-style."[85] Above all, these lessons focus on ways that the refugees' native cultures separate them from Americans and hinder their ability to fit into American society.[86]

Assumption 8: The Refugees Lack Skills They Can Contribute to American Society

The drive to change the refugees' cultural values and attitudes is motivated by the belief that Indochinese have little to contribute to American society except their manual labor. All of the refugees, regardless of their previous education or work experience, are taught that they must accept minimum-wage employment in the United States.[87] In lessons on job interviews, all of the students practice the dialogue

What did you do in Vietnam/Cambodia/Laos?
I was a farmer.

On the assumption that the refugees have only their manual labor to offer, the program teaches a specific set of skills that the program officials claim they will need in order to be employed in the United States. These skills primarily involve the ability to sort objects and carry out simple cutting and assembly tasks. Preemployment classes include lessons in which refugees sort various plastic chips according to color and size. Other lessons require students to cut different-colored wires into specified lengths, or to sort beans into plastic bags. In more advanced lessons, adults drill holes in wood, make a circuit with a lightbulb and switch, follow a pattern to make a paper hat or a box, and clean floors with electric brooms. The aim of these lessons is to prepare the refugees for assembly-line employment in the electronics industry, for janitorial service, and for other minimum-wage jobs requiring little or no English proficiency.

Such lessons teach the refugees that they must be willing to accept minimum-wage jobs regardless of their intelligence, education, or training. Thus in 1984, when Vietnamese leaving under the ODP began to reach the Philippine camp in large numbers, the officials did not revise the program, despite the fact that the first ODP arrivals were successful business owners, teachers, and professionals. A former head of a major Saigon corporation was required to attend lessons on how to write a check and to plan a family budget. In this way, the program teaches Southeast Asians that they should expect to be at the bottom of the U.S. economic ladder.

For most refugees, of course, the assumption that they must be taught to sort objects by color or shape does not apply. Hmong refugees, for instance, create some of the world's most intricately colored patterns of needlework. Other refugees, who have built traditional houses by hand using highly advanced carpentry and weaving skills, do not need to take a class to learn to cut wires into identical lengths. Many refugees were military officers, students, owners of businesses, bus drivers, and professionals with experience in Asian or American companies and the military or bureaucracy. In surveys in the Galang processing center in 1985, for instance, the refugees averaged between six and seven years of previous schooling, and the proportion of Vietnamese who had been farmers was as low as 2.5 percent.[88] Some refugees are well qualified doctors, teachers, and secretaries who lack only English-language fluency, yet they are encouraged to accept minimum-wage jobs as janitors or dishwashers rather than remain in school to improve their English. One refugee wrote that "the worst experience in my life [is] being a graduate nurse [only] to work as janitor."[89] Nguyen Zuan Hoang, who had studied biology and chemistry in college, complained that "there is nothing for me in classes." Another Vietnamese, who had a master's degree in electrical engineering, said that he was insulted by the implication that he had no skills that would qualify him for employment in the United States. Other people have limited skills but dream of being engineers and architects. Nguyen Viet Hung wrote in a class essay that "my dream is going to be an engineer. I hope my dream will come true." Yet in the refugee camps, people like Hung learn only that they must settle for unskilled jobs. Their dreams may remain intact, but the educational program established for them does not help them fulfill those dreams.

Assumption 9: The Refugees Can "Pick Up" English in the United States While Working

To convince the refugees that it is in their interest to accept minimum-wage work, the educational program tells them that they can learn English on the job and therefore work their way up to better jobs requiring greater English skills.[90] Lessons emphasize that in some states it is illegal to attend school full time while on welfare.[91] Many lessons inform refugees that "on-the-job training is one of the best ways to learn new skills, increase the level of English skills and become UPWARDLY MOBILE."[92] They are told that their American coworkers will be "quite willing to help them learn English."[93]

Studies show, however, that few refugees learn English on the job, because the minimum-wage jobs for which they are hired provide no opportunity to use English or improve proficiency. In general, refugees who work fewer hours each week seem to learn English faster, probably because they enroll in English classes during the time they have available.[94] Because few refugees who work full time either learn English on the job or are able to study enough to improve their English, highly qualified refugees often remain trapped in low-paying jobs that do not exploit their education and job skills and that offer no opportunity to learn English. As a result, in the early 1980s, the unemployment rate for Indochinese who arrived between 1975 and 1978 dramatically increased, as many were employed in "last-hired, first-hired" jobs that were eliminated in the 1982 recession.[95] Despite this evidence, the program continues to teach refugees that they should decline welfare, delay schooling, and immediately accept minimum-wage jobs where they can learn English.

Assumption 10: The Refugees' Hard Work Will Be Rewarded with Rapid Upward Mobility

The program depicts a straightforward relationship between hard work and economic advancement. Preemployment classes, for instance, teach that employers rarely fire employees who exhibit proper behavior and that the primary concern on the job should be to establish a "good work record."[96] Cultural orientation lessons teach that being a "good worker" will mean moving up to a higher-paying job.[97] Classes recommend "lateral movement" to gain varied work experience, with "hard work and perseverance" the key to upward mobility.[98] Hard-working refugees can even expect to be rewarded by being able to bring their relatives to the United States.[99]

Many lessons contrast employed and unemployed refugees in the United States by focusing on the laziness of those without work. In one lesson, Cuong works for $3.50 an hour at two jobs, knowing that "if you work hard and don't give up easily, there's always a place for you," while his friend Dung sits at home watching a television purchased with a welfare check.[100] By the end of the story, Dung realizes that he made a mistake delaying employment while he studied English, because Cuong finds a better job paying $5.00 an hour, "enough to support the kids and to pay rent and food."

In order to satisfy their employer and supervisor, refugees practice appropriate apologies in case the "boss" or a co-worker seems angry, and they learn that they must promise to do better if their performance is criticized.[101] They are taught to accept the monotony of assembly-line work as necessary for their company "to produce items of quality, keep costs low and still make a profit."[102] They do not learn how to express grievances or how to respond to unfair criticism. They practice how to follow directions, but not how to give them.[103] They are taught that a commitment to the good of their employer will lead to economic reward, personal fulfillment, and a bright future.

Assumption 11: Resettled Refugees Enjoy Equal Social and Economic Opportunity

With the exception of the lessons focusing on the refugees' racial biases, no lessons deal with discrimination. Rather, the refugees are taught that they will be treated justly and that they are to blame if they are unable to find employment or housing. Landlords will be happy to rent apartments as long as Southeast Asians maintain them properly and pay the rent on time. School officials and other authorities will be helpful and concerned about family welfare.[104] The police will be their "helpers."[105] Supervisors and coworkers will be fair and offer advice, and the refugees are encouraged to talk with them about their hobbies and invite them home for dinner.[106] In short, refugees can expect both economic opportunity and a warm welcome, provided that they strive for self-sufficiency. This official confidence in the future is conveyed most forcefully in simulations of the workplace, such as the sewing assembly room. These simulations—concrete attempts to represent the U.S. workplace—express two final assumptions about the United States.

Assumption 12: It Is Hard Work That Determines Who Gets Which Jobs

Under this assumption, if you don't have a job, it's because you did not work hard enough. The curriculum does not acknowledge that there is a structural need for entry-level workers in the United States and that race, class, and nationality play a major role in determining who has these jobs. Instead, the curriculum implies that a commitment to self-sufficiency, as expressed by hard work, will determine individual employment. In the "survival" text written by the director of the curriculum department in the Philippines and used in classes there, the refugees are given the following recommendations for success:

> Go to work on time. Don't be absent a lot.
> Work hard. Don't be lazy . . .
> Be friendly. Get along with everybody. Be nice to the other workers. . . . Smile at them.
> Be clean and neat.[107]

In *Life in the New Land*, the ICMC collection of cartoon stories used in cultural orientation classes, those refugees who are unemployed are those who are lazy, satisfied with welfare, or mistakenly enrolled in school trying to improve their English before seeking employment. Again and again, the lessons teach that there is "a good future for those who really want to succeed," while problems are due to unwillingness to work.[108]

Assumption 13: There Is Consensus in the United States on Basic American Values that Newcomers Must Adopt

In order to change the refugees' values, the educational program has had to specify the new values that will underlie their successful resettlement. These are "self-sufficiency" and a commitment to workplace productivity (as expressed by the phrase "time is money.") By teaching these values, the refugee program, like the Americanization movement, seeks to convince the immigrants to change their thinking in order to accept their position in U.S. society.

Like the Americanization movement, the refugee program was created immediately after a period of internal political conflict, during which major changes in American society polarized the country and undermined the traditional consensus on values. The Americanization movement grew in the aftermath of the Civil War and during the rapid industrialization of the United States. The refugee program grew in the aftermath of the war in Vietnam, which threatened American unity by destroying national consensus about the morality of U.S. governmental decisions.

After the war, in the 1970s and 1980s, a historic struggle continued over the shape of the country's future. But rather than recognizing, depicting, and confronting this struggle, the refugee program persists in a simplified, outdated depiction of an American consensus. Indeed, the refugees are presented a vision of life in the United States in which there is equal opportunity for all, equality and harmony on the job, and rapid upward mobility for those who work hard. Business and government harness nature for the general good, and justice results from individuals' pursuit of self-interest.

Yet the reality that refugees discover after resettlement is unemployment, layoffs due to economic forces having nothing to do with individual work effort, and a wide gulf between themselves and their American supervisors and coworkers. Though the refugees need to cope with this reality of resettlement, the program offers only a philosophy of individual self-sufficiency and a commitment to hard work.

THE PRE-EMPLOYMENT TRAINING CORPORATION

The limitations of the program's effort to prepare refugees for the reality of resettlement can be seen most clearly in the workplace simulations developed at the Galang processing center. The central feature of the simulations involves transforming the classroom into a workplace and the educational program into a simulated corporation called The Pre-Employment Training Corporation (PETCO). The corporation is intended to teach workplace rules and procedures (payroll, safety), the importance of time (being on time, working quickly), and proper workplace behavior (following directions, seeking clarification).[109] The educational administrators become PETCO managers; the teachers act as supervisors; and the students become PETCO workers. The students apply for jobs and punch time clocks. They receive paychecks, which they cash for play money and use to buy refreshments, movie tickets, and articles at a simulated department store. If they are late for class, their pay is docked. If they violate PETCO rules, they are fined. The sewing assembly simulation in Vang Nhia's class is one example of PETCO in operation; other simulations include a fast-food restaurant, a janitorial service, a variety store, an electronics assembly plant, and a small industrial production line.

The PETCO simulation is in one way a highly unrealistic depiction of work in the United States, and in another way strikingly accurate. It is unrealistic in its insistence on the benefits of hard work and obeying orders; workers in the United States "seldom are fired for lack of skills but rather due to unacceptable behavior. Employees whose skills are less than adequate, but who exhibit proper behavior, are seldom fired."[110] PETCO teaches that workers "create problems for themselves" when they do not observe company rules and that "an employer is one to turn to with bad news as well as good."[111] On the job, the refugees are taught to "measure

their value as a worker . . . in terms of meeting time and production quotas."[112] Because the emphasis on production places a high value on time,
PETCO teaches that "time is money," "time's too short," and "time is of
the essence." The goal is to ensure that the refugees accept their employers'
workplace demands and do not cause difficulties. The PETCO designers
assume that, without such training, the refugees will create "conflict and
discord in the workplace."[113]

Yet PETCO also accurately depicts, and contributes to, the powerlessness
that many resettled Indochinese experience. Though the program claims
that a major goal of PETCO is to teach the concepts of "self-reliance" and
"self-sufficiency," refugees at PETCO are given no authority to make their
own decisions.[114] They are expected to follow supervisors' orders and obey
PETCO rules; they do not elect representatives to negotiate salary, workplace rules, or any other aspect of their "employment"; and they are not
permitted to discuss their own educational needs or contribute to program
design. Instead, they are taught that their survival as employees in the United
States depends upon their ability to do what they are told.

This depiction of work in the United States closely resembles that of the
Americanization movement. It is designed to convince the refugees that
their culture and behavior is the source of their economic success or failure,
while it withholds education that might prepare the refugees for jobs offering real hope for economic well being. As Tran Minh, a young refugee
in the Philippines, learned: "We're going to have a lot of hardships . . . in
a society in which almost everybody has to exert their determination and
compete with one another just for continuing to breathe." The PETCO
simulation, like the program generally, offers Tran no alternative but hard
work. It does not teach him how to change his circumstances, nor does it
seek to empower him by working to change the economic conditions that
lead to long-term poverty. Rather, it teaches him to accept his life-long
struggle to survive, to be grateful for resettlement in U.S. society, and to
hold onto American success ideology. Though the program sets out to
describe the United States and its people to Indochinese refugees, it is
trapped by an ideology of success that is used to justify channeling refugees
into minimum-wage jobs. This is an ideology which became enshrined in
the Americanization movement; Southeast Asians are its most recent victims.

CONCLUSIONS

In its promise to help refugees, the curriculum of the U.S. refugee program proclaims a lofty goal: to prepare refugees for successful living in the
United States. Yet the curriculum does not address the massive social,
psychological, and economic problems that continue to plague resettled
refugees long after their arrival in the United States. The program claims

to provide realistic information, but instead it presents the myths and dreams of an ideology of individual self-sufficiency that fewer and fewer Americans believe fully themselves.[115] Though it claims to prepare refugees for self-sufficiency, it teaches the language of powerlessness. Though it claims to respect the traditional cultures of Indochina, in virtually every lesson it seeks to convince the refugees that their native cultures are the source of their resettlement problems. Though it claims to meet the refugees' economic needs, its solution is to assume that the refugees themselves are the source of their own inability to find jobs. Taken together, the official assumptions behind the program suggest that the underlying goal is to replace the refugees' ties to culture and community with an isolated struggle for individual material wealth. Americans who are themselves losing faith in individualism, seek to instill its principles in the newest Americans.

Keepers of the Camps

The political and military leaders of the nation taught the people to distrust the legitimacy of governmental institutions, to become cynical, and to abandon the nation's war aims. The war and its official salesmen were finally judged as counterfeit. The war's casualties were considered as political victims. The hideous bureaucracy of the war made it all seem worse.

Loren Baritz, *Backfire: American Culture and the Vietnam War*[1]

At a gathering . . . in May of this year (1985) the ICMC IESL/CO Program celebrated its fifth anniversary of service to refugees. John McCarthy, President of ICMC . . . recalled the early days of the program and looked with pride on the achievements made since 1980. Many changes have taken place since those days. Growth is the most obvious.

ICMC Program Management Plan for FY 1986[2]

The counterfeit universe presented to refugees in the educational program at the processing centers is planned and purposeful. The unrealistic vision of life in the United States, the myths of American success ideology, the denigration of Southeast Asian cultures, and the effort to change refugees' behavior, attitudes, and values result from systematic decisions by policymakers throughout the educational bureaucracy.

In order to understand why the educational program takes the shape that it does, we must look at the governmental and private agencies that organize and operate the processing centers. These agencies set goals, determine program content and methodology, and evaluate program effectiveness. They construct the counterfeit universe contained in the curriculum, and so are responsible for its long-term impact on the lives of resettled refugees.

These agencies are not the first ones to have been devoted to migration and reeducation; they are only the most recent in a string of bureaucracies charged with managing people considered marginal to American society. They are the new keepers of the camps.

PRIVATE AGENCIES AND PUBLIC POLICY

The central components in the bureaucracy of the educational program are the Bureau for Refugee Programs of the U.S. Department of State, the ICMC, and a consortium comprised of the Experiment in International Living, Save the Children, and World Education. Although it has no direct involvement in the processing centers, the Office of Refugee Resettlement of the Department of Health and Human Services regulates domestic refugee programs. Therefore it has indirect influence over the processing centers, as the overseas staff coordinates the overseas content with that of the domestic curriculum.

Primary responsibility for the processing centers rests with the Bureau for Refugee Programs, which provides funding for the centers. The bureau maintains an officer in Southeast Asia responsible for liaison with the Washington office and for oversight of program management, curriculum development, evaluation, and long-range planning. The main role of the bureau is to oversee the contracts with ICMC and the consortium and to monitor the effectiveness of the program. To these ends, the bureau establishes goals and policies and ensures that these policies are implemented. Officials of the U.S. embassies in the region also regularly visit the centers, meeting with officials and with representatives from the Washington office of the Bureau for Refugee Programs.

Under contract with the bureau, ICMC operates the main educational program in the Philippines, while the consortium operates the much smaller processing center in Thailand.[3] Together, these agencies have been responsible for planning and implementing the educational program since it was created in 1980. Because it operates the largest processing center, as well as the Orderly Departure Program (ODP) of legal emigration from Vietnam, ICMC is by far the most important agency holding a contract with the bureau. Its decisions dominate the program throughout the region, particularly in the content of the educational program. In general, the consortium's relationship with the bureau resembles ICMC's. The much smaller size of the consortium program means that it is under less scrutiny and pressure, as its effectiveness has less impact on overall statistics than the much larger ICMC program. Therefore, in order to understand the content of the program in the processing centers, it is necessary to examine ICMC's relationship with the Bureau for Refugee Programs.

As the number of refugees being processed for resettlement increased in the early 1980s, ICMC grew rapidly. From a handful of employees in 1980, the organization had expanded by 1987 to include 1,000 Americans and Filipinos on the educational staff at PRPC. Because the Philippine processing center was located far from any major population area, ICMC had to build a small city for its employees, a 4-kilometer-long company town, with classroom buildings for 10,000 students, 50 staff dormitory buildings, offices, a language lab, a video and sound studio, a resource library for teachers, meeting rooms, a training building, a guest house for visiting officials, supply rooms, a motor pool, and a photocopying building. A separate PRPC administrative organization for refugee housing and camp operations was created as well, with responsibility for UNHCR buildings; Philippine military offices and housing; food service buildings and staff housing; temporary quarters for construction crews; fuel- and food-supply buildings; a fleet of trucks, jeeps, and buses; and billets for nearly 20,000 refugees. One indication of the size and complexity of the ICMC organization is that, in 1983, the descriptions of separate job classifications in the bureaucracy at the Philippine camp included 47 different categories, running over 100 pages.[4] This list did not include the ICMC administration in Switzerland or the United States, and it was developed prior to the formation of PASS, the separate educational program for adolescents, which led in 1985 to a further expansion in the size of the bureaucracy. Perhaps a better measure of the size of the ICMC bureaucracy is the use of paper; in 1984 the number of pages of photocopies made at the PRPC copy center, not including classroom materials, was over 1.5 million. All of this expansion was funded by appropriations from the Bureau for Refugee Programs.

As it grew, the ICMC bureaucracy developed two main divisions: the educational program and operations. The operations unit was given responsibility for transportation between Manila and the camp, and for staff housing, supplies for offices and dormitories, personnel, budgets, and relations with other agencies and with the Philippine government. The educational bureaucracy was given responsibility for each of the educational components: cultural orientation, ESL, preemployment training, and preparation for U.S. secondary schools. Separate program officers were appointed for each component, with additional officers assigned to curriculum, training, and "special programs" (primarily the language lab). An overall project director was put in charge of two deputy directors, one for each division.

The educational bureaucracy was modeled after those of the military and government, rather than after the bureaucracies of universities or other U.S. educational institutions. Gradually, its terminology reflected this bureaucratic model. The personnel files of ICMC staff members, for instance, were named "201 files," a term adopted from the U.S. military. The officers in charge of the educational components gradually came to function like program officers in federal agencies rather than like department heads in educational institutions. This meant that expertise in content (ESL, cultural orientation, preemployment training) was less important than administrative experience in government. The main result is that managers are hired and promoted primarily for their bureaucratic skills rather than their educational expertise.

Although ICMC is part of a complicated web of international agencies offering refugee assistance in Southeast Asia, its phenomenal growth in recent years is due in part to its ability to operate independently of this network.[5] For instance, the single UN representative in the Philippine camps has virtually no influence over policy and operations, despite the fact that UNHCR is the most important international office influencing refugee affairs in Southeast Asia. UNHCR's lack of influence is partly a result of its focus on ensuring the principle of *nonrefoulement*—that refugees should not be forcibly repatriated. Because this is not a danger in the processing centers, UNHCR's role as protector of the refugees does not apply.[6] More importantly, because the refugees in the centers have been accepted for resettlement, major responsibility for them has shifted to the U.S. government and its contracting agencies. Therefore unlike in the first-asylum camps, where UNHCR takes responsibility for overseeing camp security and operations, the processing centers are dominated by ICMC and State Department officials.[7]

The primary means by which the Bureau for Refugee Programs influences ICMC and the consortium is through the yearly management plans. These bulky documents, running into hundreds of pages, outline major goals and expenditures for the processing centers for each fiscal year. Because they must be approved by the Bureau for Refugee Programs before funding is granted, these plans must directly reflect goals established in Washington. For instance, when Congress became dissatisfied with high unemployment rates among refugees in 1981–1982, the bureau responded by requiring ICMC to develop the preemployment training program. Later, in 1985, when Amerasians and adjustment problems among Southeast Asian adolescents began to draw the attention of Congress, the bureau required ICMC and the consortium to shift resources from preemployment training to the new secondary schools program, PASS.

Although ICMC is an independent, private agency, its dependence upon State Department funding means that it has increasingly become subject to State Department directives. Despite some effort to maintain control over educational policy, ICMC (as well as the consortium) has become, in effect, the Southeast Asian operational service arm of the Bureau for Refugee Programs. An ICMC publicity video produced in 1985 makes explicit its close relationship with the federal agency. "ICMC is ready to do its part on behalf of the United States government in this noble effort" to educate refugees.[8]

In this, ICMC is not alone, as many private voluntary agencies have developed complex, intimate relationships with the U.S. government when it has become their main source of revenue. To understand the relationship between ICMC and the Bureau for Refugee Programs, and the role this relationship plays in the content of the educational program, it is necessary to examine the growing mutual dependence between private agencies and the U.S. government.

PRIVATE AGENCIES AND THE U.S. GOVERNMENT

Since the late 1970s, private "voluntary" agencies, called "PVOs" or "volags" in the jargon of relief, have come to play a major role in the delivery of many overseas federal programs. Although there is no comprehensive list of PVOs involved in projects outside the United States, and no universally accepted definition of a PVO, most federal agencies accept the definition developed by the U.S. Agency for International Development (AID).

PVOs are: (1) formally structured (i.e., have a legal existence, a charter/constitution, staff, etc.), (2) not for profit, (3) non-governmental (although they may be "quasi-governmental"), (4) whose membership and motivations are not commercial, and (5) whose aims deal with development, population, and humanitarian activities in the LDCs [less developed countries] or have the potential of being useful in the development field. The non-sectarian service arms of the religious denominations are included in this definition.[9]

PVOs vary greatly in their philosophical and religious orientations, their operational styles, and their service specialties. There are several hundred PVOs in the United States and several thousand worldwide.[10]

About a dozen PVOs are heavily involved in resettling Indochinese refugees, with ICMC by far the largest. To some extent, their staff members move from job to job among the various agencies, the most noteworthy example being the appointment of the former director of the Bureau for Refugee Programs, James Purcell, as head of the ICM as of October 1, 1988. Transfers among the various ICMC operations are even more common. For instance, the JVA officer at the Galang camp during 1986 was a former cultural orientation supervisor in the Philippine operations; the cultural orientation officer in the Philippines during 1985–86 had previously worked in the ODP operation in Thailand; and the deputy director for operations at the Philippine center during 1985–87 was the former director of the ICMC refugee program in the Sudan, which also operates under a State Department contract.[11] For a growing number of ICMC employees, its expanding operations worldwide have provided an opportunity for rapid career advancement.

No PVO can avoid the world of politics in refugee relief and education. Therefore, in recent years, PVOs have become increasingly sophisticated in their ability to influence the formulation of refugee policy. Along with governments and the United Nations, they have become one of the major players in the game. Often, the role they assign to themselves is that of protector of refugees' interests. Thus they argue for larger resettlement quotas; they lobby the U.S. Congress for increased funding; and they perform an important public education function through their ability to publicize issues and to raise public awareness. Though PVOs do not make policy and are not in a position to eliminate the causes of refugee movements, they can have a major impact on policymakers and on program operations.[12]

The ability of PVOs to carry out these important functions depends, however, upon their independence from governments. Both the U.S. government and the PVOs recognize the advantage that formal independence provides; PVOs can gain access to regions of the world where governments are not welcome. This was one of the major reasons for the State Department's decision in the early 1970s to increase its use of PVOs in carrying out foreign aid programs. For most PVOs, therefore, it is essential to maintain the appearance of integrity and independence in the formulation and implementation of their projects.[13]

As nonprofit, tax–exempt organizations, however, PVOs must rely upon private contributions and government contracts for their income. As a result, they must satisfy private constituencies that provide their funding, as well as the U.S. government. Some agencies, such as Catholic Relief Services, one of the largest U.S. agencies, obtain the bulk of their funds from the government, most often from AID. For these agencies to carry out their work, they must maintain the support of their major source of funds: the U.S. government. But as PVOs become increasingly dependent upon government funding, they gradually lose their ability to operate independently and to represent and protect refugees' interests.

Because of important changes in federal laws in the 1970s and 1980s, PVOs have greatly increased their role in government programs overseas. The most important legislative change was "New Directions," a change in the foreign aid program known as the Mutual Development and Cooperation Act of 1973. Incorporated into amendments to the Foreign Aid Assistance Act, New Directions was the culmination of a two–year review of U.S. foreign aid policy. The New Directions philosophy emphasized reduced governmental presence and profile overseas and increased participation of American PVOs in project planning, evaluation, and implementation.[14]

A major impact of the 1973 legislation was a rapid increase in the involvement of PVOs in the delivery of foreign aid. Since 1979, American PVOs have had overseas budgets of over $1 billion, with somewhat more than one-third of this amount coming from governmental agencies.[15] The rise in use of PVOs has made it possible for organizations such as ICMC to expand their operations worldwide and to develop a close relationship with officials in the State Department. The increase in the use of PVOs has made it natural for the State Department to turn to them to plan and implement the overseas refugee program.[16]

Their growing dependency on federal funding and their crucial role in delivery of U.S. foreign aid makes PVOs especially vulnerable to the charge that their function is to implement U.S. policy. It is generally agreed that the advantages associated with independent PVOs are mitigated when the PVOs receive more than 90 percent of their funding from the government.[17] The danger, serious enough to warrant discussion in congressional hearings, is that the agencies will lose their ability to operate independently of the government agencies that provide their funds.[18]

This problem is particularly serious in the refugee program, where the Department of State provides all of the funding for the educational program in the processing centers. ICMC's complete dependence upon government funding means that it cannot be expected to operate the program in the interest of the refugees, but instead must function in the interest of the agency that provides funding.

ICMC's dependency is further exacerbated by the unusual length of the refugee program. Though traditionally considered short-term emergency efforts, refugee programs since the early 1970s have become increasingly institutionalized. Nowhere is this more evident than at the processing centers in Southeast Asia, which have operated since 1980 and are expected to continue at least through 1989. As so many people have found their jobs linked to the refugee program, those who work to resolve refugee problems have come to rely upon them for their livelihood. A common joke among staff members whose jobs were threatened by a temporary drop in the number of refugees during 1985 was, "Cheer up. There will always be refugees."

EFFECTS OF BUREAUCRATIC GROWTH

The growth of a large, relatively permanent bureaucracy for the processing centers has had two related effects upon program content. First, policy is made in Washington, D.C., far from the refugees themselves, while the teachers and others with day-to-day contact have little impact upon it. Second, the interests of individual refugees have become subservient to domestic political pressures.

In the Philippines, the growth of the bureaucracy has meant a widening gap between the Americans who formulate educational policy and the refugees whose lives are effected by that policy.[19] Upper managers have virtually no contact with individual refugees or classroom teachers. Middle managers learn that the experiences of individual refugees are irrelevant to evaluations of their job performance. Many teachers feel that policymakers are concerned with funding and congressional reaction, rather than with effective teaching or student learning. As the bureaucracy grows, the gulf widens between the well paid U.S. managers and the Filipino teachers, who receive peso salaries and handle the difficult day-to-day contact with the refugees. The bureaucrats in charge maintain their charts of the tens of thousands of refugees who complete the program, while the teachers labor in the dusty, non-air-conditioned, asbestos-polluted classrooms. Like the low-level members of many bureaucracies, the teachers often feel that they must implement policy formulated by bureaucrats who know nothing about the people whom the program is supposed to assist. Gradually the individuals within the organization lose the ability to ensure that it will achieve the goal for which it was established: the education of Indochinese refugees.

As the policymakers become removed from the people affected by their decisions, program goals increasingly reflect domestic policy concerns rather than the refugees' real needs. Two major domestic concerns have come to determine program goals and content: reducing the refugees' use of public assistance and ensuring that they do not compete for jobs with middle-class and working-class Americans.[20]

Though these goals do not necessarily benefit the refugees, they appear throughout the refugee bureaucracy. One of the most explicit statements is contained in ORR regulations requiring refugees to take jobs as soon as possible after their arrival in the United States; in practice, this means that they are required to accept minimum-wage employment, a fact that the ORR regulations explicitly recognize.[21] Similarly, in testimony before Congress, James N. Purcell, Jr., former director of the Bureau for Refugee Programs, argued that the program should have the goal of placing refugees in jobs immediately upon their arrival. To this end, the bureau has supported efforts to restrict aid to refugees through existing welfare mechanisms.[22] In this way, ensuring that refugees take minimum-wage jobs has become the primary goal of the processing centers as well as of domestic resettlement agencies.

INSIDE THE EDUCATIONAL BUREAUCRACY

How does the educational bureaucracy operate in order to sustain the counterfeit universe it presents to refugees? After all, many Americans and host country nationals, with widely varying points of view, work in the processing centers. To some extent, these individuals are able to present their own views to individual refugees outside of meetings and classes, but there is remarkably little debate about class content or about the appropriateness of channeling refugees into dead-end jobs. This is due to a system of hierarchy and sanctions that restricts individual creativity and initiative and creates powerful pressure to conform to official goals and methods.

There are in fact two parallel hierarchies within the processing centers.

One is the formal bureaucratic hierarchy determined by the list of job levels, with upper managers at the top, followed by middle managers (program officers and others in charge of curriculum, teacher training, and special services), and then supervisors, teachers, and support staff. The second hierarchy is organized according to nationality: Americans are at the top, followed by "host-country nationals" (Filipinos or Thais), with Indochinese at the bottom.

One of the main factors affecting the hierarchy of nationality is the large difference in pay between "local hire" (Filipino or Thai) and "direct hire" (U.S.) staff members. At PRPC, Filipino employees are paid salaries, in pesos, that are somewhat above the average for similar jobs in Philippine society. U.S. employees are paid dollar salaries that are approximately ten times greater than the salaries paid to Filipinos for the same jobs. The pay differential also applies to per-diem payments for staff members on official business in Manila; again, Americans are paid approximately six times as much as Filipinos.[23] In theory, Americans hired in the Philippines are supposed to be paid "local-hire" salaries, but these Americans are permitted to travel to the United States to be rehired as "direct-hire" employees. The resulting tenfold increase in salary easily pays the expense of travel to the United States. In the ICMC Management Plan for 1983, the issue of unequal pay for equal work was termed "very sensitive."[24] The proposed solution was to recognize the contribution of staff members with long employment records (in most cases Filipinos) through parties, certificates, and awards.

But the distinction between U.S. and Filipino staff members is not limited to salary; it is rigidly maintained throughout the bureaucracy. Separate meetings to discuss employee concerns are held for local-and direct-hire staff members. Jobs are specified as either local or direct hire. Virtually every official act, including committee appointments, housing assignments, budget requests, and transportation priorities, maintains the distinction between U.S. and Filipino staff members.[25]

An additional source of division involves gender differences within the hierarchy. Most of the U.S. managers have been male, while most of the teachers have been Filipino females. Many of the American men, including some program officers, frequent the notorious bars and massage parlors of the Ermita section of Manila near the ICMC office, as well as the sex clubs around the U.S. military bases, about one hour's drive from the refugee center. Occasionally, the Americans bring bar girls to stay with them in their houses in the village of Morong near the camp. In the small-town atmosphere of the processing center, where individuals' actions are widely known and discussed, many Filipino women resent the Americans' actions.

Division also results from the Filipinos' awareness of the gap between conditions inside the camp and in the rural areas of Bataan Province in the surrounding area. Malnutrition is widespread in the barrios and in the town of Morong nearby. Each day, impoverished Filipinos living along the road to the camp see large trucks bringing free food to the refugees. Several times each week, they see busloads of refugees transported to Manila for their flights to the United States.[26] In contrast, hundreds of Filipinos line up each day at the U.S. embassy on Roxas Boulevard in a desperate attempt to gain an entry visa for the United States. For the tens of thousands of Filipinos wishing to emigrate to the United States, the special treatment offered the refugees is a source of resentment. Many Filipino teachers inside the camp gates identify with the feelings of the Filipinos outside who are seeking to emigrate to the United States.

Mistrust and tension also characterize relationships between the U.S. and Filipino branches of the camp administration. The Filipino military and civilian authorities oversee the actual site and handle construction, maintenance, security, transportation, and supplies, including food. They also process the refugees when they arrive and depart, and they control the work-credit system, which requires the refugees to complete two hours of employment each day in addition to their classes. State Department and ICMC officers attempt to exercise authority in these areas, though they do not control actual operations.[27]

An important result of this split between Americans and Filipinos is that relationships are characterized by extreme formality and an overriding concern with avoiding conflict. Thus the staff members constitute a pseudo-community: a group in which the primary dynamic is conflict-avoidance and denial of difference. In such a group there is enormous pressure to conform, because open diversity would endanger the pretense of community by threatening to reveal the atmosphere of distrust and competitiveness under the surface.[28] This is especially the case in the intense and isolated atmosphere of the refugee camp. In this way, officials are able to formulate and implement policy without having to deal with organized staff opposition.[29] In short, the hierarchy of nationality results in pressures to conform and to avoid open conflict, thereby serving the interests of bureaucrats who wish to formulate policy without the active involvement of a critical professional staff.

In addition to the hierarchy of nationality, the formal bureaucratic hierarchy also ensures that individuals within the organization conform to bureaucratic policy. In the Philippines, a system of privilege encourages individuals to link their own work with the goals and procedures established by policymakers and program managers.

The system of privilege begins when new staff members leave Manila for their trip to the refugee center. The drive between Manila and the processing center is a long and difficult one, over narrow and dangerous mountain roads that may be partly washed out during the monsoon season, yet the trip is the primary means by which staff members stock up on food and personal supplies. Different vehicles are assigned to individuals at different job levels, varying systematically according to comfort, safety, availability, and frequency.[30] Many other examples of the hierarchy of petty privilege fill the daily life of the ICMC staff members, as job levels determine menus at public events, frequency of paid trips, access to a swimming pool and bowling alley, availability of medical services in the camp clinic, access to paper and photocopying, and style of furniture in dormitories. A textbook written by the curriculum officer was used in the camp, despite serious criticisms of it in a review of survival English texts.[31] As one Filipino teacher said: "Every day in every way we are reminded who is important and who isn't."

But the system of privilege is not limited to matters of convenience. Assignment to asbestos or nonasbestos housing is made according to job level. Top officials who establish housing assignment priorities live in private houses made of nonasbestos materials, while program officers are assigned private rooms in a special concrete-block dormitory. Other middle managers are assigned similar private rooms in a separate concrete-block dormitory. In contrast, lower-level supervisors and teachers are assigned shared rooms in structures made of asbestos. As a result of this system, most Americans occupy nonasbestos housing, while most Filipinos live in asbestos structures.

The assignment of privileges emphasizes for employees the importance of the bureaucratic hierarchy, where every individual has a supervisor. As the bureaucracy grows in importance, staff members become increasingly attentive to the need to please their supervisors. Indeed, this can eventually become a greater imperative than the overall goal of the organization. At ICMC, this shift in priorities was brought about in part by adoption of a detailed, strictly hierarchial system of supervisory responsibility. Called the ICMC Supervision Model, this system ensures that each level of the bureaucracy seeks the approval of the next-higher level for its actions. Adopted in mid–1983, the Supervision Model includes a strict schedule of formal evaluations, specific forms and procedures to be used in all evaluations, 12 hours of training in use of the system for every member of the staff, and periodic system reviews that require several hundred hours of staff time. The system was approved by the Bureau for Refugee Programs in 1984 and led to rapid promotion to deputy director of the individual most responsible for its design and implementation.[32]

The effect of the new system on the staff was profound. Individuals quickly learned that whether refugees acquired English or cultural orientation and preemployment skills was subordinated to the need to please one's boss. In fact, the pressure to gain a supervisor's approval is often at odds with accurate analysis and prediction, particularly at the higher levels of the bureaucracy, where upper managers are held responsible for the overall success of the program.[33] ICMC employees learned that requests for a comprehensive testing program, or other program changes, might be interpreted as criticisms of management. Most importantly, because the program lacked a system for assessing student learning, there was no objective measure of success. All that mattered was what officials said. In such circumstances, officials gained enormous power to pursue policies and make decisions that are not easily subject to critical analysis.

In bureaucracies, the need to demonstrate success and to maintain funding often leads to manipulation and distortion of data. In place of open debate, bureaucrats may substitute "facts" designed to show that progress is being made, that the bureaucracy is working. Truly objective, scientific data can be dangerous to a bureaucracy, insofar as it may reveal a failure to achieve stated aims. Thus bureaucracies often misuse scientific data and procedures to justify their actions and sustain programs and funding.

Like officials everywhere, ICMC managers seek "objective" measures to support their decisions. Two examples of such measures reveal their role in decisions in the Philippine center since 1983[34]: (1) an evaluation of the ICMC Instructional Model[35]; and (2) a student opinion survey that found serious student dissatisfaction with the preemployment training program.[36] These studies failed to meet accepted scientific standards in several ways. Most importantly, the questionnaires were not tested before use, and they were designed to elicit particular answers. Moreover, the individuals in charge of data collection and analysis had no training or experience in such studies, and they had a personal stake in the outcomes. Despite such problems, these studies were the basis for important decisions regarding classroom practices, supervision and evaluation of teachers, and course content.

One of these decisions was to delay use of communicative curricula in preemployment training, a decision justified by the conclusion of the student opinion survey that there was serious student dissatisfaction with PET classes using the communicative approach. In the survey, 11 out of 151 respondents expressed some form of dissatisfaction with PET classes, while the remainder expressed satisfaction. Though no comparative figures were gathered for cultural orientation or ESL classes, this finding was declared "significant" and the conclusion of the report emphasized the students' "anti-PET attitude." Moreover, the report claimed that B-level students, from the largest of the five levels in the program, were especially unhappy with PET, although in the survey only 10 B-level students out of a total B-level population of nearly 3,000 expressed any form of dissatisfaction.

In a similar manner, officials sought to justify their decision to require specific teaching practices with a survey of teachers' opinions.[37] When the survey unexpectedly uncovered misgivings about these practices, the project director responded with a memorandum that staff members called the "you are all fools memo."[38] The memo praised the deputy director who had developed the list of required teaching practices, and it warned the staff not to criticize them. Faced with such a memo, the ICMC staff members realized that further discussion of the teaching practices would damage their careers with ICMC. In such circumstances, teachers and low-level staff members are made to understand that the highest priority is to support official decisions. The result is a cynical realization that the goal of the ICMC bureaucracy is not to ensure learning, but to ensure continued funding.

THE FIELD OF ENGLISH AS A SECOND LANGUAGE

One final factor makes it possible for the educational bureaucracy to sustain its counterfeit universe: the lack of qualified staff in high positions in the processing centers. Since the field of English as a second language (ESL) developed as a separate discipline in the 1950s, it has become widely accepted that ESL instructors and administrators must have specialized training in the nature and structure of language, theory of language learning, and theory and methods of teaching. Several dozen universities now offer M.A. degrees in ESL, and a growing number of the best universities in the country offer doctoral programs.

In the 30 years in which ESL has been recognized as a separate discipline, the overseas refugee program has been arguably the single most important undertaking in the field. The Philippine processing center is the largest ESL program at one site anywhere, and its impact upon the lives and futures of its graduates is enormously important. Therefore it is perhaps surprising that the leading theoreticians, planners, and practitioners in the field have had virtually no involvement in the program.[39] Of 33 members of the executive and editorial boards of Teachers of English to Speakers of Other Languages (TESOL), the international organization of ESL professionals, only two visited the overseas camps, both as short-term consultants, between 1981 and 1986. Many of those individuals who are hired have little or no training in ESL or other relevant areas of education. Of the twelve managers in charge of various instructional components in the Philippines between 1983 and 1986, only two had graduate degrees (M.A.s) in ESL or linguistics; another, in charge of the cultural orientation component, was a graduate student. The deputy director with responsibility for the instructional program did not hold a degree in ESL or linguistics. Though hiring has recently improved, the program has been slow to incorporate the most recent advances in language teaching, such as communicative texts and methods, and has instead employed techniques that recent research has shown to be ineffective.[40] To some degree, this results from the difficulties involved in finding individuals willing to relocate and to work under difficult conditions. But virtually all ESL professionals know about the processing centers and the job openings in them, and the salaries exceed those for comparable positions in the United States. American supervisors with virtually no previous experience receive approximately $15,000 per year. Since most employees do not pay U.S. income tax, this amount is comparable to a much higher salary in the United States. Also, staff members receive paid airfare, free housing in camp, and transportation between Manila and the camp. With every fifth week off, most American staff members travel extensively in the region and still return to the U.S. with some savings after one year of employment. Filipinos are paid about one-tenth the American salaries.

However, developing a competent, effective staff within the refugee program would threaten the ability of the bureaucracy to achieve its stated goals. By maintaining a relatively inexperienced and underqualified core of middle managers and supervisors, officials of ICMC and the Bureau for Refugee Programs retain a freer hand to formulate and implement decisions.[41] When a system of hierarchy and sanctions is accompanied by enormous pressure to get along in an isolated company town far from anywhere, and many staff members have inadequate professional training, the result is a single-minded bureaucracy with uncritical commitment to a counterfeit universe.[42]

Thus ICMC bureaucratic structure, along with its total dependence upon federal funds for its operations in Southeast Asia, ensures that the content of the program responds to ORR and State Department dictates rather than to the refugees' needs. Inexperienced individuals within the bureaucracy lack vision and responsibility to the refugees whom they serve, and they are rewarded not for creative ability to educate refugees, but rather for loyalty to their supervisors. Therefore they remain blind to the fate of the refugees completing the program: minimum-wage jobs offering long-term economic crisis.

The rigid hierarchy in the processing centers is ironic in light of the emphasis on individual initiative in the lessons for refugees. The refugees are told that Americans value self-reliance, independence, creativity, and personal initiative, yet the Americans and Filipinos working in the program must navigate through complex bureaucratic structures in which the ability to manipulate others is essential for individual success. While the refugees are taught that Americans value their ability to think for themselves, staff members discover that they must be cautious, distrust program managers, and view colleagues as rivals and individual initiative as a threat to standard operating procedures.

Like the content of the classes, the structure of the camp bureaucracy teaches the refugees their place in American society. This structure—rigidly hierarchial and highly specialized—ensures that the program channels refugees into the minimum-wage jobs for which they are needed. It does this by blocking alternatives, by precluding open debate about program goals, and through tight restrictions on the ability of individual refugees or staff members to affect program content.

RACISM AND THE BUREAUCRACY

Dillon S. Myer, the bureaucrat in charge of the internment of U.S. citizens of Japanese descent during World War II, later became head of the Bureau

of Indian Affairs. Then, in early 1961, he directed the Cuban refugee program for the U.S. government, and afterward served in an unknown role
in Vietnam.[43] Myer's smooth transition from one office to another suggests
an underlying similarity in his career responsibilities: In the internment
program, in the Bureau of Indian Affairs, and in the refugee program, he
was responsible for implementing policies of dispersing groups of people
considered marginal to U.S. society and to the official conception of what
it means to be an "American." As his biographer, Richard Drinnon, has
shown, Myer's life was a crusade to limit the influence of Japanese, Indians,
and Cubans in American society. Through his work, he brought consistency
to U.S. policy. And he also brought racism.

Admitted racism such as Myer's no longer characterizes official statements
about refugee resettlement, yet a narrow conception of what it means to
be an "American" continues to be a troubling feature of policy and practice.
Occasionally, this perspective becomes public. At the 1987 convention of
the international association for TESOL, the State Department organized
a meeting to bring ESL professionals up to date on the overseas program.
The first two hours included slides and videotapes of the centers in Southeast
Asia. Then the director of the program for Eastern Europe immigrants,
who had previously worked as an associate director in Thailand, showed
slides of the processing centers in Austria. She concluded her remarks with
the question: "What strikes you about these photos?" After a moment of
audience silence, one of her assistants gave the desired response: "They look
so different from the Indochinese. They look just like Americans!"[44]

Indeed, the Eastern European refugees were white, wore middle-class
clothing, and smiled directly into the camera. But millions of Americans
do not fit this description. The comments by the State Department officer
expressed a severely restricted definition of "American," one that excludes
ethnic Vietnamese and Chinese, Khmer, Lao, Hmong, Mien, and other
Southeast Asians, as well as many other people. It is not surprising that
educational policy formulated from such a perspective would include efforts
to change the identity of Indochinese refugees, to help them "become American." The cost to the refugees is enormous: tradition, community, and
identity, but the loss is America's as well: the opportunity to learn from
differences, to rediscover tradition, and to recover community.

Keeping the Charts

I am working more than 60 hours each week, but do not make enough money to meet all my expense. Because of my hours I cannot attend English classes. Also have problem with high cost of medical care. . . . My job provides me no health insurance.
> Refugee quoted in *Making It on Their Own*[1]

Victory is very near. I'll show you the charts. The charts are very good.
> Walt Rostow to Daniel Ellsberg, 1967,
> in David Halberstam, *The Best and the Brightest*[2]

In 1953, General Henri Navarre, commander of the French forces in Indochina, first uttered the now infamous statement that he could see victory in Vietnam "like a light at the end of the tunnel." A year later, in May 1954 at Dien Bien Phu, the French were defeated. During the U.S. war, as the years dragged on and the death toll mounted, one official after another issued optimistic forecasts about the course of the fighting. Sent on a mission to obtain firsthand information about the situation, General Maxwell Taylor, appointed Chairman of the Joint Chiefs of Staff by President Kennedy, cabled from Vietnam in 1961 that it was "not an excessively difficult or unpleasant place to operate."[3] In April 1975, only days before the evacuation of U.S. personnel from Saigon, Graham Martin, the last U.S. ambassador to South Vietnam, claimed that $700 million would be sufficient to shore up the faltering South Vietnamese forces and turn back a Communist victory. Henry Kissinger presented this argument to the U.S. Congress on April 15, just two weeks before the collapse of the government of South Vietnam.

The persistence of such actions is a result of two major forces at work in government bureaucracy: field officers manipulating data to make themselves and their programs look good, and widespread lying to further policy goals.[4] Policymakers in Washington are under constant pressure to be successful, which means that they must demonstrate that their programs are achieving their declared aims. Field staff members who are responsible for implementing policies, however ill conceived or unreasonable those policies might be, recognize that their career advancement depends upon their ability to successfully achieve policy objectives. Their task, in other words, is to demonstrate success, and so they are understandably reluctant to question objectives or tell their superiors when programs are not working as planned. Since policymakers depend upon field staff for data, policy formulation is ultimately undermined.

A related difficulty involves selecting appropriate criteria for measuring progress. During the war, it rarely occurred to Americans to find out what the Vietnamese considered "progress" in the war. It was far easier, and seemed only natural, to measure progress in terms that mattered in U.S. domestic politics. This measure was the body count.

The Americans failed to see the issue from the perspective of the Vietnamese. Because North Vietnam was a poor country, it fought with its greatest resource: people. The failure of U.S. officials to investigate and understand the other side's notions of progress and success was due in part to the traditional American assumption that other cultures and other people are just like us, or wish that they were just like us.[5] It was also due to American ignorance and unwillingness to learn about the culture, politics, language, and history of the Vietnamese.[6]

So when bureaucrats come under pressure to demonstrate progress, they devise technical measures, such as the body count, that may be useless in the effort to evaluate the fairness, wisdom, and effectiveness of a policy. The war in Vietnam showed that irrelevant measures of progress, ignorance of other cultures, and the bureaucratic imperative to demonstrate success will ultimately lead to failure of policy.

OFFICIAL STATEMENTS

Evaluation of the refugee education program has been extensive in recent years, with studies carried out by private evaluation firms under contract to the Bureau for Refugee Programs, by the Center for Applied Linguistics, and by staff members of the private agencies that operate the programs. The main conclusion of these studies, as well as of more informal evaluative reports by State Department officials, is that the educational program is an unqualified success.

Purcell, then director of the Bureau for Refugee Programs, testified in 1985 before the Subcommittee on Immigration, Refugees, and International

Law of the House Judiciary Committee that "the results have been re-markable—in some cases, even extraordinary."[7] Purcell's testimony, like many official statements about the effectiveness of the refugee program, included a description of one particular refugee whose individual resettle-ment was unquestionably remarkable: Jean Nguyen, who was introduced by President Reagan during his State of the Union Address. Less than ten years after leaving Vietnam, Nguyen graduated from West Point, and thus presented a striking model for other Vietnamese. The repetition of her story by high government officials was not without political significance. She had left Vietnam and joined the U.S. Army, the very army that had fought in her country. Her action was therefore politically useful because it implied an acceptance of U.S. involvement in the war by a Vietnamese refugee whom Americans could easily welcome and respect. Purcell cited other extraordinary successes as well, in particular "the numerous Indochinese high school valedictorians we read about each graduation season."

Other State Department officials present similar views of the effectiveness of refugee education. Ann Morgan, the officer in charge of monitoring the processing centers, stated in late 1985 that the educational program had reduced the time required for refugees to attain employment in the United States.[8] Morgan praised the program not only for its success in achieving its stated goal of preparing refugees for employment, but also for providing leadership in adult language education and for fostering a positive relation-ship with the three countries in which the processing centers were con-structed.[9] Other Department of State reports, such as one by the Inspector General's office, support this official view of program success. "The ESL/CO program has successfully achieved its goal of providing Indochinese refugees with at least survival skills in English and a basic introduction to American culture."[10]

Official claims that the educational program effectively prepares refugees for resettlement suggests that a measure of "successful resettlement" has been established, that this measure has been correlated with refugees' per-formance in classes and on standardized tests, and that the resulting data demonstrate that the overseas program has a direct positive influence on the refugees' resettlement. In fact, this has not been done, as there are enormous difficulties involved in showing any relationship between edu-cational programs and success in resettlement.

The resettlement program declares that its goal is to help refugees achieve self-sufficiency as soon as possible after their arrival in the United States. In practice, self-sufficiency is defined as employment. As the former deputy coordinator for refugee programs in the U.S. embassy in Manila declared in 1984, the goal of classes is "keeping refugees on a track into employment rather than on to welfare rolls or other government assistance."[11] Similarly, the Philippine cultural orientation curriculum states that "a broad objective of our classes is to prepare our students for the American job market so that they will more quickly become self-sufficient."[12] The preemployment curriculum declares that preemployment training "is designed to enable refugees to better function in any entry-level job in the U.S."[13] The key role of overseas education in achieving the goal of reducing the refugees' unemployment and use of public assistance has been one of the primary arguments given by State Department officials for continued funding of the program.

Because both official statements and program documents declare that the main goal of the educational program is to prepare the refugees for employment, one measure of evaluating program effectiveness is how well it has achieved this goal. A second measure is evaluation of the goal itself.

EARLY RESEARCH ON RESETTLEMENT

In the first six years of Indochinese refugee resettlement, researchers sought to describe the fate of newly arrived refugees.[14] The main aim of this early research was to determine which factors affect employment, public assistance, and income levels—the primary concerns of Congress, the Bureau for Refugee Programs, and ORR. Comparisons of these early studies are difficult because they relied upon different sources for their data and different measures of employment, income, and public assistance. Taken together, however, they suggest that approximately 40 percent of heads of household were employed, and that most employed refugees received minimum wage or only slightly above. Approximately 60 percent of all households received some form of public assistance, in most cases for several months after their arrival, with subsequent income coming from a combination of earned income and public assistance payments.

These early studies depict refugees struggling to become self-sufficient, relying upon welfare during their early months in order to avoid economic catastrophe, and moving to low-paying jobs as time passed. Though few refugees were found to be above the poverty line, the general trend seemed to be toward employment, and therefore it was assumed that economic self-sufficiency was possible for most families within a short period. These studies implied that the effort by the processing centers to speed refugees' employability could be expected to have a long-term positive effect on resettlement.

More recent findings, however, suggest something quite different; that the program in the centers does not lead to employment for many refugees and that employment does not help refugees avoid long-term poverty. These conclusions come from a careful reading of data provided by public and private agencies involved in refugee resettlement. We now turn to these reports.

THE RMC STUDY

The RMC study was contracted by the Bureau for Refugee Programs with the RMC Research Corporation of Hampton, New Hampshire, to assess the impact of overseas education on resettlement in the United States.[15] The study is widely cited by State Department officials as evidence that the overseas program is an unqualified success. For instance, when confronted with congressional criticisms of the Philippine educational program at hearings conducted in 1985, Purcell effectively silenced his critics by citing the RMC study.[16] The conclusions of this report also have been the basis for claims that current programs and funding should continue.[17]

The RMC project was an elaborate undertaking, involving site visits, a battery of tests, interviews with refugees and staff members in refugee programs in Southeast Asia and the United States, and complex data analysis. The study included visits to the processing centers by RMC staff, tracking of two samples of refugees (one that had completed overseas classes and one that had not) for a period of six months after their arrival in the United States, and in-depth interviews and case studies of 50 refugees, half of whom had not taken classes in the processing centers. In addition, telephone and site interviews were conducted with a large number of service agencies involved with Indochinese refugee resettlement.

When it was issued in October 1984, the RMC report was the first major scientific study of the effects of the educational program, and its conclusions were good news for those who supported continuation of the program without major changes. The most important conclusion was that the refugee education program had a major impact on the English proficiency of incoming refugees and that this impact was sustained well into the second year after arrival in the United States. The study also stated that domestic resettlement and service agencies strongly supported the overseas program and that the refugees themselves expressed similar support in interviews. The study concluded that "pre-entry training should be regarded as an *essential* element of refugee resettlement and should continue to be funded at whatever level is necessary to maintain its current level of high quality instruction."[18]

The RMC report provides important information about the unemployment and public assistance rates of resettled refugees. The study compared the employment and welfare rates of two groups of refugees: one group of 259 people, the "trained" sample, was resettled after completing overseas classes, while a second group of 103 people, called the "untrained" sample, was resettled without the benefit of education in the processing centers. If the processing centers have had a significant impact on employment and welfare rates, the group resettled without benefit of overseas education should exhibit higher rates of unemployment and use of public assistance.

The RMC report found, however, that "there is no significant difference between trained and untrained refugees in terms of the number employed or the number participating in various public assistance programs."[19] Specifically, the study found no difference during the first six months after arrival between the trained and untrained samples in the proportion of refugees receiving food stamps, cash assistance, aid to families with dependent children, unemployment compensation, supplemental security income, and other programs.[20] Research conducted in different studies reaches similar conclusions about the impact of overseas education on unemployment and public assistance rates. All studies find that the proportion of refugees requiring public assistance has remained high since the late 1970s, despite the implementation of the educational program in the processing centers in 1980.[21]

Despite the evidence that refugees' unemployment and public assistance rates have not been affected by overseas education, the RMC report concluded that the program is effective. To reach this conclusion, the study presented a complex argument based on unreliable data and on an assumed, though empirically unverified, relationship between language proficiency and employment.

The most important part of the RMC argument was that the study had found statistically significant differences between the test scores of the trained and untrained samples of refugees. The two sample groups were given the Basic English Skills Test (BEST), which assesses competence in five language areas: listening, communication, pronunciation, fluency, and reading/writing. The major finding of the RMC study was that six months after arrival in the United States, the trained group scored higher than the untrained group in all skill areas except pronunciation.[22] Furthermore, it found no differences among trained refugees from the separate program sites in Thailand, Indonesia, and the Philippines. Because the report assumed that increased proficiency in English leads to an increased probability of employment, it held that these higher scores constituted strong evidence that refugee education aids in employment.

Indirectly . . . there is evidence to suggest that pre-entry training could be making a contribution toward refugee self-sufficiency. This study and others have established a strong link between English proficiency and employability. Since pre-entry training is having such an enormous effect on English proficiency, there can be little doubt that its impact would extend to the area of employment.[23]

The logical argument of the RMC study is simple and appealing: Refugees with higher English language proficiency are more likely to obtain employment; overseas education leads to significant gains in English language proficiency as measured by the BEST test; therefore overseas education increases the likelihood that refugees will find employment. This argument is repeated in many public statements about the successes of the refugee education program and is widely accepted by staff members in most language and cultural orientation programs in the United States, as well as by most staff members in the processing centers.[24]

But the argument is fundamentally flawed, both empirically and logically. The empirical basis for the argument is the RMC finding that trained refugees scored higher on the BEST test than untrained refugees. Unfortunately, the RMC project did not undertake the most basic procedure needed to establish that overseas education improves English proficiency: a longitudinal study of test scores before and after classes. In fact, the trained sample of refugees was not tested before the educational program at all. Instead, both samples were tested only one time, after they arrived in the United States. Although as a group the trained refugees scored higher on the BEST test than the untrained group, it is impossible to determine whether their higher average score on the BEST test was due to their overseas classes or to other factors. It is entirely possible that the trained sample had a higher average English proficiency before beginning classes. In fact, the RMC report acknowledges this possibility. "Because we had no measure of English proficiency or previous training among untrained refugees, there was no way to insure that the trained and untrained groups were equally matched with respect to prior exposure to English."[25] If it cannot be demonstrated that the trained and untrained samples were equally matched prior to language classes, then it is possible that the trained sample would have had a higher overall language proficiency even without taking classes. Therefore no conclusion can be drawn from the data about the effectiveness of education in the refugee processing centers.

Moreover, the report includes indirect evidence that the trained and untrained samples were in fact quite different in crucial ways, apart from the classes. One important difference between the samples was that 70 percent of the trained group had relatives in the United States, while only "about half" of the untrained group did.[26] The report notes that refugees joining these "anchor relatives" perform better in many ways. Caseworkers who were surveyed report that these refugees are more independent of government and private agencies upon arrival in the United States; that they become more knowledgeable about American culture; that they are more eager to learn English; that they make more rapid progress toward adjusting to life in the United States; that they have fewer problems finding stable employment; and that they participate in fewer cash assistance programs.[27] Teachers also report that refugees with relatives already in the United States learn English more quickly and experience less stress than other refugees, and analysis of BEST test results shows that refugees with relatives improve their English proficiency at twice the rate of unattached refugees.[28] Taken together, these findings suggest that the trained sample had a great advantage over the untrained sample in having relatives in the United States, that the trained sample had significant advantages in English-language learning, and that this advantage may account for its higher score on the BEST test.

A second empirical problem with the RMC data involves sampling procedures. The procedures for selecting individual refugees for the trained and untrained samples differed markedly, generally favoring refugees with higher proficiency for the trained sample and lower proficiency for the untrained sample. The trained sample was selected by voluntary agencies in the United States, after the RMC researchers requested that the agencies seek volunteers who would be willing to cooperate fully on the study. It is likely that only refugees with intermediate or advanced proficiency would be willing to volunteer to work with U.S. researchers for an extended period of interviews and questionaires. The untrained sample was selected through a somewhat more complicated procedure. Initially, the State Department asked for volunteers among refugees in the processing centers, but few refugees volunteered to resettle without taking classes. (The documents do not explain their reluctance to do so.) Those who did volunteer generally were people with relatively high levels of English proficiency. Therefore, in order to avoid having an untrained sample with an unusually high English proficiency, the State Department selected additional refugees for the untrained group only from those refugees who did not have advanced English proficiency. As the RMC report admits, "this group was limited to those with moderate, low, or no proficiency."[29] In other words, the trained sample was selected in a manner that was likely to result generally in high English proficiency, while the untrained sample was selected in a manner that was likely to result in low English proficiency. Therefore the higher average scores on the BEST test among the trained sample may be due to the selection procedure rather than to the effects of the refugee education program.

In addition to empirical problems, the argument that the overseas program increases refugees' self-sufficiency is logically flawed as well. Though the RMC report admits that the data on refugees' unemployment and public assistance rates do not demonstrate the effectiveness of overseas education, the report assumes that these rates are affected by increases in the refugees' English-language proficiency. Essentially, the logical argument is as follows: Low unemployment rates are associated with high English-language proficiency; therefore programs that increase English-language proficiency will result in lower unemployment rates. This argument has tremendous intuitive appeal. It suggests that a factor that is within programmatic control, namely language education, can have a direct impact upon the refugees' unemployment and use of public assistance. By implication, this view also holds that refugees whose English proficiency improves, but who fail to obtain jobs, should be held responsible for their own unemployment.

One of the fundamental principles of scientific reasoning is that correlation does not demonstrate causality. In other words, showing that two phenomena are statistically correlated does not constitute proof that one phenomenon caused the other. Instead, it is possible that the correlated phenomena are the results of other factors. This means that a correlation between language proficiency and employment rates does not prove that one causes the other. It is possible that both may be the result of a third factor, or that some other, more complex relationship between language and employment may be involved. Investigating this relationship requires a highly complex analysis that was not carried out in the RMC research project. Nevertheless, the RMC report made the undocumented claim that is translated into program policy: Teach English, and refugees' employment levels will increase.

The relationship between language proficiency and employment has been examined by Robert L. Bach, perhaps the foremost analyst of refugee and immigrant employment. Bach forcefully rejects this simplistic view of the solution to high unemployment, arguing that reliance on correlational data may lead to ineffective policy.

Obviously, to the extent that policy or program decisions are influenced by such [correlational] analyses, judgements may be based more on personal biases in selecting the one or two variables that seem important than on the strength of more supportable analytical inferences.[30]

The problem in sorting out the effect of language on employment is that English-language proficiency is related to many other characteristics of the refugees and their resettlement experience. In particular, there are strong correlations between the refugees' education, former work with U.S. personnel during the war, and language proficiency. The task for researchers is to distinguish the various effects on employment of language, previous education, and former work with U.S. personnel. The question is whether English proficiency is highly correlated with employment independent of all other factors. If it is, then the belief that it promotes employment is placed on solid scientific ground. Bach's analytical tool, the statistical procedure called "multiple regression," provides insight into all of these factors relative to each other.

Multiple regression analysis suggests that previous education in the home country has by far the strongest predictive power for employment. Each additional year of education prior to arrival in the United States increases the probability of employment by 3 percent, a much stronger effect than English-language proficiency. This finding suggests that refugees who had high social and economic standing and high levels of education in their home countries are in a much stronger position to successfully compete for jobs after arriving in the United States.[31] This means that English proficiency may not be an indispensable skill for employment, but instead a symbol of status in the home country indicative of other advantages, such as education, that lead to employment in the United States. Bach's conclusion is that there is no empirical basis for the belief that increasing English proficiency, apart from education generally, will improve the probability of employment. "These results . . . do not support claims that English proficiency is essential to early participation in the labor market and to the successful acquisition of a job."[32]

This conclusion was presented to ORR in August 1984 and has been widely disseminated through the Department of Health and Human Services. Bach's report also has been read by staff members in the refugee processing centers and was distributed to upper- and mid-level managers, supervisors, and curriculum developers at regional planning meetings, including the meeting of preemployment training staff members in Singapore in late 1985. Yet officers and curricular staff members have not revised the program in light of Bach's findings, and State Department officers continue to insist that there is a direct causal relationship between English proficiency and employment.[33]

TESTS BY THE CENTER FOR APPLIED LINGUISTICS

In addition to the RMC report, a second major basis for claims that the overseas program is working are tests administered to a sample of refugees at the processing centers by the Center for Applied Linguistics (CAL). In 1985, for instance, in response to congressional criticism of the overseas educational program, the director of the Bureau for Refugee Programs cited the CAL tests as evidence that the refugees were making satisfactory progress.[34]

The CAL tests are administered to approximately 10 percent of the refugees entering classes, and again as students finish the program. The tests are designed to assess "proficiency on skills that are essential to survival in the U.S."[35] These skills consist of four broad types: ESL listening and speaking, ESL reading and writing, cultural orientation, and preemployment.[36] These four skills areas are assessed by four tests: the intensive ESL core test for listening and speaking (known as the core test); the reading and writing test; the cultural orientation test; and the PET test. All the tests assess functional competencies, which are also called "survival competencies" in CAL testing reports.[37] Thus the tests reflect the competency-based approach used in the curriculum.

In order to be useful measures of students' learning, these tests must be valid. Validity is normally measured in three ways.[38] For the first measure, content validity, the key issues are whether the content of the tests is a direct reflection of what is being measured, and whether the content was derived in a scientific manner. The process for developing the CAL tests involved asking staff members in the processing centers and in refugee programs in the United States for their recommendations. Job developers, job counselors, and employers of refugees were also consulted for the PET test. In addition, items from the Basic English Skills Test, which is widely used in the United States, were adapted. This process is similar to the process used for developing the curriculum, and it has the same weakness, namely that the content validity of the tests rests solely upon the judgments and beliefs of the individuals who are consulted. The test items were not derived through scientific procedures, but rather through an informal opinion survey.

The second way to assess validity is theoretical or logical. What is the underlying theory or logic behind the test? The logical basis for the CAL tests is as follows:

1. Refugees who have greater functional competence do better at surviving in the United States.

2. Refugees who do better at surviving in the United States perform better on the CAL tests than those who do worse at surviving.

3. Therefore refugees who are more functionally competent perform better on CAL tests than those who are less competent.

This logic requires that performance on the tests must be positively correlated with "survival": refugees who "survive better" must be those who receive higher scores on the test.

Several measures of "survival" are possible, such as physical and mental health, family reunification, and maintenance of native language and culture. These are not the goals of the refugee education program, however, so there is no reason to expect the CAL test scores to be related to any of these factors. The appropriate measures for the program are its stated criteria: refugees' rates of employment and need for public assistance. To prove that the CAL tests actually assess refugees' functional competence for survival, it is necessary to prove that the test scores correlate with employment and public assistance rates; refugees with higher test scores should have lower unemployment rates. Unfortunately, the refugee program has not shown any relationship between the test scores and employment or public assistance rates. In fact, the Center for Applied Linguistics has not shown a relationship between test scores and any measure of resettlement success or survival. Therefore there is no way to assess the logical validity of the tests.

The third way to assess validity is empirical. Do students who score well on the test demonstrate a greater ability to carry out related tasks than those who score poorly? For the refugee program, this again means that it is necessary to show a relationship between test scores and some measure of resettlement success. Again, no such correlation has been found.

CAL testing reports admit that major difficulties would be involved in trying to show a relationship between test scores and successful resettlement.

There is no "standard of acceptable proficiency" (i.e., passing score) established across ethnic groups on any of the tests. . . . Setting such a score would take a very large study involving validation of the score in a variety of U.S. situations with arriving refugees from all ethnic groups.[39]

The difficulty is that unemployment and public assistance rates, or any other serious measures of resettlement success, are affected by many factors other than refugees' competence in English, cultural orientation, or preemployment skills. Thus it would be difficult and expensive to demonstrate that the CAL tests are valid measures of refugees' employment and survival skills.

These difficulties with the CAL testing program mean that the CAL tests do not provide a basis for the claim that the refugee education program has prepared refugees for employment. Without a validated test to assess progress in the functional competencies required for "survival" or "successful resettlement," it is impossible to assess the effectiveness of the program in terms of its ability to reduce refugees' unemployment and public assistance rates.

RECONSIDERING PROGRAM GOALS

Public assistance is the central concern for planners in the refugee program, yet the overseas program has been unable to demonstrate a positive effect on refugees' rates of unemployment and public assistance. Ironically, at the center of the failure to design an effective program is the goal itself, which is based upon an obsession with welfare that leads to irrational analyses of the process of resettlement and to a strange logic in which welfare is both the problem to be solved and the excuse for the program's inability to affect welfare rates. Moreover, reducing welfare is not only the stated program goal, but it is also the means to achieve the broad social aim of assimilating Indochinese people into U.S. society.

Purcell, then director of the Bureau for Refugee Programs, outlined this view in testimony before the Subcommittee on Immigration, Refugees, and International Law of the House Judiciary Committee in April 1985, and it has become the basis for regulations issued by ORR to all state refugee programs. Purcell's testimony, intended to praise program successes and make the case for continued funding, painted an inspiring picture in which "Indochinese refugee communities across the nation are revitalizing aging inner-city areas through hard work and investment in small commercial enterprises."[40] The only barrier to the success of most refugees, Purcell claimed, is welfare. "A major obstacle to refugee self-sufficiency and the overall success of the resettlement program has been the high benefit structure of the welfare system in some states." Purcell claimed that voluntary agencies have the ability to place refugees in jobs but are frustrated by the lure of welfare.

Purcell's testimony is enormously revealing. It assumes that refugees have a choice between welfare and employment and that they choose welfare. It also suggests that the Bureau for Refugee Programs views employment not only as a fiscal issue, but also as a means to assimilate refugees socially and culturally. "The draw of public assistance thwarts . . . efforts to promote refugee social and cultural assimilation through early entry into the work force."[41] In short, Purcell suggests that the emphasis on employment in the resettlement program is intended to put an end to the social and cultural distinctiveness of Indochinese cultures in the United States.

In a sense, this logic means that the resettlement education program cannot fail. Although the primary aim is to reduce refugees' unemployment and public assistance rates, when these rates remain high, the program is not judged to be ineffective. Instead, the welfare system itself and the refugees who "chose" to remain unemployed are held responsible. From this perspective, the education program is not held accountable; if it does not have the desired effect, then uncooperative refugees and the "high" benefits of welfare are to blame for frustrating program efforts. And because employment is the means to achieve the assimilation of refugees into U.S. society and culture, this overriding goal is frustrated as well.

At the heart of resettlement policy is a concern with "welfare dependency," a vague term expressing the feeling that refugees somehow are side-tracked in their progress toward "becoming American" by the welfare life-style. Officials repeatedly express their alarm about welfare dependency. H. Eugene Douglas, U.S. Coordinator for Refugee Affairs, testified before Congress in 1983, "Despite all our efforts over the past years, significant problems persist in the domestic refugee program. Refugee costs remain high, as reflected by welfare dependency rates."[42] Two years later, Douglas repeated this concern, asserting that there is consensus on the nature of the problem. "We are all familiar with the major disappointment of the past few years in the domestic program—the utilization and expense of the public assistance programs which provide financial assistance and resettlement services to refugees."[43] More recently, the Senate Judiciary Committee expressed deep concern about public assistance rates among refugees, citing an unacceptably high 54 percent of refugees who have been in the United States less than three years as being on some form of cash assistance. "Continued high rates of refugee welfare dependency are harmful to individual refugees and unhealthy for the domestic resettlement program."[44] Officials often argue that high welfare rates are a result of refugees' abuse of the welfare system. In 1982, Douglas presented this view in testimony on proposed refugee admissions for fiscal 1983.

I am seriously concerned . . . about the apparent misuse or over-utilization of our refugee public assistance programs. Many refugees appear to regard public assistance as an entitlement. Voluntary resettlement agencies and local welfare officials often do little to discourage this attitude.[45]

Voluntary agencies that resettle refugees are given much of the blame. In 1985, the House Judiciary Committee criticized voluntary agencies for helping refugees to obtain welfare soon after their arrival. Citing the important role of the agencies in encouraging self-sufficiency, the committee complained that "in many cases, refugees are placed on welfare within days of their arrival in this country. . . . It should be viewed only as a last resort."[46] Even officials outside government repeated this concern. Elizabeth Tannenbaum argued that education cannot reduce welfare rates as long as welfare is available and refugees are "encouraged" to apply.

There is little that the pre-entry training program can do to significantly reduce the rate of refugee welfare dependency as long as public assistance is available to refugees and as long as friends, relatives, and others encourage them to enroll.[47]

The inescapable conclusion of this logic is that only two courses of action can reduce welfare rates: making welfare unavailable or preventing "friends, relatives, and others" from encouraging refugees to apply for it. Because the second course of action does not seem feasible, the most effective means of reducing welfare rates, in this view, is to limit eligibility for welfare. In other words, reduce welfare rates by reducing the number of people eligible for it. This action is unrelated to educational programs, and ultimately means that educational programs become irrelevant to the goal of reducing refugees' use of public assistance.

The Office of Refugee Resettlement (ORR) has followed this logic by adopting regulations for state-administered refugee resettlement programs designed to achieve this goal. Declaring that self-sufficiency means "gainful employment in non-subsidized jobs with at least 90-day retention and receipt of a wage adequate for the basic economic needs of the person and family without reliance on public assistance," ORR regulations require refugees to accept minimum-wage jobs, and they forbid language or job skills training if minimum-wage employment is available.[48] ORR's first priority is "strictly applying sanctions in cases where recipients refuse to register and/or accept appropriate employment, including entry-level and minimum wage jobs."[49] At the end of 1987, ORR proposed new rules designed to save $14 million and to provide newly arrived refugees "stronger incentives" to rapid self-sufficiency. Under the new rules, eligibility for special refugee cash assistance was cut from 18 to 12 months. The effect is to force more refugees into general assistance programs, which in some locations are considered loans that must be repaid by doing work for county governments.[50]

The effect of ORR regulations is to pressure refugees into minimum-wage employment even when the wages are insufficient to support the refugees' families or when the refugees possess advanced employment skills. ORR rules state that English-language education must emphasize the language required for entry-level jobs and may not teach other language skills.

The State English language training program for refugees shall be developed and/or structured to increase basic survival language proficiency, as opposed to academic language proficiency. . . . Services other than employment services and English language training such as orientation, child care, information and referral, interpretation and translation, social and cultural adjustment-oriented activities, etc., shall be provided to refugees only if it is shown how such services contribute directly to economic self-sufficiency and effective resettlement.[51]

This rule means that domestic English-language programs may provide virtually no classes for refugees other than "survival" ESL, regardless of the previous education, training, and job skills of the refugees. For those refugees with significant previous training and employment experience as clerks, mechanics, nurses, engineers, bus drivers, teachers, doctors, technicians, or dozens of other professions, ORR regulations forbid "academic" English-language preparation. For refugees who are unable to obtain employment in these fields only because their English proficiency is inadequate, ORR regulations do not permit language education that would help them to find higher-paying jobs, despite the success of specialized programs for nurses and other medical professionals.[52] In short, refugee education is designed to prepare refugees for minimum-wage employment regardless of their previous education and experience by precluding educational programs other than those considered appropriate for minimum-wage work. Continued high welfare rates are not blamed upon the failure of the program designed to reduce them, but rather upon refugees' alleged unwillingness to cooperate with these regulations.

But what precisely is "welfare dependency?" Though it is widely viewed as a serious problem, it is rarely defined with precision. In one attempt to provide a statistical measure of welfare dependency, the Office of Refugee Resettlement developed a formula for the "refugee dependency rate." This measure is based upon a ratio of two indicators, the "potentially employable recipients" (PER) and the "potentially employable population" (PEP). Potentially employable recipients are refugees receiving assistance who are eligible for employment (i.e., not aged, disabled, or blind). The potentially employable population comprises the refugees between the ages of 18 and 64. The Office of Refugee Resettlement defines the "adjusted refugee dependency rate" as the ratio of PER to PEP.[53] Because the PER is the segment of the refugee population that ORR has targeted for its welfare reduction efforts, the adjusted refugee dependency rate can be used to assess the effectiveness of steps to reduce refugees' "welfare dependency."

The ORR statistical measure of dependency is an exception, however, in that it is a precisely defined use of the term. More often, dependency refers to a set of assumptions about the attitudes, values, and character of the refugees. The key assumptions are that refugees will not work unless forced, that they expect a handout, and that they are not grateful for what they have received. These assumptions have been expressed repeatedly in congressional testimony by government officials, and also by many resettlement agencies.[54]

Lance Clark, a researcher at the Refugee Policy Group, has outlined this implicit view of refugees. "Refugees are often described as unmotivated, lacking in initiative, as being unappreciative of the kind of assistance given to them, looking to others to solve their problems."[55] In this view, refugees are responsible for their own inability to find employment and for their high rate of public assistance. Refugees themselves, in other words, are unwilling to seek self-sufficiency, which is the goal of the refugee education program.

But is this the case? Are refugees unwilling to seek employment unless forced to do so by government regulations and pressure from their sponsors? Although this is the prevailing view among federal officials, there is now a growing body of data on the process of achieving self-sufficiency that provides strong evidence that the "refugee dependency syndrome" is a myth.

DEPENDENCY AND SELF-SUFFICIENCY

The most important analyses of refugees' self-sufficiency are a 1985 ORR study by the Institute for Social Research of the University of Michigan[56] and a 1983 study by the Church World Service (CWS) Immigration and Refugee Program in collaboration with Calculogic Corporation, a consulting firm with experience in social science research.[57] These studies represent efforts, by the major government agency responsible for domestic refugee programs and one of the most important private voluntary agencies that sponsors refugees, to assess the refugees' welfare dependency. Though a government agency and a sponsoring agency might have different priorities, the two studies reach strikingly similar conclusions: that most refugees do everything possible to become self-sufficient, that refugees' attitudes and values do not lead to welfare dependency, and that the process of achieving self-sufficiency is a long and difficult one in which public assistance plays a crucial and justifiable role.

The ORR study covered 1,384 households of Vietnamese, ethnic Chinese from Vietnam, and Lao refugees who had arrived in the United States after 1978. Because the study focused on five urban areas, the findings may not be wholly applicable to refugees living in towns or rural areas. Yet the degree of commonality across the five sites surveyed suggests that the findings may be broadly generalizable to the Indochinese refugee population at large.

The CWS study involved a mail survey of cases sponsored by CWS denominations during fiscal 1980, through the first half of fiscal 1983. The survey, conducted during the summer of 1983, yielded data on 2,189 cases, of which 40 percent were single refugees, 13 percent groups of two, and 25 percent groups of five or more. Because the survey covered a sample of all refugees resettled by CWS, approximately 30 percent of the cases were not Southeast Asians. Nevertheless, there were few significant differences between the Southeast Asian refugees and those from other countries. The most important difference was that the Southeast Asians had a generally lower English proficiency upon their arrival in the United States.

Both studies found a higher rate of employment than is generally assumed. In the CWS survey, the proportion of cases in which no one was employed was 46 percent for fiscal 1983 arrivals, but only 14 percent for fiscal 1980 arrivals. The ORR study found that 58 percent of all adults who wanted to work had jobs. More importantly, the two studies found that virtually all refugees who had stopped looking for work had done so for reasons that are widely considered to be acceptable. In the CWS study, less than one-third of the adults were unemployed and not seeking work. Of these, at least 29 percent and perhaps nearly 50 percent were mothers staying home to care for young children.[58] Another 25–50 percent were students enrolled in school. Only 2 percent of the sponsors reported that the refugees did not seek employment because they did not want to work, and only 1 percent cited the use of public assistance as a cause. Similarly, the ORR study found that 81 percent of the adults not looking for work intended to do so in the future. Nearly 60 percent were classified as housewives or mothers with young children, and over 40 percent were in school learning English or other skills. Most of those not looking for work were more recent arrivals. In other words, except for mothers with young children, most refugees not looking for work were attempting to acquire language and other skills that they believed would help them obtain employment. In fact, 24 percent of all the adults were students in high schools, community colleges, and adult education programs.[59] Furthermore, the ORR survey suggests that the refugees are wise to improve their skills, because the proportion of those who had been laid off their jobs was extremely high: nearly 35 percent of all those who had ever been employed. Refugees in minimum-wage jobs clearly suffer from the difficulties associated with being "the last hired and the first fired."

Both studies found strong evidence that the refugees' attitudes and values did not lead to a "dependency syndrome." The ORR study found no evidence that refugees prefer public assistance to employment; rather, the study concluded that public assistance is used primarily as transitional support until jobs can be found, and that the rate of use drops steadily as time passes and the refugees improve their English, job skills, and ability to locate jobs. The report rejected the argument that public assistance should be reduced in order to force more refugees into jobs, because the survey found that "in fact they get off [welfare] as soon as they can in any case. The Southeast Asian refugees . . . may be trusted to be self-reliant."[60] Similarly, the CWS study found that Indochinese refugees are precisely the kind of population welfare is supposed to assist. "It is real service needs, not refugees' attitudes, which are at the root of the problems refugees face in achieving self-sufficiency."[61] In the words of one refugee who completed the CWS mail survey, "Living upon welfare is a shame for me. I am looking for a position in a post office or in the education system . . . in order to better living conditions. I believe that, sooner or later, I will reach my goal, a so simple one to everybody."[62] Thus, the two studies found no evidence supporting the belief that refugees abuse the welfare system by using it as a substitute for employment, not did they find evidence that refugees possess a poor work ethic or other attitudinal problems.

This view coincides with that of Bach, who has concluded from his study of refugee employment that there is no evidence to support the "mythology" in which "refugees' problems in achieving self-sufficiency [are] interpreted as refugees' lack of, or poor progress toward, learning American values, including its work ethic."[63] Bach found that the employment problems of Southeast Asian refugees, like those of other immigrants and minorities, have their roots in the nature of their connection to the labor market and their conditions of employment, not in their preferences or mentality. In fact, Bach found that the refugees are much less likely than the U.S. population as a whole to cite household responsibilities as a justification for not looking for a job. He concluded that use of public assistance declines when people find jobs, not that people will find jobs when they are cut from public assistance rolls.

Yet the refugees' use of public assistance continues to be much higher than for the U.S. population generally. The ORR study found that nearly all refugees begin their lives in the United States on welfare. In the study sample, 65 percent of the households were receiving some form of assistance. The CWS report found a steady decline in the use of welfare as time passes; yet nearly half of all cases were receiving some form of assistance.

Why is the refugees' use of public assistance so widespread? The answer to this question appears to be quite simple: It takes time for refugees to find work that will support their families. On average, it took the refugees in the ORR sample 11 months after their arrival to find their first job, and those refugees living solely on public assistance are the most recent arrivals. Yet after two to three years in the United States, the refugees achieved approximately the same rates of unemployment and public assistance as U.S. minority groups generally. The CWS report argued that the process of achieving self-sufficiency is extremely difficult, requiring great effort on the part of the refugees over a period of two to four years. Given a realistic understanding of the difficulties involved, the CWS report suggested that the refugees' public assistance rates are remarkably low, reflecting their extraordinary effort to survive. Yet, as we have seen, belief in the myth of welfare dependency remains.

REFUGEE POLICY AND THE MYTH OF WELFARE DEPENDENCY

Why is the myth of welfare dependency so persistent? Why are federal officials so critical of the refugees' use of public assistance, even though the ORR and CWS reports conclude that the refugees use public assistance in an appropriate manner, and only until they are able to find jobs? Why do federal officials argue that the refugees lack the American work ethic and so choose public assistance over employment, while studies show that in fact the refugees do everything possible to get off of welfare as soon as possible?

In part, the issue involves a difference in expectations. Federal officials expected the refugees to become self-sufficient very quickly; in fact, the overseas educational program was unrealistically expected to make the refugees employable within six months after their arrival in the United States. In contrast, sponsors who work closely with refugees during their first months in the United States may have more realistic expectations, based on their understanding of the difficulties the refugees face: language problems, extreme emotional stress, transportation difficulties, differences in social organization and bureaucratic procedures, and lack of transferable job skills.

But there is more involved than differences in expectations. The official view that refugees have a dependency mentality expresses deep-seated American assumptions about the source of individual success and personal wealth. One important assumption is that the American character is responsible for the U.S. riches. This traditional view is that hard work and proper attitudes (a work ethic) are the source of the nation's wealth. If the American character is what makes the United States a wealthy nation, then Americans can take credit for their riches. The implication is that the poor are responsible for their own poverty because their poor work ethic prevents them from enjoying the wealth that is available to them.

This belief assumes as well that the United States is a land of riches available to all, a view that is threatened if refugees who work hard in fact fail to become self-sufficient. It is easier to deny that hard-working people remain impoverished than to admit the contradiction of the ideology of self-sufficiency. But refugees call attention to it. As one respondent wrote in the CWS survey, "As a matter of fact America is not Land of Honey and Money, but I changed myself to be a machine, working day and night, competing with different kind of people in different kind of job."[64] This refugee does not present a flattering image of becoming an American: becoming a machine, competing with others, struggling to make it. And the struggle often does not end in success.[65] Even with jobs, refugees may be deeply unhappy. In the words of one agency staff member, "I have met many refugee families . . . in a very discouraging situation. They are almost completely isolated, having a very hard time in everyday life."[66]

This bleak picture of resettlement reveals that good intentions may not be enough to bring about the goal of refugees' self-sufficiency. Like the U.S. war effort, the resettlement program is proclaimed to be an extraordinary act of national generosity, yet many of the recipients of that generosity continue to suffer. Americans want their efforts on behalf of Southeast Asia to be rewarded with successful, happy, grateful refugees. When that does not happen, many blame the refugees for their own difficulties, concluding that they must not be willing to help themselves, or that they are ungrateful. As in the war, this reaction helps to preserve belief in America's generosity, innocence, and virtue.

So refugees threaten the fundamental beliefs that there is a direct relationship between hard work, a virtuous character, and material wealth; that the United States offers economic opportunity for all who want to work for it; and that the humanitarian efforts we choose to make will be sufficient to alleviate the suffering of those we choose to assist. By upholding the myth of the refugees' welfare dependency, policymakers can uphold these beliefs and thereby justify policies that are harmful to the refugees. To protect these beliefs and policies, much about the resettlement experience must be denied: the extraordinary difficulties, the risks, and the lack of guaranteed success.

Ultimately, the myth of dependency absolves officials of responsibility for the outcomes of their decisions. Despite its many problems, the educational program is not being redesigned, because the refugees and the welfare system—not the program—are believed to be at fault. In addition, the educational program plays an important role in the effort to restrict the refugees' access to domestic public assistance, by providing an essential link in the argument that the federal government has done everything it can for Southeast Asians and that drastic steps, such as restricting access to welfare, are therefore justified.

But restricting access to welfare is not the only step taken to date. In late 1985, the program in the processing centers began to shift some of its resources away from preparing refugees for employment and toward skills for what the program calls "homebound" refugees. This action builds into the program the assumption that many refugees will be unable to obtain employment. In a lengthy justification of this shift in policy in late 1985, the State Department officers in charge ordered the agencies in the processing centers to begin to prepare revised curricula.

The fact is that many of the A–B [lower] level students *will not* or *cannot*, by virtue of their circumstances, seek employment immediately. . . . If we have done as much as we can for these groups with respect to providing survival English instruction, . . . we should consider turning our attention to the realities of the resettlement experience they are likely to have. If these groups are not necessarily going to be a part of the labor force immediately, perhaps they should get heavier doses of household safety, nutrition, family planning, medical care, income-producing opportunities for the homebound, etc.—rather than spending a hefty percentage of time on employment-related skills which they may not use in the early months of resettlement.[67]

This memo argued, oddly, that the educational program should reduce its emphasis on employment because many refugees remain unemployed. If the program had effectively prepared the refugees for work and had reduced their rate of unemployment, then faith that the program had done everything possible for them would be a credible basis for turning attention to education in other areas. But there is no evidence that the program has affected the refugees' unemployment, which remains high long after their arrival in the United States. Therefore the shift to "homebound" skills can only be viewed as an admission of programmatic failure.

The insistence that the refugees choose to remain on welfare furthers the belief that their cultures lead them to prefer a handout to a paycheck. Bach recognized the power of this argument.

Actively seeking work . . . is both an attitude and a behavior. Too often, however, it is interpreted solely as an attitude: the person outside the labor force does not want or need to work. When this kind of interpretation is applied to refugees, . . . the relatively large numbers of people who are not actively seeking work (in the labor force) are seen as lacking the mentality to work. And this mentality is then interpreted as a welfare mentality.[68]

If the refugees are unemployed because they possess inappropriate attitudes and values, then it follows that the educational program designed for them must foster "American" attitudes and values that will help them gain minimum-wage employment and assimilate into American society and culture. Finally, therefore, the myth of dependency is the basis for channeling the refugees into minimum-wage jobs offering little room for advancement and for the effort to undermine the refugees' communities, to change their values and attitudes, to reeducate them.

EMPLOYED REFUGEES

The strongest evidence that the myth of welfare dependency is used to justify policies that harm the refugees comes from information about what happens to the employed refugees. They are the success stories of the educational program; they have attained the goal set by policy. Yet, contrary to the claims of the educational program, the 1985 ORR report found that employment does not help the refugees avoid long-term poverty. Indeed, the report presents a disturbing portrait of employed Southeast Asians in permanent economic crisis.

The good news of the ORR study is that as refugees spend a longer time in the United States, their unemployment rate drops steadily. Nearly 90 percent are unemployed after four months, but only about 35 percent are unemployed after three years.[69] But while the percentage of families living above the poverty line increases during the same period, the increase is not nearly as great as the increase in employment. About 20 percent of families live above the poverty line after four months in the United States, while about 57 percent do so after three years. In other words, an increase in the percentage of Indochinese refugees employed is *not* associated with an equivalent decrease in the percentage of families living in poverty.[70] These figures mean that many employed refugees remain below the poverty level. The ORR report admits that "while the general direction of change in economic status . . . is upward, the picture is not nearly as dramatic as might be expected based on the data on changes in unemployment over time."[71]

To explain these findings, we must examine the kinds of jobs refugees obtain. The ORR study divided employed refugees into three job categories: "professional or managers"; "clericals, salespeople, or craftspersons"; and "operatives (e.g., of machinery), service workers, or laborers." The study found that approximately 80 percent of all employed refugees are in the category with the lowest wages (operatives, service workers, and laborers).[72] Moreover, these jobs contrast with their occupations in Southeast Asia, where only 14 percent had held such jobs.[73] For the vast majority of refugees, resettlement in the United States resulted in significant downward mobility.

Downward mobility is most apparent among individuals who were professionals, officers, and managers in Southeast Asia. While they are more likely than other refugees to be employed, they are primarily in low-paying, unskilled or semi-skilled positions. The same is true of clericals and salespeople. Fewer than 4 percent find similar work in the United States. Others work as janitors, maids, and assemblers. Nearly half are unemployed.[74]

These findings show that few refugees have been able to make full use of their background skills to improve their economic circumstances. For example, refugees with experience as machine operators in Southeast Asia are comparatively unsuccessful at finding similar jobs in the United States; only 25 percent are employed.[75] The ORR report concludes that employment rates do not give an accurate picture of the refugees' resettlement experience.

Moreover, most of the refugees who are employed find themselves in jobs that are quickly eliminated during economic slowdowns.[76] The ORR study found that more than half of all employed refugees are working in "peripheral" jobs, which are irregular, seasonal, and part time, with low average salaries and virtually no opportunity for advancement.[77] The study's pessimistic conclusion: "In addition to being unemployed and underemployed, the refugees tend to hold dead-end jobs, . . . low in wages, status, and any possibility of upward mobility."[78]

One additional observation is relevant to the assertion that service agencies should discourage refugees from seeking welfare during their early months in the United States. The ORR study found that 80 percent of refugees in the country less than four months live below the poverty line, in part because they are not able to quickly obtain public assistance payments due to difficulties in getting on the rolls and waiting for applications to be processed and checks sent. The report notes that these people must depend upon friends and voluntary agencies for food, clothing, and shelter. The report concludes that refugees' first months in America are "difficult" and "dismal," made a little easier only upon the arrival of the first public assistance payment.[79]

THE ROLE OF THE PROCESSING CENTERS

We can now use the findings of the ORR study to understand the role that the processing centers play in the total resettlement process. The centers offer an educational program designed to convince the refugees that they have no alternative but to accept minimum-wage jobs. They train the refugees for these jobs by teaching basic employment skills, attitudes of subservience, and limited English competencies such as apologizing and following orders. Also they exclude alternatives such as specialized job training or general English language that might offer greater opportunities for long-term economic well being. In short, they play a crucial role in preparing the refugees to be efficient, manageable workers in minimum wage jobs.

In fact, this view of the function of the educational program is supported by the program officials themselves. Despite the official claim that the content of the educational program is based upon an analysis of refugees' economic needs, the primary references used by program staff to justify the curriculum are in fact studies of employers' needs. Preemployment training refers in part to a survey of employers' reactions to Indochinese refugees as workers in the electronics industry and other fields.[80] A reference cited for the PET curriculum is a handbook for training industrial workers that recommends that needs assessors answer questions employers want answered.[81] A study of refugee ESL funded by the Office of Refugee Resettlement emphasizes language skills that will make refugees satisfactory employees.[82] Most striking is a summary of general principles for determining refugees' needs that appears in the State Department journal *Passage*.

This summary declares that refugees' "employment needs" are best determined by assessment of the needs of their employers.[83]

In the survey of employers' needs used to write the preemployment curriculum, employers said that they seek workers who are hard working, industrious, productive, dependable, and punctual and who do not "over-emphasize" salary and benefits.[84] It is the job of the educational bureaucracy to ensure that the refugees fit this description. The transformation of the educational program into a simulated PETCO corporation graphically symbolizes its role as a representative of industries employing Indochinese refugees. The emphasis on workplace rules and behavior, on following directions without complaint or protest, on working quickly to maximize productivity, and on accepting minimum-wage employment without regard to background skills is a direct response to what employers want in their employees. In short, the program is designed to prepare refugees for long-term employment in dead-end, minimum-wage jobs.

THE BODY COUNT

Without validated measures of learning or successful resettlement, the only measure of success available to program planners is an updated version of the body count. In the war, the body count was intended to measure U.S. military success; in the refugee program, it is supposed to measure U.S. generosity. In the central administration building in the Philippine processing center, huge charts on the walls show the "Daily Status Report on Refugee Processing and Deprocessing." At a glance, everyone knew on July 20, 1984, that 136,366 refugees had been processed, of whom 64,760 were Vietnamese, 52,506 Cambodians, and 19,100 Laotians; that the camp population on that day was 17,105, of whom 6,940 were Vietnamese, 7,986 Cambodians, and 2,179 Laotians; that 2,095 babies had been born since the camp opened, while 130 refugees had died. Though the charts looked good, no one on the staff knew to what degree program graduates had learned English, achieved cultural orientation, or acquired preemployment skills. No one knew whether the time the tens of thousands of refugees had spent in class had been worthwhile. No one knew how many considered their own resettlement to be "successful." No one had any way of knowing.

Humiliation and Danger

A woman who had been granted asylum in the USA refused to leave
the camp with the eight children she had brought out of Vietnam. She
was alone, and felt that she could not provide for so many children in
the USA. Four of the children were adopted, and she told the camp
authorities that she could only take with her the four children who were
her own. This was a very difficult decision for her to make. The result
was that she was put into prison in the camp.

John Knudsen, *Boat People in Transit*[1]

Refugees are not permitted to leave the confines of the processing centers
without written permission. In Indonesia and Thailand, permission is rarely
granted, even for medical emergencies, while in the Philippines, program
officers are occasionally allowed to take small groups on afternoon outings
to the beach or to Morong. Some refugees travel without permission to
Morong to buy food or even to Balanga, an hour's drive from the center,
to phone relatives in the United States. But for the vast majority, the
perimeter fences, for six months or more, define the boundaries of their
lives. Therefore, in the closed and isolated world of the processing centers,
officials have an extraordinary opportunity to regulate people's activities.
The aim of this regulation is to reeducate by reinforcing attitudes, values,
and behaviors taught in class. As we shall see, the effect also is to increase
the risk to the refugees' physical and emotional well being.

THE PLAN TO "TRANSFORM" THE REFUGEES

Like the classes, regulations affecting daily life in camp are intended to
prepare the refugees for living in the United States. The system of regulation

has the stated purpose of transforming each resident from a "displaced person" to an "individual well equipped for life in his country of final destination."[2] The Community Action and Social Services Development Group (CASSDEG), which is responsible for camp rules, summarizes the scope of this planned change:

The refugee's transformation involves his total development as a person. This takes into consideration his physical, social, political, cultural, intellectual, religious and economic needs. All these needs are being met to enable him to regain confidence and self-worth; to encourage him to become a productive, participative individual; and to prepare him for a new life in his adopted country.[3]

According to CASSDEG, this transformation of personal identity has three phases, lasting a total of about 16 weeks, the minimum required stay in the processing centers:

—*Adaptation* (2 weeks), which is geared to produce a well-adjusted refugee, able to cope with and adjust to his new physical and social environment.
—*Capability building* (12 weeks), which transforms the refugee into a highly motivated temporary resident.
—*Disengagement* (2 weeks), which is the refugee's final transformation into a prospective immigrant, equipped for integration into the culture and society of his host country.[4]

To bring about this transformation in the relatively short period the refugees are in camp, the officials have developed a detailed and pervasive system of regulation and sanctions affecting most aspects of daily life, including housing and sleeping arrangements, food preparation and consumption, work, sanitation, health, and personal hygiene. Its three main mechanisms are a complex array of refugee committees, a work credit system, and a system of penalties for violating camp rules.

THE COMMITTEE SYSTEM

The committee system is organized according to building and neighborhood. At PRPC, buildings are grouped into 10 neighborhoods, which hold an average of 1,800 people each when the camp is full. Each neighborhood is led by a "neighborhood leader" and a "neighborhood committee" made up of individuals chairing separate committees for food distribution, kerosene distribution, sanitation, sociocultural activities, peace and order, mail, special training, and women and youth. Within each neighborhood, buildings contain ten separate rooms, called "billets," holding up to ten individuals each. Every building has a representative responsible for food and kerosene distribution, sanitation, and so on within the ten billets in that building.

The declared aim of the committee system is to develop the refugees' sense of social responsibility. The assumption is that involving many refugees in the day-to-day operation of the camp will generate a renewed commitment to community. "On a general level, community organization is used to assist the refugee in reviving his sense of community through participation in the Center's activities."[5]

Though hundreds of refugees are involved in these committees, the authority of the committees is limited primarily to distributing supplies and informing the camp population of changes in official policies. The officials can unload food for up to 18,000 people per day at the central supplies depot and then rely upon neighborhood and building representatives to divide and transport the supplies throughout the camp. The officials can also ensure that directives are posted in native languages in every billet in camp within hours after they are issued. Occasionally, sociocultural events such as concerts and dance demonstrations are arranged by the neighborhood committees.

THE WORK CREDIT SYSTEM

Distributing food and kerosene is one way to fulfill the requirement of the "work credit system," CASSDEG's mechanism for involving all refugees in camp operations. Other ways to fulfill the requirement include cutting grass to keep poisonous snakes away from residential areas, fumigating buildings with liquid malathion and other chemicals, washing latrines and sidewalks, clearing drainage ditches, translating and typing documents, maintaining records, and assisting teachers in classes. Organized by CASSDEG, the system requires that all refugees work directly under work crew supervisors (normally Filipino staff members employed by CASSDEG or one of the voluntary agencies) throughout their stay in camp. At the central office of the work credit system, records for every individual over the age of fifteen ensure that anyone who fails to complete two hours of work, six days a week, is not permitted to leave for the United States.

In official statements, the purpose of the work credit system is declared to be educational: to help the refugees become productive in the camp, and thereby to develop habits that will make them productive in the United States.[6] The reward for successfully completing the work credit requirement is resettlement, while the penalty is delay in departure for the United States. The system also, however, has the unstated function of providing free labor for the operation of the camp. In his studies at PRPC, the Norwegian anthropologist John Knudsen found that most refugees believe this to be the primary purpose of the system. For them, "it is individual work done to avoid being held back in the camp."[7]

The work credit system, and the delay in resettlement that it can impose, is used to enforce camp rules. For instance, members of the military patrols that provide security can require additional work as punishment for minor offenses. Refugees who leave their billets after the 9:00 p.m. curfew may be required to work several extra hours cleaning up the communal areas, while anyone caught leaving the camp may be required to do a double shift on a work crew.

Like the educational program, the work credit system assumes that the refugees must be taught to be productive, that they will not feel responsible for their communities unless coerced, and that they do not already possess productive, participative competencies. That is, it assumes that their cultural background does not give them a basis for productive work. This assumption is implicit in CASSDEG's action statement, which declares that the system is intended "to encourage [the refugee] to become a productive, participative individual," and in the statement of ICMC policies given to refugees upon arrival: "Soon you will be going to the U.S. One trait you will need to develop there is self-sufficiency. We encourage you to begin practicing it here at PRPC by assuring that rules are respected."[8]

Despite CASSDEG's hope that the work credit system will encourage the refugees' sense of belonging, few refugees feel that it is their system or that it is designed to encourage community responsibility. This may be because the system was designed and is maintained without refugee involvement, and because the sanctions against those who fail to follow its requirements are imposed by camp officials rather than by the refugees themselves. In contrast, in the Vietnamese first-asylum camp in Palawan, also in the Philippines, the refugees operate the work credit system and impose their own sanctions for those who fail to participate adequately. As a result, most feel responsible for the system and believe that it reinforces Southeast Asian cultural norms supporting productive work. As the refugee-operated Palawan camp newsletter states:

Ours is a people of long civilization. We have great faith and pride in our own people. We earnestly believe that, through our own labour and efforts, we will be able to pay our debt of gratitude to the adopting countries, to the people who give us the chance to start a new and free life.[9]

SANCTIONS

Violating camp rules and failing to complete the work credit requirement are only two of the many reasons officials may impose the ultimate sanction—delaying or cancelling departure for the United States. The threat of "administrative hold" is also used to enforce class attendance, to ensure that all interviews and examinations are completed, and to guarantee that cooking utensils and other supplies are returned. During orientation, for instance, refugees are told that three or more absences from class may lead to administrative hold (though they are assured that "this is not a punishment.")[10]

Unruly or impolite classroom behavior or any other problem that teachers may identify can also result in administrative hold. Anyone giving a false birth date to the authorities can be held for six months; if they give a false name, they can be held for one year. Visiting staff members in their private rooms, suspicion of involvement in "communistic" activities, and participation in public protests or demonstrations also may result in this sanction.

Administrative hold may be used as punishment for anyone suspected of criminal behavior. For example, one young man accused of rape was sentenced to one-to three-years administrative hold, though the rape was never proven.[11] Another man accused of physically abusing his adopted daughter was held for three months, until the authorities decided there was serious doubt about the reliability and motives of his accusers; nevertheless, records of the allegations were forwarded to the man's resettlement agency in the United States.[12]

A second category of delays in departure is medical reasons. Reasons for medical hold include tuberculosis, venereal disease or other progressive disorder, pregnancy beyond 32 weeks (families of newborn babies are held for two weeks after birth), and failure to complete the required physical, laboratory, radiographic, and dental examinations.

The most controversial category of medical hold is for "mental conditions" diagnosed during cursory examinations in first-asylum camps or after arrival in the processing centers.[13] For instance, one man arrived in the Philippines from a Malaysian refugee camp with records indicating "schizophrenia." As a result, he was required to remain in the processing center for over a year until officials were satisfied he had gotten over his problems.[14] Refugees diagnosed as depressed also may be placed on medical hold. Although studies show that feelings of uncertainty, isolation, loneliness, and intense anxiety are universal responses to the trauma of flight and resettlement, anyone seeking psychiatric help for these conditions risks being placed on indefinite medical hold. Of course, the aim of medical hold is to ensure that the United States does not accept individuals with emotional or psychiatric problems. The official assumption seems to be that refugees will be able to solve their personal problems if they are detained in the camp, even though camp conditions may be one of the primary reasons for such problems. Unfortunately, the inadequate facilities for treating these disorders mean that refugees on hold are largely on their own in solving their psychiatric or emotional problems.[15]

The use of psychiatric and somatic diagnosis as justification for the serious sanction of holding refugees in camp has three major effects. The first is that refugees hide their physical and emotional problems from the authorities. Knudsen cites the case of a woman who did not report dizziness and other potentially serious problems to medical authorities out of fear that she would be held in camp, which "she knew . . . would not help as she was sure that it was the stay in camp that had made her ill."[16] To some extent, this fear of discovery is a holdover from first-asylum camps, where tuberculosis is cause for being excluded from resettlement opportunities.

The second effect of medical holds is that refugees hide their feelings and their physical and emotional needs from other refugees out of fear that such information could eventually be used against them. The man accused of abusing his adopted daughter, for instance, was brought to the attention of the authorities by neighbors with whom he had had a variety of conflicts. As his neighbors were interviewed, it became increasingly uncertain whether they were telling the truth about the abuse. Of course, the need to protect oneself through the privatization of feelings only intensifies the sense of isolation and meaninglessness that is the source of many physical and emotional disorders.[17] Refugees trying to survive six months in camp without relying on others for intimacy demonstrate that the need for privacy outweighs the need for community in the processing centers.

The third effect of using diagnosis to impose medical holds is that the refugees who suffered the heaviest trauma in flight (rape, torture, death of family members from murder, starvation or dehydration, and confinement in the asylum camps having the worst conditions of safety and sanitation) tend to be those who suffer most in the processing centers. Those with the worst emotional problems often are adolescents, young adults, and the elderly left alone after family members perished during flight. These individuals are the most likely to be placed on psychiatric hold, and therefore must endure longer stays in the camps without proper treatment.[18]

Although refugees trying to minimize their stay in the camp work hard to maintain their privacy, the relief bureaucracy does not. Medical records are telexed without the refugees' permission to resettlement sponsors for any condition that may require follow-up in the United States. Suspicions about psychiatric disorders or criminal behavior also may be sent to sponsors in the United States.[19]

Administrative and medical holds are two of the most serious of the sanctions used to regulate and control life in the processing centers. Another is imprisonment in the camp jail, called the "monkey house." (During many months in the processing centers, I never heard the terms "jail" or "prison.") Operated by the military units that provide camp security, the jails have the authority to hold refugees indefinitely without charges or hearings. As many as 60 people may be held at a time, accused of crimes, political subversion, or violations of petty camp rules. During the Marcos regime in the early 1980s, Philippine military authorities were especially tough on suspected communists, due to the strength of the communist New People's Army guerrillas in the countryside of the Bataan Peninsula. In 1982, for instance, 16 alleged members of the "Sequeo Gang" were imprisoned by the Philippine authorities in the PRPC jail.[20]

Yet most refugees who are imprisoned are held for suspected violations of minor camp rules. Anyone alleged to be caught drinking alcohol (which is forbidden to refugees but not staff members) can be imprisoned for up to three months; assaults usually result in longer prison terms. The specific length of confinement depends upon decisions by camp officials. In 1981, for instance, the penalty for drinking was only seven days in jail.

Other refugees are imprisoned for refusing to follow bureaucratic resettlement requirements. One woman who had arrived at PRPC with four adopted children as well as four of her own children was afraid that she would not be able to support all of them in the United States, and so refused to take the adopted children with her. She was placed in jail as a way of forcing her to take all eight children to the United States.[21]

When refugees are imprisoned, no trials or other hearings are held, and prisoners do not have the right to confront their accusers or to demand proof of the alleged violations. As a result, some staff members threaten to report poor classroom attendance, work-credit violations, or other punishable offenses as a way of extorting money, goods, and personal or sexual favors. The problem is sufficiently serious that fully one-quarter of the ICMC policy statement given to arriving refugees consists of warnings about such extortions.

Refrain from giving gifts—food, clothing, money, valuables—to any ICMC staff members. . . . Your obligations as a student are limited. . . . Outside the classroom you have no inherent obligation to work for or serve an ICMC employee, for example by cooking, gardening, or carrying books and bags, etc. . . . Any and all forms of sexual harassment or seeking of sexual favors, explicitly or implicitly, are strictly forbidden, whether inside or outside the classroom.[22]

Despite such policies, most refugees give gifts to teachers and supervisors at the end of classes, when attendance records are being readied for final review prior to departure.[23]

In addition to suffering extortion of belongings and personal favors, refugees imprisoned in the jail reportedly have been beaten and robbed. Among women, imprisonment is particularly feared, due to reports of sexual abuse of female prisoners. Family members who visit prisoners are also at risk. Because the jail does not provide food for prisoners, family and friends must bring it each day. Guards have reportedly extorted cigarettes, money, and sexual favors for the right to deliver food to hungry prisoners.

At times, the system of work-credit requirements, administrative and medical holds, and imprisonment in the camp jail becomes a source of conflict. In 1985, for instance, a group of several dozen angry Cambodians gathered at the central administration building because they believed that one of their members had been unjustly placed on administrative hold due to an inaccurate attendance record. Troops aimed loaded weapons at the angry crowd, until two Cambodian leaders apologized in Tagalog to the ranking Philippine military officer and demonstrated supplication by touching the officer's hand to their foreheads in the traditional Philippine act of subservience. Satisfied that he was in control, the military officer ordered the troops to lower their weapons and allow the refugees to leave peacefully. In other instances, troops have reportedly fired warning shots and sprayed hoses to disperse crowds.

Such incidents demonstrate the powerlessness of those confined in the processing centers. Indeed, it is refugees' powerlessness that makes the system of sanctions so effective in controlling their behavior. Officials can order the arrest and imprisonment of any individual without supplying proof. They can use the threat of imprisonment or administrative hold to intimidate refugees who resist. They can copy or send records anywhere without obtaining permission. They can require refugees to carry out work that they are unwilling to do themselves: collecting garbage, spraying pesticides, or working with asbestos materials without respirators or protective clothing. Although hundreds of refugees serve on official committees, none are involved in establishing policies, enforcing sanctions, or maintaining order. As one refugee complained, "We are refugees. We cannot demand anything."[24]

An additional reason for the effectiveness of sanctions is that most refugees have one primary goal: to stay in camp as short a time as possible. They recognize that their circumstances bring about their feelings of insecurity, loneliness, powerlessness, and uncertainty about the future, as well as their somatic and psychosomatic disorders. The immediate solution to these problems is to get out of camp. To do so, they must obey the rules. Unfortunately, their understandable caution leads them to isolate themselves from each other and to avoid organizing to increase their rights and their power. In this way, regulated camp life intensifies rather than resolves the refugees' personal problems.

LIVING WITHOUT POWER

Other aspects of regulated camp life contribute to the refugees' sense of powerlessness. Housing presents some of the most serious problems. The housing units are simple, with each building holding ten billets designed for up to ten people each. Each billet has a large wooden platform used as a bed, a table with two benches, and a shelf for the cookstove. The structure is made of single-wall hardboard sheets with wooden shutters, but no windows. There is no insulation, though there is an electric light. (Electricity to the refugees' billets, but not to staff housing, is cut off at curfew.) A sleeping loft is attached near the ceiling to accommodate people who cannot find space on the bed or the floor at night. When full, the billets provide less than 30 square feet of living space per person. Residents are not permitted to leave their billets after 9:00 p.m., nor to sleep anywhere but in their assigned spaces.

Housing assignments are made so that family members stay together in a single billet. Unrelated refugees who were together during their flight from home or in first-asylum camps are usually broken up when housing assignments are made. Because most refugees are cautious about forming new friendships in camp, the effect is to further isolate those who are not accompanied by immediate family members.

Each billet is expected to be a cooking team, with food, cooking pots, and cooking oil distributed to the residents as a group. Individuals are given chopsticks, mosquito nets, antimalaria tablets, straw sleeping mats, and blankets.[25] Refugees cannot leave the camp until they return these items or pay for them. In some cases, arriving refugees may sign for more items than they receive, or not receive anything at all after signing forms they do not understand. In some instances, teachers have paid for items so that refugees could leave for the United States.

Sanitation around the housing areas is inadequate due to the design of the latrines. Each neighborhood contains a common latrine building, with separate stalls assigned to each billet. The waste falls into open channels in the floor, with no water for washing it away. During the rainy season, ground water often floods the buildings, spreading the waste throughout the area, even into the billets. The only facility for bathing and laundry is a few faucets outside the latrine building. Because the taps are in full view of the billets and nearby roads, refugees bathe with their clothes on in order to avoid public embarrassment. Without a drainage system, water from the faucets runs between the buildings, creating large muddy areas around the latrines. These areas also serve as breeding grounds for mosquitos. Up to 10 malaria cases are reported each week to the clinic.[26]

Isolation is intensified by the mail system. Most of the refugees have networks of correspondents at home and in the United States who try to send much-needed information about family members and the resettlement process, as well as money for food, medicine, and clothing. Yet mail is often stolen by staff members at the camp post office. In the Philippines in 1984, several employees were forced to resign after investigators charged that they had stolen thousands of dollars from envelopes arriving during the Tet holiday. Refugees call the post office the "lost office," and contrast it with the well-run postal service in Palawan, which is operated by the refugees themselves.

Just as the refugees have no choice in housing assignments, they also have no choice in food. Fish or meat (usually chicken), vegetables (usually some sort of lettuce), and fruit (usually bananas) are distributed every day. Several days' supply of rice is distributed each week. Official records indicate that the average daily per capita calorie count of all food arriving in the camp is approximately 2,070.[27] The difficulty is knowing how much of the food actually reaches the refugees. Once or twice a week during 1983 and early 1984, for example, PRPC staff sold "surplus" chickens off the main loading dock. By the middle of 1984, corruption had become so widespread that UNHCR nutritionists concluded that the amount of food being delivered encouraged theft. Therefore a 40 percent reduction in food supplies was ordered as a way of reducing the food available to corrupt officials. The immediate effect upon the refugees was to force many to shop in the public market for food or to scavenge in the surrounding forests for lizards, snakes, and edible plants. Some staff members violated camp policy by giving money to refugees to buy food.

Water for cooking and drinking presents a constant problem throughout the camp. Because the well water is contaminated by bacteria, amoebas, and other parasites, staff members boil it for cooking and drinking, but the refugees have inadequate supplies of kerosene and firewood and so must drink unpurified water. As a result, intestinal disorders are common, especially among children. The problem is most acute during the rainy season, when runoff from the latrines is most likely to affect drinking water. During the dry season, water may be available only an hour or two a day in some neighborhoods.

In order to assure a supply of water when the faucets are dry, refugees collect rain as it runs off their roofs. Although this provides a much-needed backup supply, there is a major health hazard: The roofs are made of asbestos, and so the water potentially contains asbestos particles, which can cause stomach cancer. A report by the Centers for Disease Control recommended for this reason that runoff water not be used.[28] However, camp officials have not taken steps to ensure that this recommendation is implemented, and uninformed refugees continue to collect roof runoff.

ASBESTOS

The decision to use asbestos in the construction of the processing centers was made to avoid the disastrous fires that often strike refugee camps around the world. As an alternative to bamboo or plywood, asbestos offers excellent fire protection in living areas where families cook over open fires in crowded conditions.

Yet asbestos presents serious health risks if it is inhaled or ingested. The most common asbestos-related diseases are asbestosis, a chronic disease of the lungs causing shortness of breath similar to emphysema; mesothelioma, a fatal cancer of the abdomen or chest; and lung cancer. While asbestosis and cancer are often associated with prolonged exposure over many years, certain kinds of asbestos are known to significantly increase the risk after exposure as short as one day. The most dangerous form is crocidolite; just a few inhaled fibers can cause mesothelioma. Although federal agencies for many years listed standards for exposure to asbestos in the workplace, it is now agreed that there is no safe level of exposure to the material. The key to minimizing health risks is to strictly limit the chance of inhaling or ingesting fibers.

The buildings in the processing centers are constructed of a hard fiberboard material containing varying proportions of asbestos. The wallboards used in refugees' billets, staff dorms, classrooms, and some offices can be broken by hand and easily scratched with a fingernail. They contain 10–30 percent asbestos, primarily amosite and chrysotile. The roofs, which are much harder than the wallboards but can be scratched with a knife and broken if struck forcefully, contain up to 40 percent asbestos, primarily crocidolite and chrysotile.[29]

In solid form, these materials present little health risk. The risk becomes much greater, however, when the roofs or walls are scratched, cracked, or broken, resulting in release of asbestos fibers that may be inhaled or swallowed. This occurs primarily during construction, remodeling, and demolition, or when the buildings are damaged or deteriorate from storms, accidents, and everyday use. Discarded building materials also present a hazard if they are left open to weather and wind, or if they affect the water supply. Because the roofs contain crocidolite, the most dangerous form of asbestos, damaged roofs and discarded roofing material present the greatest risk to health.

In the Philippines and Thailand, construction, remodeling, and demolition take place periodically as the camps grow and as necessary repairs are made. In addition, many buildings have damaged roofs and walls. At both sites, classrooms contain a high level of dust, which can be observed falling from ceilings and walls. Concern over the health risks at both sites has led some staff members to seek expert assistance to reduce the risk. The history of these efforts, and the administrative response, began with the first flurry of concern in September 1982.

On September 9, 1982, a petition to the ICMC administration, signed by 45 ICMC employees, requested that dust flaking off the walls be analyzed for asbestos content, that construction crews be provided safety equipment, and that no new buildings be constructed with asbestos.[30] Attached to the petition were photocopies of articles from *Time* and *Newsweek* about the carcinogenic effects of asbestos. Although Americans made up only 10 percent of the staff at that time, nearly half of the petitioners were Americans. Most of the Filipinos on the staff, who provide essential income for large and extended families, were unwilling to jeopardize their employment with ICMC by signing the petition.

Conrad Spohnholz, the ICMC director at that time, did not respond to the petitioners directly, but a month later he wrote to Joseph Gettier, the refugee coordinator at the U.S. Embassy in Manila, noting that the "bad press" asbestos was receiving had led staff members to be concerned about levels of asbestos dust.[31] Spohnholz's memo played down the risk to refugees by noting that they remain only about six months, while some staff members were hired as far back as late 1980. Spohnholz suggested that someone from the Centers for Disease Control (CDC) might be asked to visit the site, but his suggestion was not followed. When one of the leaders of the petitioners reported that she had been threatened with dismissal if she continued to speak publicly on the asbestos issue, the group of petitioners disbanded.

For nearly seven months, the issue was rarely discussed in public, though a few staff members circulated articles about asbestos and tried privately to build support for further action. Finally, in May 1983, a group of teachers' supervisors (one level above teachers in the ICMC hierarchy) wrote to Spohnholz, repeating the proposals made in the earlier petition and asking that he renew his request for CDC analysis. The supervisors justified their letter by quoting ICMC's program management plan for the year, which had listed as a priority a "more conducive atmosphere for healthy working and living relationships."[32]

After receiving no reply to their letter, the leaders of the supervisory group decided to seek help outside the ICMC bureaucracy. A representative who had helped draft the letter to Spohnholz visited a colonel of the Philippine military command to request that he intercede on their behalf. This brief meeting led to further visits to an attorney and to a doctor in the PRPC clinic. Though none of these people took action directly, the discussion of asbestos had been moved beyond a few low-level ICMC employees to other agencies in the camp. As a result, Spohnholz wrote a note to the leaders of the group, assuring them that the Philippine military command, UNHCR, the State Department, and ICMC were looking for somebody to undertake a hazard analysis. Spohnholz also said that he would ask if ICMC could partially fund the analysis.[33]

Yet months passed without action. In November 1983, two months after arriving in the Philippines, I wrote to Matt Henrikson, the ICMC staff director in Manila, noting the health risks of asbestos and requesting that experts be asked to evaluate the processing center site. He responded by stating that working in the Third World always involves greater health risks than in the United States, but he promised to do what he could.[34]

Meanwhile, I decided to seek expert analysis of building materials and air samples from dormitories. At that time, staff members wondered whether painting the wallboards would reduce the number of fibers released into the atmosphere. Therefore I collected air samples from a room with painted walls, and sent it along with pieces of roofing and wallboard to Dr. Lee Montieth of the University of Washington Department of Environmental Health. Montieth's analysis showed that the air sample (collected by the primitive means of leaving an open jar on a shelf) was free of significant concentrations of asbestos fibers, but that the roofing material contained crocidolite, the most dangerous form of asbestos.

Unlike Spohnholz's futile efforts 13 months earlier, Henrikson's promise to seek professional advice eventually led to concrete results. In January 1984, a team of specialists from the National Institute for Occupational Safety and Health (NIOSH) prepared to visit the processing centers. While still at NIOSH labs in the United States, the team analyzed wallboard and roof samples from the centers. This analysis documented the fact that the walls and roofs contained asbestos concentrations of 10–40 percent of total material. Moreover, the samples "released fibers readily with light hand rubbing," suggesting to investigators that "some exposures are occurring" in the processing centers.[35] Robert Knouss, director of the Office of Refugee Health, asked investigators whether the centers should be closed immediately, or if a phased renovation could be safely conducted.[36] Richard Leman, head of the team preparing to visit the processing centers, reported that he could not assess the immediate health risk without additional data to be collected during the site visit. Nevertheless, his preliminary report warned of the serious risk from asbestos exposure:

The absence of a threshold or safe level is . . . indicated by the dramatic evidence of asbestos-related disease in members of asbestos-worker households and in persons living near asbestos contaminated areas. These households and community contacts involved low level and/or intermittent casual exposure to asbestos. Studies of duration of exposure suggest that even after very short exposure periods (1 day to 3 months) significant disease can occur.[37]

Aware of the potentially serious health risks in the processing centers, the NIOSH team alerted officials to the potential for press attention that could result from their visit.[38]

In February 1984, the NIOSH team visited Phanat Nikhom in Thailand and the Philippine processing center. Their visit, documented in a report issued April 10, 1984, confirmed that both walls and roofs contained asbestos, with crocidolite making up 10–20 percent of some samples.[39] The investigators were concerned primarily with measuring the degree to which fibers shed from building materials. Their report contained both good news and bad news for residents.

The good news in the NIOSH report was that air samples taken from staff dormitories, classrooms, offices, and refugees' billets contained fiber concentrations below federal occupational limits. The highest concentration, (0.015 fiber/cubic centimeter), found in two staff dormitories, was well below the federal minimum for crocidolite of 0.2 fiber/cc. In Thailand, where conditions were generally better than in the Philippines, the highest concentration was 0.011 fiber/cc., measured in the clinic. Samples of dust wiped from ledges and other locations inside buildings also showed absence of asbestos or low levels in accumulated dust. Of course, Leman's warning that there is no safe level of exposure implied that the low concentration of fibers in the air presented some increased risk of asbestos-related disease.

The bad news in the NIOSH report was that a significant health risk existed if building materials were damaged or broken or used in such a way that fibers could be released. The investigators noted that adhesive tape pressed on walls resulted in shedding of fibers, as did scratching with fingernails. Wallboards also dissolved in water, indicating that rain or other moisture could release fibers. Their report noted that exposures occurred when residents unknowingly used pieces of asbestos. "Roof and wall materials were scattered all about the processing centre grounds including roadways and play areas. One child was observed using a piece of wallboard as chalk."[40] Not mentioned in the report was the fact that staff members often observed slates of building material being used as chopping blocks in food preparation and as laundry boards.

Investigators made several recommendations to reduce the risk of exposure to released fibers. They recommended that damaged walls or roofs should be repaired or covered with a nonasbestos material, and that grounds should be thoroughly cleaned and policed frequently to ensure that all asbestos debris, as well as the existing stockpile, was removed and destroyed. The report particularly noted that housing used by food service workers, drivers, and other low-level staff "is in a state of great deterioration and is in immediate need of repair. . . . Large sections of the buildings containing asbestos wall board and ceiling tile are damaged and should be replaced." The report emphasized that any repair or removal should be carried out only with dust suppression, such as wetting or vacuum cleaning, by workers wearing high-efficiency particulate respirators. The report also recommended that drainage from roofs not be used for drinking or cooking. The report stated that no further construction or repair should be carried out with asbestos materials.

The NIOSH report noted that the greatest health risk is to workers involved in construction and repair, normally carried out by refugees and by Filipino or Thai crews. As the investigators noted in their preliminary risk assessment before the site visit, "There is increased risk of developing mesothelioma after extremely brief exposures (1 or 2 days) to high concentrations of asbestos."[41] Because the investigators did not observe any construction or repair during their brief visit, however, they did not attempt to quantify the risk presented by normal construction procedures used in the centers.

Children were also presumed to be at increased risk, due to their youth and "long life potentials," though the report optimistically noted the relatively short time refugees spend in the centers. "The risk while not quantifiable, is probably quite low, . . . since most live in [the centers] less than six months." Finally, the report ended with a warning:

Even though the health risk to residents in both these processing centres can not be quantified, it should be noted that present knowledge indicates that exposure to

inhaled asbestos fibers, of any type, increases the risk of subsequent cancer development. The selection of asbestos containing materials in construction of these
processing centres should not be allowed in future processing centres construction
or repair. By following the listed recommendations in this report, a lower risk for
future cancer development among refugees and residents of the two processing
centres is possible but can not be assumed to be entirely eliminated.[42]

    Although the NIOSH report did not attempt to quantify the risk to
refugees or staff, Leman provided Knouss with a quantitative risk assessment based upon the samples of construction materials analyzed before the
site visits. Lemen based that assessment upon the Environmental Protection
Agency's risk estimates for children who attend schools containing friable
asbestos building materials (i.e., materials that are easily crumbled or reduced to powder). Lemen adapted the EPA model to conditions in the
processing centers by assuming an exposure of six months, the typical time
refugees remain there. His assessment concluded that the number of asbestos-induced cancer deaths would be between 1 and 58 per 100,000 refugees, with the "most reasonable" estimate being 9.3 per 100,000. With
over 250,000 refugees having lived in the centers, this assessment predicts
between 2.5 and 131 cancer deaths, with 21 as the most reasonable estimate.[43]
Leman did not attempt to quantify the risk to staff members, who remain
in camp (along with their families) much longer than refugees.
    Lemen's estimates did not take into account two factors. First, there is
significant variation in the friability of the materials used in construction.
In some buildings the wallboards flake quite easily, while in others, paint
and paper taped on the walls virtually eliminate fiber release. In general,
dormitories occupied by the ICMC educational staff are safest, while those
occupied by food service workers, drivers, and other low-paid staff members and by refugees are the most subject to flaking.
    Lemen's estimate also did not take into account "peak exposures" during
demolition or other activities involving intensive release of asbestos fibers.
Such peak exposures could be expected to significantly increase the number
of asbestos-induced cancer deaths.
    When the NIOSH report reached the ICMC officers, they distributed to
staff members only those sections from the report that compared air samples
to similar samples taken in Bangkok and in a variety of locations in the
United States, such as automobile toll booths. Memos declaring "good
news" implied that the report had given the centers a clean bill of health.[44]
Noting that government standards allow no safe level of asbestos exposure,
one memo asked, "How is that for a real scientific position from experts?"[45]
    While the ICMC managers sought to reassure the staff, NIOSH officials
expressed their concern to refugee program bureaucrats in the United States.
In May, Knouss reported the NIOSH findings to Purcell, then director of
the Bureau for Refugee Programs. Knouss's letter noted that the refugees

in Phanat Nikhom, who are required to repair and demolish buildings under the work credit system, are at greater risk of developing cancer than other refugees. Knouss emphasized the importance of the NIOSH recommendations, although he cautioned that, even if the NIOSH recommendations were stringently followed, the risk for future cancers "cannot be assumed to be entirely eliminated."[46]

At Purcell's request, Knouss prepared a sample warning statement for staff members in the processing centers. Sent to Purcell on May 9, 1984, the statement declared that "the refugees who perform construction work with this material will experience more intense exposures and, therefore, are at greater risk of subsequent cancer development than the other refugees in these centers."[47] The statement was not distributed to the teachers at the Philippine center.

Although the NIOSH recommendations were intended to minimize the risk of exposure to released fibers, two years after the NIOSH report was issued, peak exposures would dramatically increase as major renovations began.

During the two years between the NIOSH report and the beginning of renovations, staff members tried to force the officials to carry out its recommendations. In July 1984, three months after the NIOSH report had been issued, rumors spread through the camp that the Philippine military commander, General Gaudencio Tobias, would order that asbestos be discontinued in new construction at PRPC. Steve DeBonis, who had been the first to protest use of asbestos back in 1982, prepared a statement warning all potential employees about the asbestos health risks at PRPC. (Until that time, new ICMC employees had not learned that they were to live and work in asbestos buildings until they arrived in the center.) The statement was never used, although some time later orientation materials sent to newly hired staff members just before their departure from the United States noted that they would live in asbestos dormitories.

In the middle of July, ICMC staff members were taken to Tagaytay, a lake resort outside Manila, for a retreat. First conducted at Kamaya Point the previous year, when the Instructional Model was introduced, the annual retreat was intended to renew staff enthusiasm and commitment and to introduce changes in teaching practice and bureaucratic organization. But at the Tagaytay retreat, complaints of continued failure to carry out NIOSH recommendations were expressed openly. Over a period of several days, supervisors and teachers for the first time organized themselves for the purpose of confronting program managers. Angered at the officials' failure to act on the NIOSH report, they formed the new Asbestos Task Force.

After returning to PRPC, the task force held its first meeting at the center on August 9, 1984, with more meetings held during August and September. With many Filipinos concerned about their jobs, the task force was dominated by Americans. Steve DeBonis, one of the task-force members, wrote to Gregg Beyer, the UNHCR representative, asking him to take action to implement the NIOSH report. After receiving no response, DeBonis wrote twice more to Beyer, first pleading, "Please write and say that you've read the Environmental Survey and are concerned,"[48] and then again, "To try and let you know that I'm not an alarmist, . . . my reasons for concern are not based on whimsey."[49] Finally, on August 31, Beyer wrote to Ted Gochenour, the new ICMC director in the camp, attaching a copy of DeBonis's first letter and noting that a UNHCR specialist had reached similar conclusions to the NIOSH report after quietly visiting PRPC in May.[50] Beyer's letter suggested no specific action, however, stating merely that he had not forgotten the NIOSH report.[51]

Upset that the task force had circumvented the ICMC bureaucracy by contacting the UNHCR representative directly, Gochenour responded with an angry letter to DeBonis criticizing him for using ICMC stationery and demanding that any future letters be cleared by Gochenour. Gochenour's letter did not mention the NIOSH recommendations.[52] Later, after DeBonis asked whether any action would be taken on the recommendations, Gochenour answered vaguely that Beyer had promised UNHCR funds for the asbestos situation.[53]

Meanwhile, the asbestos task force tried a new approach: to teach the refugees directly about the hazards of asbestos. Don Ronk, a task force member who had lived in Laos and Vietnam during the war, prepared information for cultural orientation instructors that emphasized the seriousness of the risk. "The DON'Ts of asbestos are not matters of debate and . . . *should be taught as rules.*" Ronk's rules suggested the range of exposure to asbestos that the refugees continued to suffer.

Don't collect rain water from roofs for drinking, cooking or washing.
Forbid children to play with bits of asbestos sheeting, particularly using it for chalk.
Toys constructed of asbestos should be thrown into the land-fill.
Asbestos sheets should never be used for chopping boards or wash boards.[54]

The task force also began efforts to teach refugees working as assistant teachers about the risks of asbestos, in hopes that they would translate the warnings into the refugees' native languages in classes. Task-force members went to teachers' meetings to urge them to include materials on asbestos in their lessons, and they posted warnings in dorms and classrooms. Some members contacted refugee neighborhood leaders to enlist their assistance in ending dangerous practices in the billet areas. The task force also wrote to ICMC asking once again for compliance with the NIOSH report, as well as for new ceilings in the classrooms to catch falling dust and for supplies of paint to be applied to all exposed asbestos surfaces.

But the energy of the task-force members dissipated when Gochenour announced on August 22, 1984, that new dorms to be constructed to handle increases in staff would be made of concrete blocks rather than asbestos. Gochenour's memo blamed delays in dorm construction, which had led to overcrowding in staff housing, on the asbestos controversy and promised that steps would be taken within 60 days to complete new concrete-block housing. Because priority for the new dorms would be determined by position in the bureaucratic hierarchy, most U.S. task force members would be able to move into the concrete block dorms. With the hope that the situation would improve by the end of the year, task-force members turned their attention back to their heavy schedule of teaching and meetings, relieved that confrontation with the ICMC and PRPC administration had been avoided.

During 1985, enough new concrete block buildings were constructed to accommodate the middle-level ICMC managers. (Upper managers had always lived in houses constructed of nonasbestos materials.) Nothing was done to repair the refugees' billets or the housing for low-level staff members. But as older asbestos housing continued to deteriorate in the fierce storms and intense tropical sun, facilities managers eventually could no longer delay major repairs. During April and May of 1986—two years after the NIOSH report was issued—rumors spread that major renovations of deteriorating housing would finally take place. Concerned that the renovation procedures might increase the risk to refugees and employees, Steve DeBonis offered Dennis Nihill, a former ICMC supervisor now in charge of housing, a copy of an EPA publication on controlling friable asbestos and also reminded Nihill of the NIOSH report. Nevertheless, when the renovations began in late May, it was reported that the air around unprotected demolition crews was filled with asbestos dust, that loads of discarded asbestos were being dumped next to the Morong High School, that pulverized asbestos was being scattered along the road to Morong, and that piles of broken asbestos littered the camp. After the crews had used camp buses to transport the broken asbestos, staff members reported finding thick layers of dust on floors and seats when the buses picked them up after work. Teachers reported that work crews tore off asbestos roofing while residents were inside.[55]

The response among staff members was immediate and angry. A petition called for a halt to all work until experts were called in to oversee the operation. The petition also demanded safe disposal of the asbestos already removed, periodic free cardiopulmonary checkups for employees, and an investigation into the reasons for failure to implement the two-year-old NIOSH report. Jon Darrah, the ICMC Director, who had replaced Gochenour a year earlier, agreed to provide dust masks for the workers.

Angered at the inadequate response, close to 200 ICMC employees attended a rally to demand compliance with the NIOSH recommendations.

Led by Filipinos who charged that the U.S. administrators considered Filipinos "expendable," the rally was attended by Morong residents, who demanded that the town not be used as a dump for PRPC asbestos. Both Darrah, the new ICMC director, and Hank Cushing, the U.S. embassy official responsible for the refugee program, attended the rally. Staff members who attended report that they were told that individuals were free to leave if they did not like the health conditions in the camp. Some Filipinos reportedly protested that economic pressures forced them to remain, while others noted that the refugees were not free to live elsewhere. Finally, Darrah agreed to suspend renovation work and to call in outside consultants.

Under the supervision of Steve Cook, the deputy ICMC director for operations, the Asbestos Removal and Disposal Unit from the U.S. Naval Base at Subic Bay visited PRPC on May 20, 1985, to assess the renovation project. Cook reported their recommendations in a May 29 memorandum to all ICMC staff, assuring them that the Subic team was qualified to conduct its survey and that its recommendations would be followed. Those recommendations were simple: to rope off areas under construction, to provide gloves and approved masks for workers, to avoid breakage of materials, and to bury the asbestos at a safe location. Melchor Morales, head of the Subic team, also agreed to monitor fiber content in the air during a test renovation of two staff dormitories on June 3–4.

The air samples collected on June 3–4 showed that fiber concentrations at ten locations around the construction sites varied from 0.002 to 0.098 fiber per cubic centimeter, just under the OSHA "action level" cited by the Subic team of 0.1 fiber per cubic centimeter.[56] The report recommended that additional caution be used to minimize breakage, that the disposal site be located away from any area of landslide risk, and that the site be inspected regularly to prevent scavaging. No refugee billets were involved in the test.

The results of the report were summarized in a memorandum from Darrah to all ICMC staff on June 16. Concerned that the memo left many questions unanswered, Bill Twyford, the only program officer involved in the asbestos protest, asked Darrah to attend a June 21 meeting of the newly formed "environmental concerns group" to respond to questions about renovation and disposal procedures and about heavy dust concentrations still in buildings renovated before the Subic team conducted its tests. On July 5, Darrah announced that the Subic specialists would return to test the interior of these buildings. These tests, conducted July 7–8, showed concentrations ranging from 0.002–0.010 fiber per cubic centimeter.[57] Again, no refugee billets were tested.

Despite assurances that the recommendations of the NIOSH and Subic team reports would be followed, when renovations resumed in July, some construction areas were not cordoned off, and asbestos was discarded in open piles in Neighborhoods 5 and 8, near refugees' residential areas. Monitoring the situation for the environmental concerns group, Twyford insisted that Nihill and Darrah follow procedures and explain why violations continued to occur.[58]

Eventually, the renovations to ICMC dorms were completed, and the discarded asbestos, including the material that had been dumped near the Morong high school, was buried. For nearly six months, the issue faded, until in December 1986 another major project began—new roofs for dorms occupied by food service workers, drivers, and other low-level PRPC employees. These were the dorms that the NIOSH investigators had noted in February 1984 were "in a state of great deterioration and in immediate need of repair."[59] Now, 34 months after that recommendation, the repairs had begun.

During several weeks of repair and renovation, broken asbestos was piled uncovered in residential areas, and in some cases, the old asbestos roofs were reportedly reinstalled, despite the policy against using asbestos in construction and repair.[60] Although some ICMC employees continued to pressure the administrators to enforce safety rules, the residents of the buildings under renovation did not protest. As the lowest-paid employees with no job security, they had little choice.

THE HIERARCHY OF POWER

The story of the asbestos problem reveals the importance of the hierarchy of power in the processing centers. American upper managers have always lived in nonasbestos structures, while American and Filipino middle managers and supervisors, after some protest, were able to obtain rooms in concrete-block dormitories. Though virtually all of the Americans now live in nonasbestos buildings, most Filipinos do not. At the bottom of the hierarchy, the refugees have no possibility of escaping their asbestos billets. By mid–1988, most asbestos in ICMC dorms—but not in the refugees' billets—had been painted over to reduce flaking. Thus the hierarchy of power is also a hierarchy of safety. Those with power are able to protect their long-term physical well being, while those without power are at increased risk of asbestos-related diseases.

The risk from asbestos, as well as the work-credit system and substandard housing, food, water, and sanitation result from deliberate decisions by program managers at ICMC, in the Bureau for Refugee Programs, and in the Philippine military command. These managers exercise total control over the camp life, work requirements, and pedagogical objectives, as well as the materials and methods used in building construction and renovation. Although formally required to participate in camp life through the system of committees and work credits, the refugees in fact have no authority. In class, they study the language of powerlessness; outside of class, they must practice it.

The bureaucracy offers little reason for hope, as its officials know that there is no reward for proposing change. To implement the NIOSH recommendations or to fundamentally change the organization of camp life would require that care be shown for people who are in no position to complain. It is easier to ignore their needs and the effects of camp life on their physical and emotional well being.

But there is another insidious effect. The processing centers claim to foster individual responsibility, self-sufficiency, and commitment to democratic principles within an active and organized community. Yet instead they fail to protect civil liberties or individual autonomy, and they employ an undemocratic hierarchy within a potentially harmful environment. The refugees learn an important lesson from this gulf between word and deed: that the practice of democracy is quite different from its principles and that many Americans do not believe that individual responsibility, democracy, and self-sufficiency apply equally to all. In its zeal to reeducate, the U.S. refugee program ultimately undermines precisely those principles that it claims to represent.

The Future and the Past

In any case, the war was our responsibility. So is the aftermath.
Loren Baritz, *Backfire: American Culture and the Vietnam War*[1]

I would like to share with all of you the warm-hearted humanity between us. So that we can be happy in our struggle for life together.
Tran Minh, in a letter written to the staff
at the Philippine Refugee Processing Center

The relationship between the United States and Vietnam, Cambodia, and
Laos has continued for nearly a generation. Though the story of that relationship is enormously complex, two crucial chapters can be distinguished:
the war, which had its origins in the 1950s, and the postwar refugee crisis,
beginning in 1975. While distinct, these two chapters are closely related.
The conditions created by the war are what led people to risk their lives to
find a new home; many of the individuals, private agencies, and federal
bureaucracies in the war have also been involved in the refugee program;
and the underlying political conflicts that made the war so protracted and
so devastating continue to block a political solution to the refugee problem.

But there is an additional connection that has gone largely unnoticed.
That is the role of the refugee program in America's memory of the war.
In the struggle to shape the nation's memory, the refugees have become
voiceless pawns in a political debate over the future of U.S. foreign policy.

THE REFUGEE PROGRAM AND THE VIETNAM WAR

All communities have a collective memory, which offers the historical
continuity and historical ecology within which individuals find meaning

and identity. Central to this memory are stories of shared suffering that bond the community together: migrations, wars, famines, ancestors' struggles against oppression, and other hardships.[2] But if it is not balanced by stories of suffering inflicted on others, the memory of shared suffering can disintegrate into violent nationalism, as it did in Germany after World War I.

Memory of suffering inflicted is one basis for a community's hope, for its vision of the future. The aspirations that this vision generates provide a moral framework for the individual's sense of contributing to the common good. For the United States in the first half of the twentieth century, the greatest story of suffering inflicted was slavery. Memory of the injustice it entailed helped to generate the vision of society that Martin Luther King, Jr., articulated in the U.S. civil rights movement.

In the second half of the twentieth century, Vietnam is potentially America's great story of suffering inflicted. The memory of the devastation the United States inflicted upon Southeast Asia, and the consequences of the war for U.S. society, can help to create a vision of the use of power for constructive purposes rather than to wage war. Yet increasingly, public rhetoric identifies *Americans* as the primary victims of the war, thereby transforming Vietnam into a story of suffering shared.

This revisionist memory of Vietnam as a story of suffering shared takes many forms. One is the image of Vietnam as a quagmire that dragged an innocent and reluctant United States into an incomprehensible conflict it did not want in a land it could not understand.[3] Another is the argument that American idealism—a desire to help Asians in need and an alleged reluctance to use violence—was responsible for the war and North Vietnam's victory.[4] Discussion of events unrelated to Vietnam reflects the view of America-as-victim as well. For instance, when introducing a report on Soviet troops in Afghanistan, a network news reporter asked, "Is the war in Afghanistan doing to the Soviet Union what Vietnam did to us?"[5] Like many American discussions of the impact of the war, the question assumed that something terrible happened to the United States in Vietnam and ignored the other victims of the war, the peoples and societies of Southeast Asia.

The debate over the "lesson" of Vietnam is not simply a continuation of the argument between hawks and doves; it is a battle for control of America's shared memory, for control of history.[6] Because historical memory is the source of the assumptions and beliefs that guide national policy, the battle is also for control of the nation's future. Therefore we must ask, What are the consequences of viewing Vietnam primarily as a story of suffering shared?

A central assumption of such a memory is that U.S. policy, though ultimately unsuccessful, was nevertheless based, not upon perceived self-interest, but rather upon a desire to help the peoples of Southeast Asia resist

Communism. Closely connected to this assumption is the belief that Communists create refugees, while Americans help them. For instance, Secretary of State George Shultz, in testimony before Congress, summarized his view of the refugee situation. "The root cause of the refugee problem in Southeast Asia is clear. . . . [It] is a direct result of the imposition of communist oppression on the people of those countries."[7] In official State Department papers, refugee movements are attributed to "human rights abuse in communist Vietnam" and a desire by refugees to escape Communism.[8]

Such statements are not merely politically motivated expressions of sympathy for today's refugees; they are an effort to recast history. Thus State Department officials use the refugees to fondly recall the days in South Vietnam under Thieu.

The Thieu government was sensitive to and restrained by public opinion both at home and abroad. The representative political bodies in South Vietnam . . . were . . . instrumental in the preservation of an important degree of political freedom and expression and would have contributed further to democracy if they had not been eliminated by the communists in 1975. . . . The South Vietnamese people under Thieu were generally free to travel . . . abroad without restriction. . . . Since 1975, as many as 1 million refugees have fled their native homeland to escape the brutal and repressive totalitarian regime.[9]

The simplistic depiction of refugees as victims of Communism denies U.S. responsibility for creating refugees prior to 1975; for destroying the land and the social systems of Indochina, thereby creating the economic conditions that have motivated large numbers of refugees to leave their homes; and for opposing economic assistance that could strengthen the economies of Indochina and reduce the number of refugees. Though the governments of Southeast Asia clearly must share responsibility for the refugee crisis, the nonhistorical interpretation of refugees that has come to dominate official U.S. rhetoric plays a central role in the revision of memory that overlooks U.S. responsibilities and the consequences of U.S. actions. By not recognizing the war as an event of suffering inflicted, this transformed memory will help to sustain the assumptions and policies that led to the war, and preclude the war from ever generating a vision of the peaceful and responsible use of power.

The shift in America's memory about the war can be seen most clearly in the change that has taken place in the image of Vietnam veterans. From guilt-ridden executioners in the 1970s, they have come to be seen as heroes of a war fought with good intentions and as victims of weak political leaders who were unwilling to do what was necessary to win. As Arthur Egendorf, a veteran and nationally recognized expert in treating war trauma, says, "sympathy for the Vietnam veteran has now joined motherhood and apple pie as a hallmark of true Americanism."[10]

INDOCHINESE REFUGEES AND AMERICA'S VIETNAM VETERANS

The change in America's view of its Vietnam veterans has been profound. Virtually all accounts of U.S. soldiers returning from the war in the 1960s and 1970s emphasize the unwillingness of family and friends to associate themselves with people whom they believed had inflicted suffering senselessly. Though talking about Vietnam is crucial to the process of healing from the war, they were reluctant to ask questions about Vietnam or to listen to the veterans talk about their experiences. Until the mid–1980s, this refusal to readmit veterans to U.S. communities increased the veterans' isolation as well as the psychological struggles they faced in adjusting to life back home.[11] As a result, many returning soldiers felt isolated and alone in a country that they did not understand, and that did not understand them. The parallel to Southeast Asian refugees is striking; in an article appearing in 1981, Erwin Parson called the veterans "America's boat people," abandoned to their private uncertainty, despair, and pain.[12]

Isolation is not the only similarity between the experiences of Vietnam vets and those of Indochinese refugees. A major study of U.S. soldiers found that in Vietnam they had a constant sense of being "uprooted, transplanted, and dislocated to a strange planet."[13] Like refugees in flight and in first-asylum camps, these soldiers confronted a hostile, violent world that they could neither understand nor control. Their response—profound mistrust, numbing, and denial—also paralleled the refugees' reactions.[14] Though they longed to escape the conditions in which they found themselves, both vets and refugees faced a life after Indochina that was more bewildering than they had expected. For both groups, the journey to the United States was another profound shock, the start of a life-long struggle to survive.

Adjusting to life in the United States has created similar social and psychological stresses for both Vietnam veterans and Indochinese refugees. After the life-and-death intensity of Indochina, the details of daily life, such as filling the gas tank, appearing at appointments on time, and shopping at the supermarket seem trivial, even silly. But, paradoxically, because they seem so unimportant, these decisions become enormously difficult to make.[15] Both groups also exhibit symptoms of posttraumatic stress disorder.[16] Many families of vets and refugees experience similar difficulties: children becoming "symptom bearers," high rates of depression, alcoholism and drug use, and divorce.[17] Survivors may feel a powerful bond with their comrades who died, and guilt that they lived.[18] As a result, many refugees and veterans become cautious in personal interactions in order to protect themselves from being misunderstood.[19]

Yet ultimately the two groups differ significantly in the reception they have been given and their prospects for recovery. Since the dedication of the Vietnam Veterans' Memorial in 1982, public attitudes toward vets have shifted dramatically. Oral histories of the war have become best sellers; television and film vividly depict the U.S. soldiers' experience.[20] Veterans' groups offer an effective means of integrating the experience of Vietnam with life in the United States.[21] But for the refugees, a tremendous outpouring of sympathy in 1978–79 quickly evaporated, so that the long struggle of resettlement has attracted little sympathy and less and less attention. As Senator Mark Hatfield observed in 1984, "in just four short years, the same public which embraced the refugee with open arms is perceived to have become fatigued, discouraged, burnt-out."[22] For Indochinese refugees, the passage of time has meant increasingly hostile American communities, reduced funding for adjustment programs, and no end in sight to their social, psychological, and economic difficulties.

This essential difference in America's response to the veterans and the refugees is part of the ongoing transformation of memory about Vietnam. Though the refugees, like the veterans, can lay claim to some of the rights and privileges of heroes, they remain more stigmatized than heroic, "foreigners" lacking "self-sufficiency." The United States does not acknowledge that many of them fought alongside the U.S. soldiers. Perhaps most importantly, while the United States has apologized to its Vietnam veterans, it still denies it has any reason to apologize either to the refugees or to the people of Southeast Asia.

While both the veterans and the refugees are seen as victims, only the veterans have come to be seen as heroes. Thus the transformation of Vietnam from a story of suffering inflicted to a story of suffering shared involves simplistic patronizing of refugees, simplistic explanations for refugee movements, and exclusive glorification of America's—but not Indochina's—veterans. Though few of the refugees care whether they are seen as heroes, like the veterans they need understanding, they need their stories heard and their contribution recognized. As long as the transformation of memory continues, these needs will not be satisfied.

RECOMMENDATIONS

The refugees are also like the veterans in that they need more than understanding. They need jobs, education, child care, improved health care, and adequate housing. They need to have U.S. communities offer hope, rather than long-term economic crisis. Unfortunately, even attempts to "understand" may contribute to inaction. As Art Huddleston, a Vietnam veteran and teacher of refugees, argues, posttraumatic stress disorder too often is "extended to encompass all reactions . . . to currently unreasonable conditions by ascribing them to events located in the past."[23] Action as well as sympathy is necessary to change the "currently unreasonable conditions" facing refugees.

To that end, the following recommendations are offered. They include general recommendations to guide a renewed discussion of refugee issues and specific recommendations for the overseas processing centers, for federal refugee policy, for Southeast Asian communities in the United States, and for programs to educate Americans.

General Recommendations

1. Prevention of Refugee-creating Policies. Policymakers must adopt policies that ensure people do not become refugees in the first place. This means, first of all, that the United States should not fight wars that lead to movements of refugees and, second, that U.S. foreign policy should have as a major priority the resolution of refugee situations around the world. At present, refugees are seen as an unfortunate by-product of foreign policy, or they are used as pawns by competing sides, as in the stalemate over Cambodia. A commitment to avoiding and resolving refugee situations would reduce the probability of long-term suffering, such as continues in Southeast Asia.

2. Historical Perspective on Refugees. Any reanalysis of refugee policy must start with an insistence upon a historical perspective toward refugees. Historical perspective reminds us that refugee movements in Southeast Asia did not begin in 1975, that a resolution to the refugee crisis will require creative solutions to long-term political conflicts, and that most refugees experience significant downward mobility upon their arrival in the United States.[24] Moreover, historical perspective reminds us of the sources of America's beliefs about the purpose and content of immigrant education, and warns of the danger that educational programs will serve the interests of employers rather than those of the refugees.

3. Refugees' Empowerment. If the refugee program is to enhance refugees' independence, resettlement policies in the camps and the United States must support refugees' empowerment. Currently, the life of a refugee in camp is strictly controlled for the benefit of the bureaucracy, while in U.S. communities, refugees are expected to make major life decisions in order to accommodate budgetary needs. An alternative approach to resettlement is for refugees to determine for themselves their needs and the goals of the programs that affect them, and to operate local programs for the benefit of their local communities.

Specific Recommendations

The Processing Centers

1. Reorganize life in the processing centers. At present, refugees have virtually no control over key aspects of their daily lives. This must change. Refugees need material support and other forms of assistance, but not a

transformed identity. They deserve safe and sanitary living conditions, a life free from humiliation and danger, and the right to make for themselves the dozens of decisions that comprise everyday adult life: where to sleep, to bathe, to rest, and to work; when to sleep and to eat, and with whom; what to read and to study. The right to make such decisions is central to true self-sufficiency.

2. Reconsider the competency-based approach to ESL. The current fascination with competency-based education contributes to a two-tiered educational system in which some people are educated, while others practice limited vocational and survival "competencies." CBE also creates the illusion of "objective" assessment, when in fact refugees require a far broader conception of successful resettlement than CBE offers. Alternative pedagogies that empower refugees should be adopted, particularly problem-posing approaches that promote action outside the classroom.[25]

3. Revise curricula. Curricula should reflect refugees' varying educational, employment, and sociocultural needs. Most importantly, revised curricula should reflect a more flexible definition of "successful resettlement" than simply minimum-wage jobs. This definition would include maintenance of language and culture, preservation of traditional family structures, and employment appropriate to refugees' previous education, skills, and experience.

4. Transfer authority for the centers from the Department of State to ORR or the Department of Education. Because the Department of State is not designed to handle a large educational program, it is not able to offer effective educational leadership. In contrast, ORR has long had responsibility for domestic programs. If additional funding is made available for education, the Department of Education may offer a reasonable alternative to ORR.[26]

5. Review the institutional structures of the overseas centers, with the aim of reducing expensive bureaucratic systems and augmenting support for education.[27] At present, the Philippine center is operated by an agency that has not demonstrated an ability to educate refugees for resettlement. Alternative proposals should be solicited from educational institutions with demonstrated success in innovative approaches to adult education. In addition, salaries should be increased for host country nationals, who currently handle the bulk of teaching and supervisory duties, in order to reflect the importance of their work in the centers.

6. Recruit former refugees for administrative positions. Both the operational and the educational aspects of the processing centers, particularly the design of the educational program, should include significant participation by former refugees.

7. Construct housing and classrooms of nonasbestos materials. Under the supervision of the Centers for Disease Control, the processing centers should immediately remove existing asbestos structures in a manner that

does not endanger the refugees, staff members, or residents of the surrounding area and replace these structures with buildings of concrete block or other suitable materials. In addition, the CDC or other appropriate agencies should track the potential effects of asbestos among resettled refugees and staff members, and offer free treatment to those affected by asbestos-related diseases. Because Filipinos and Thais have spent the greatest amount of time in the centers, the Centers for Disease Control should assist the Philippine and Thai governments in establishing similar health programs, funded by the United States.

Federal Refugee Policy

1. Eliminate policies that channel refugees into minimum-wage jobs. Long-term language education, job training, and other services should ensure that skilled refugees find employment paying a livable wage, and that refugees with limited English proficiency are not forced into employment before they have the opportunity to gain fluency in English.

2. Eliminate regulations that require states to spend the bulk of their funds on employment services, and adopt policies reflecting goals other than minimum-wage employment. Policies should be designed to protect Southeast Asian languages and cultures, to maintain extended families, and to foster Southeast Asian social, recreational, and political organizations. Funding should be provided for programs that support health care, transportation, child care, and a range of language classes beyond "survival English."[28] Measures of effectiveness should be adopted that reflect these revised goals. Above all, local programs should have the purpose of building Southeast Asian communities capable of exercising effective social and political power in the interests of their members.

3. Eliminate existing "multiple-wage-earner" policies, which ensure that households will need the incomes of several members to survive. At present, regulations pressuring refugees into minimum-wage jobs often mean that adolescents and young adults are unable to attend school, that young children are left without proper care during working hours, and that families are placed under enormous economic pressure. The resulting damage to family structure contributes immensely to the social and psychological problems of resettled refugees.[29]

4. Whenever possible, transfer decision-making authority within refugee programs to the refugees themselves, as in the Mutual Assistance Associations (MAAs). Refugees should play a central role in decision making at all levels within the programs. They should determine program goals and content and fill key positions in the refugee bureaucracy.

5. End efforts to disperse Southeast Asians around the United States. Though the policy of dispersal no longer dominates the programs, policymakers should ensure that refugees are not penalized for moving to regions with existing concentrations of Southeast Asians.[30]

6. Encourage states and local communities to recognize education, training, and professional certification earned in institutions in Southeast Asia. At present, highly qualified refugees are often denied access to jobs because their previous training and experience are not recognized by U.S. institutions.[31] Such practices, which contribute to underemployment, should be discouraged.

Southeast Asian Communities in the United States

1. Form political alliances with other members of the working poor. Refugees have much in common with other minorities and the working poor in the United States, but have limited their political activity primarily to anti-Communism.[32] As a result, many Indochinese support U.S. political leaders who oppose social programs that benefit refugees. By reconsidering their political alliances, Southeast Asian communities can better influence their political agenda, above all in obtaining a livable wage.

2. Insist upon respect for Southeast Asian languages and cultures. Indochinese community leaders should play an active role in public schools to ensure that their children grow up with an understanding and a respect for their social and cultural institutions, and to insist that Americans respect cultural diversity.

3. Encourage service providers, particularly schools, to hire bilingual staff members and employ Indochinese as social workers, community-service police officers, county health officers, and other technical specialists.[33] In areas where Southeast Asians have been trained and recruited for such positions, the entire community has benefited.[34]

Educating Americans

1. Explore ways for Southeast Asians to be resources in U.S. institutions. Former refugees should be recruited to teach languages and to contribute to historical, sociological, and anthropological analyses of Southeast Asia. In addition, innovative efforts should be undertaken to ensure that existing institutions accommodate traditional cultures.

2. Fund courses in adult schools, high schools, and colleges and universities about the recent history of Southeast Asia. These courses should focus on the U.S. role in creating and sustaining flows of refugees, as well as the long-term historical involvement of the United States in Indochina and the contributions resettled refugees are making to U.S. society.

3. Build broad public support for refugee resettlement programs. Programs should be funded that bring information about refugees to the general public, particularly in areas with large numbers of Southeast Asians. Above all, U.S. communities need to be shown that multilingualism is an asset, not a threat, to the community.[35]

THE GOSE REFUGEE CAMP

One irony of the refugee program is that Americans are trying to teach self-sufficiency to people who have already demonstrated their ability to survive some of the most difficult challenges human beings ever face. It is when they arrive in the asylum camps and processing centers that refugees become powerless, as they confront a rigidly hierarchical organization that denies them the right to make even the simplest decisions of daily life. Though the Americans claim to teach self-sufficiency, by their actions they teach acceptance of a bureaucratic hierarchy that subjects the refugees to an unprecedented loss of individual autonomy. A final irony is that the Americans responsible for this system accuse the refugees of developing a dependency syndrome.

But it is the Americans who are dependent. They depend upon an image of themselves as supremely knowledgeable about what refugees need; they depend upon not having to confront their own ignorance of the languages and cultures of Southeast Asia; and they depend upon a hierarchy that places them in charge. An alternative approach to refugee education, one that truly sought the refugees' self-sufficiency, would require that Americans give up these dependencies.

Such an alternative was offered by the Gose camp, operated for the Vietnamese who arrived in Japan during the early 1980s by Caritas, a Catholic group.[36] Caritas recognized that people become refugees by circumstance, not by character. Thus they need assistance, but they do not need to be reeducated. Refugees at Gose were permitted to move freely in and out of camp. There were no written rules; instead, the camp residents held group meetings to resolve conflicts and to set policies, thereby recovering the collective responsibility that had characterized life in Vietnam. Cooking, cleaning, shopping, and other daily activities were organized and carried out by the residents themselves, rather than under a work–credit system operated by camp officials. Most residents over the age of sixteen were employed outside the camp and contributed their wages to cover the costs of their stay. The living accommodations were clean and well lighted, with hot and cold showers, lavatories, washing machines, a kitchen and dining room, and a hobby room.

These conditions not only expressed a true commitment to the refugees' self-sufficiency, but also an abiding belief in their dignity. In its zeal to reeducate the refugees, the U.S. refugee education program in Southeast Asia denies both self-sufficiency and dignity. The program assumes that the refugees are aliens who must be transformed before they can be welcomed into U.S. society. But it is the program that is alien to the principles it claims to represent. The result is that the processing centers are another step on the refugees' torturous road "from dignity to despair."[37] Yet it is not too late for changes in policy and practice for the thousands of future refugees who will be caught up in the alien winds of forced migration and reeducation.

Epilogue: Thinking of Hung

But I didn't believe to hope of humanity. Because I was a witness.
                                          Tho Nguyen, refugee from Vietnam,
                                  in an essay written in the Philippines

The heart of the work is finding what we have in common.
                                                  John Wheeler,
                  Touched with Fire: The Future of the Vietnam Generation[1]

I accompanied Hung on his long walk to the departure area on the hot, humid morning he left PRPC for the United States. He would stay overnight at the refugee transit center at the Manila airport before his flight the next morning to Seattle, where he would change planes bound for Georgia. We talked about our first meeting, when I had delivered Tien's letter, and we made plans to see each other in six months when I would return to the United States.

At the waiting area, I chatted with other refugees as Hung completed the predeparture ritual: returning his cooking utensils, completing one last physical examination, verifying his class attendance and work-credit records, and receiving his departure number and the documents that would identify him to authorities throughout his journey. Then we waited in the shade for the buses from Manila, which would drop off another group of arrivals before taking Hung and the others to the airport. We calculated that it had been exactly two years, eleven months and five days since he had left Vietnam. He had studied ESL, cultural orientation, and PET and had asked a thousand questions. But now his biggest concern was about changing planes in Seattle; it would be 50 degrees colder than he had ever felt, and he had no coat.

I looked around at the 150 people waiting with us. Some were Vietnamese who had survived harrowing journeys across the South China Sea. Others were Cambodians who would never forget the horror of Khmer Rouge rule. A few were Laotians who had made the swift, desperate swim across the Mekong River to Thailand. All had lived for months, perhaps years, in the first-asylum camps of Malaysia, Thailand, Singapore, Hong Kong, Indonesia, or the Philippines before coming to PRPC six months before. On this day, their lives as homeless refugees were about to end.

Yet it was not a day of joy. Departure meant leaving friends who had shared the journey to asylum and the struggle to survive this far. It meant leaving the fragile yet familiar PRPC to live among Americans, whom they did not understand. To Hung, it meant the final, bitter end to the hope that he would ever see his family again. Tomorrow, from Manila, he would leave Asia, perhaps forever. In two days, he would be in Georgia, alone at seventeen.

After nearly three hours, four buses finally arrived. Exhausted men, women, and children stepped off and filed silently into the arrival area to begin processing. Hung's compassionate expression reflected the uncertainty and fear etched on the faces of the new arrivals. Suddenly, the loudspeaker announced that the departing refugees were to line up as their numbers were called. Hung was first, and so we stood quickly, shook hands, and embraced before he turned and walked away.

Within minutes, the buses to Manila, rented from a large Philippine company, were packed with refugees and their meager belongings. Hung sat at the window directly above the company's name, painted red against a white background, Victory Liner. A hand-painted sign in the front window announced to oncoming traffic: "Refugees—Do Not Delay." Silently, three of Hung's friends reached up through the window to touch his hand one last time. Tears came to Hung's eyes, and cries of final goodbyes filled the air. Black smoke poured from the exhaust. With a roar, the buses pulled out. Hung did not look back.

Four years later, in spring 1988, the State Department eliminated funding for *Passage*, its official journal about refugee education. The final issue describes new reading material used at PRPC. In a sample lesson, a cartoon strip depicts an unattractive, overweight, bearded man in a T-shirt who is mugged by a handsome, clean-shaven man in a suit. Upon hearing the victim's cries for help, a police officer arrives, only to mistakenly arrest the victim, who is taken to jail as the thief goes free. A dialogue leaves no doubt about the intended message:

TEACHER:Why did the police bring the big man to the police station?

STUDENTS: Because he looks very dirty. . . . He looks like a robber, and he doesn't speak English very well. . . .

TEACHER: So that you will not be mistaken as a robber, what will you do?
STUDENTS: Look clean and wear clean clothes.[2]

In 1988, Hung lives in the Midwest, where he recently had his first contact with American police: a traffic ticket that he felt he should not have been given. He took his case to trial before a judge and, acting in his own defense, using a language he had only recently and imperfectly learned, in a judicial system he did not understand, he convinced the judge that the traffic cop was wrong. Telling me about this on the phone, he laughed as he described his courtroom speech, and spoke with pride about his own courage. "Imagine," he said, "me, a lawyer in an American court! And I won! I won! Imagine."

Notes

INTRODUCTION

1. Frances Fitzgerald, *Fire in the Lake* (New York: Vintage, 1972), p. 565.

2. The phrase "becoming American" is often used to describe the changes in behavior, values, and attitudes that refugees and immigrants are believed to undergo. For instance, a widely distributed film about Hmong refugees is entitled "Becoming American." The phrase is used in many popular publications, such as in the article "Learning to be American," by Barbara Garner, in the *Brown University Alumni Magazine* (1986), pp. 43–45.

3. This figure includes 130,000 "official" refugees under the protection of the UN High Commissioner for Refugees (UNHCR) and 265,000 "displaced persons" assisted by the UN Border Relief Operation. See *Refugees* 48 (Geneva: UNHCR, December 1987), p. 27.

4. Under the Khmer Rouge, Cambodia was called Democratic Kampuchea, which was adopted by the United Nations as the official designation of the country. Under the Heng Samrin government, the country became the People's Republic of Kampuchea. In the fall of 1984 the United Nations decided to use Cambodia as the designation. That is the term used in this book. "Khmer" refers to ethnic Cambodians, the largest ethnic group in the country, as well as to their language. The country also contains other ethnic groups, such as Chinese, Chams, and various highland groups, all of whom are also called Cambodians. In Laos, ethnic Lao, also called lowland Lao, are a slight majority of the population, the rest of which consists of other ethnic groups, usually classified into highland or midland Laotians. These include the Hmong, Mien, and Tai Dam. In this book, the term "Lao" refers to ethnic Lao people, while "Laotian" refers to any person from Laos.

5. William Shawcross, *The Quality of Mercy: Cambodia, Holocaust, and Modern Conscience* (New York: Simon and Schuster, 1984).

CHAPTER 1: INTO THE CAMPS

1. UN Convention (1951) and Protocol (1967) Relating to the Status of Refugees.

2. Refugee Act of 1980, U.S. Public Law 96–212.

3. Figures on Cambodian resettlement in the United States are from *Refugee Reports* (Washington, D.C.: American Council for Nationalities Service), December 12, 1986, p. 7, based on data in Linda W. Gordon, "Southeast Asian Refugee Migration to the United States" (Washington, D.C.: U.S. Department of Health and Human Services, Office of Refugee Resettlement, September 1984).

4. There is wide disagreement about the number of Cambodians who died of starvation, disease, torture, and execution during the period of Khmer Rouge rule, from 1975 to 1978. See Judith Bentley, *Refugees: Search for a Haven* (New York: Julian Messner, 1986), p. 31, which cites a high figure of between 2 and 4 million out of a population of 7 million. Few analysts of Cambodian affairs accept estimates of over 50 percent of the total Khmer population. Gil Loescher and John A. Scanlan, *Calculated Kindness: Refugees and America's Half-Open Door, 1945–Present* (New York: Free Press, 1986), p. 148, state that "between 1 and 3 million Cambodians—one-seventh to nearly one-half of the nation's entire population—died from executions or from preventable malnutrition." These figures are suppported by the Vietnam-backed Cambodian government, which stated in July 1979 that the population had dropped during Khmer Rouge rule from 7.25 to 4 million. See *Kampuchea: Decade of the Genocide—Report of the Finnish Inquiry Commission*, edited by Kimmo Kiljunen (London: Zed, 1984), p. 30. But in a detailed analysis of population estimates from various sources, Michael Vickery, *Cambodia: 1975–1982* (Boston: South End Press, 1984), pp. 186–88, argues that the drop in population that occurred between April 1975 and January 1979 was probably no more than about .4 million. Vickery concludes that "although there is no evidence which permits the extrapolation of the worst death tolls—2–3 million—bandied about in the anti-DK [Democratic Kampuchea–Khmer Rouge] press, the number of deaths over normal, from whatever cause, are a serious indictment of a regime committed to the regeneration of its country" (p. 144). It is now widely believed that in 1979 the Heng Samrin government and the Vietnamese probably exaggerated the number of Khmer Rouge victims in order to justify the Vietnamese invasion. This belief is based on the 1981 population census by the Cambodian Ministry for Planning and the Exhibition of Permanent Achievements (see *Kampuchea: Decade of the Genocide*, p. 31), which lists a total population of 6.8 million. If this estimate is correct, then it is improbable that the number of excess deaths during Khmer Rouge rule was in the millions. For additional discussion of the inaccuracy of some holocaust claims, see William Shawcross, *The Quality of Mercy: Cambodia, Holocaust, and Modern Conscience* (New York: Simon and Schuster, 1984), pp. 207–24.

5. For an account of the lobbying effort on behalf of Cambodian refugees, see Loescher and Scanlan, *Calculated Kindness*, pp. 152–54.

6. For an account of the forcible repatriation of Cambodians during April 1979, see Shawcross, *Quality of Mercy*, pp. 84–85.

7. See Loescher and Scanlan, *Calculated Kindness*, p. 158.

8. For example, see "Deathwatch: Cambodia," *Time*, November 12, 1979, pp. 42–48.

9. Loescher and Scanlan, *Calculated Kindness*, pp. 162–63.

10. Ibid., p. 167.

11. *Refugee Reports*, December 16, 1988, p. 10.

12. For further information on the Cambodians being held in UNBRO holding centers in Thailand, see *Cambodians in Thailand: People on the Edge*, issue paper

prepared by the U.S. Committee for Refugees (Washington, D.C.: American Council for Nationalities Service, 1985), pp. 13–15.

13. See Shawcross, *Quality of Mercy*, pp. 230–31.

14. For an interesting discussion of the varied reasons for movement of Cambodian refugees toward Thailand, see Vickery, *Cambodia: 1975–1982*, pp. 29–31.

15. *Refugee Reports*, December 12, 1986, p. 7.

16. For a summary of the use of the parole authority to admit Indochinese refugees to the United States, see Loescher and Scanlan, *Calculated Kindness*, pp. 123–36.

17. Ibid., pp. 129–31.

18. Ibid., p. 136.

19. Ibid., p. 140.

20. For an account, see Barry Wain, *The Refused: The Agony of the Indochina Refugees* (New York: Simon and Schuster, 1981).

21. Announcement by UN Secretary-General Kurt Waldheim. See Loescher and Scanlan, *Calculated Kindness*, p. 145.

22. Ibid., p. 146.

23. *Refugee Reports*, December 12, 1986, p. 7.

24. For a description of the resettlement program in China, see *Refugees* 13 (Geneva: UNHCR, January 1985), pp. 19–32.

25. Estimates of the number of prisoners held in reeducation camps vary widely. Though the United States has considered resettling some prisoners, to date no agreement has been reached between the United States and the government of Vietnam. See "Overview of Refugee Situation in Southeast Asia," hearings before the Subcommittee on Asian and Pacific Affairs of the U.S. House Foreign Affairs Committee, April 5, 1984 (Washington, D.C.: Government Printing Office, 1984), pp. 6–7.

26. The estimate of 8,000 Amerasians was made by Vietnam's Vice Foreign Minister, Ha Van Lau. James Purcell, former director of the U.S. Bureau for Refugee Programs, estimated between 6,000 and 8,000 Amerasians. See "Overview of Refugee Situation," p. 63.

27. See "Amerasians: Dust of Life," in *Refugees*, April 1985, pp. 35–36.

28. H. Eugene Douglas, Coordinator for Refugee Affairs, in hearings before House Judiciary Committee on the Refugee Admissions Program for fiscal 1986, September 19, 1985 (Washington, D.C.: Government Printing Office, 1986), p. 9.

29. ODP departures to the United States dropped from 6,697 in fiscal 1984 to 1,125 in fiscal 1985 and 880 in fiscal 1986. See *Refugee Reports*, December 12, 1986, p. 5.

30. The United States processes the largest number of ODP cases, while Canada and Australia also have substantial programs. From January to September 1986, the numbers of ODP cases for countries other than the U.S. were Australia, 2,220; Canada, 2,095; France, 685; West Germany, 472; Great Britain, 210; and all others, 574. See *The Orderly Departure Program: The Need for Reassessment*, prepared by the Migration and Refugee Affairs Committee of InterAction (Washington, D.C.: U.S. Catholic Conference, Migration and Refugee Services, 1986).

31. *Refugees from Laos: In Harm's Way*, issue paper prepared by the U.S. Committee for Refugees (Washington, D.C.: American Council for Nationalities Service, 1986), p. 5.

32. For a brief discussion of disagreement between UNHCR representatives and the U.S. government during 1976–1978 over the motivation of Laotian refugees, see Loescher and Scanlan, *Calculated Kindness*, pp. 126–27.

33. "Refugee and Migration Problems in Southeast Asia," staff report, Subcommittee on Immigration and Refugee Policy, Senate Judiciary Committee, August 1984 (Washington, D.C.: Government Printing Office, 1984).

34. *Refugees from Laos: In Harm's Way*, p. 13.

35. Ibid., pp. 1, 12.

36. *Refugee Reports*, December 12, 1986, p. 5.

37. *Refugees from Laos: In Harm's Way*, pp. 15–16.

38. In 1986 the description of the preemployment training program was changed to "work orientation." The change did not indicate a fundamental shift in content or purpose.

39. Several books are available that chronicle various aspects of refugee movements in Southeast Asia since 1975. Two useful descriptions of the major refugee flows in 1979–80 are Keith St Cartmail, *Exodus Indochina* (Auckland, New Zealand: Heinemann, 1983); and Wain, *The Refused*. The best analysis of the world's effort to respond to the Cambodian crisis is Shawcross, *Quality of Mercy*. Widely differing views of events inside Cambodia during the period of Khmer Rouge rule are presented in Francois Ponchaud, *Cambodia: Year Zero* (New York: Penguin, 1977); Vickery, *Cambodia: 1975–1982*; and George C. Hildebrand and Gareth Porter, *Cambodia: Starvation and Revolution* (New York: Monthly Review, 1976). An introduction to the refugee situation generally is available in Bentley, *Refugees: Search for a Haven*. Two excellent analyses of U.S. refugee policy are Loescher and Scanlan, *Calculated Kindness*, and Norman L. Zucker and Naomi Flink Zucker, *The Guarded Gate: The Reality of American Refugee Policy* (San Diego, Calif.: Harcourt Brace Jovanovich, 1987).

CHAPTER 2: SURVIVORS

1. Joseph Campbell, *The Hero with a Thousand Faces* (Princeton, N.J.: Princeton University Press, 1968), p. 218.

2. There is some uncertainty about the proportion of northern refugees who were Catholic. Ellen Hammer, in *Vietnam Yesterday and Today* (New York: Holt, Rinehart, and Winston, 1966), p. 50, says merely that "most of the . . . refugees who fled to the south" were Catholics. Francis J. Corley, in "Vietnam since Geneva," *Thought* 33, (Fordham University Quarterly, 1958–59), pp. 515–68, gives a figure of 676,348 Catholics out of a total of 860,206. Joseph Buttinger, in *Vietnam: A Dragon Embattled*, vol. 2 (New York: Praeger, 1967), p. 900, cites official statistics of the government in Saigon that 794,000 were Catholics, though he suggests that the number "might have been as low as 600,000."

3. Hammer, *Vietnam Yesterday and Today*, p. 50.

4. Buttinger, *Vietnam: A Dragon Embattled*, pp. 900–901, 1117.

5. Ibid., p. 900.

6. As the model for the Ugly American, Lansdale has been the focus of major debate. See William J. Lederer and Eugene Burdick, *The Ugly American* (New York, Norton, 1958). *The World Almanac of the Vietnam War*, edited by John S. Bowman (New York, Bison Books, 1985), p. 38, credits Lansdale with motivating many

Catholics to leave, in addition to providing the logistical support necessary to transport nearly one million people. One claim was that Lansdale encouraged Catholic priests to tell their followers that anyone remaining in the north would be condemned to hell, while other reports suggest that he spread the rumor that the north would be annihilated by atomic weapons (see Buttinger, *Vietnam: A Dragon Embattled*, p. 900). In contrast, Stanley Karnow, in *Vietnam: A History* (New York: Viking, 1983), p. 223, argued that "his role has been inflated in some accounts."

7. *World Almanac of the Vietnam War*, p. 38.

8. See John D. Montgomery, *The Politics of Foreign Aid: American Experience in Southeast Asia* (New York: Praeger, 1962), p. 85.

9. Though the specific numbers of refugees in the new villages cannot be determined precisely, it is widely agreed that the program successfully established settlements for several hundred thousand people. The program has been called "the most widely acknowledged success of the Diem regime" (*World Almanac of the Vietnam War*, p. 46), though critics point out that the program was only "an effective crash program of American aid [that] had little to do with the ability of the Diem government to develop the economy as a whole." See Robert Scheer, *How the United States Got Involved in Vietnam* (Santa Barbara, CA: Center for the Study of Democratic Institutions, 1965), quoted in Buttinger, *Vietnam: A Dragon Embattled*, p. 1129.

10. Buttinger, *Vietnam: A Dragon Embattled*, p. 922.

11. See Hammer, *Vietnam Yesterday and Today*, p. 197.

12. See Buttinger, *Vietnam: A Dragon Embattled*, pp. 859–60.

13. Ibid., p. 1128.

14. The struggle by aid agencies to avoid being used for political and strategic gain became especially acute during the effort to aid victims of the famine in Cambodia after the overthrow of the Khmer Rouge by Vietnamese troops. See William Shawcross, *The Quality of Mercy: Cambodia, Holocaust, and Modern Conscience* (New York: Simon and Schuster, 1984).

15. *World Almanac of the Vietnam War*, p. 124.

16. Frances Fitzgerald, *Fire in the Lake* (New York: Vintage, 1972), pp. 460–61.

17. Ibid., p. 465.

18. *World Almanac of the Vietnam War*, p. 158.

19. Fitzgerald, *Fire in the Lake*, pp. 569–70.

20. *World Almanac of the Vietnam War*, p. 196.

21. Ibid., p. 324.

22. This description of refugee camps near Da Nang relies upon Fitzgerald, *Fire in the Lake*, p. 571.

23. Gloria Emerson, *Winners and Losers* (New York: Penguin, 1976), p. 357.

24. Fitzgerald, *Fire in the Lake*, p. 573.

25. Arnold R. Isaacs, *Without Honor: Defeat in Vietnam and Cambodia* (New York: Vintage, 1983), p. 161.

26. Ibid., p. 162. See also William Shawcross, *Sideshow* (New York: Washington Square Press, 1979), p. 211.

27. *Christian Science Monitor*, March 14, 1970, cited by Isaacs, *Without Honor*, p. 162.

28. *Far Eastern Economic Review*, January 8, 1972, cited by Isaacs, *Without Honor*, p. 162.

29. W. E. Garrett, "The Hmong of Laos: No Place to Run," *National Geographic* (January 1974), pp. 78–111, cited by Isaacs, *Without Honor*, p. 162.

30. Isaacs, *Without Honor*, p. 162.

31. *World Almanac of the Vietnam War*, p. 258.

32. Elizabeth Becker, *When the War Was Over* (New York: Simon and Schuster, 1986), p. 34.

33. Figures from Economist Intelligence Unit, *Quarterly Economic Report, Annual Supplement, 1975*, cited in *Kampuchea: Decade of the Genocide—Report of the Finnish Inquiry Commission*, edited by Kimmo Kiljunen (London: Zed, 1984), p. 6.

34. Becker, *When the War Was Over*, p. 34.

35. Ibid., p. 166.

36. Shawcross, *Sideshow*, p. 227.

37. Ibid., pp. 318–19.

38. General Accounting Office, Report to the Senate Refugee Subcommittee of the Judiciary Committee, "Problems in the Khmer Republic (Cambodia) concerning War Victims, Civilian Health and War-related Casualties," February 2, 1972.

39. Becker, *When the War Was Over*, p. 183.

40. The experience of U.S. soldiers who were newly arrived in Vietnam is summarized in Joel Osler Brende and Erwin Randolph Parson, *Vietnam Veterans: The Road to Recovery* (New York: New American Library, 1985), pp. 42–45.

41. "Malaysia's Fight Against Piracy," *Refugees* 10 (Geneva: UNHCR, October 1984), pp. 17–18. Keith St Cartmail, *Exodus Indochina* (Auckland, New Zealand: Heinemann, 1983), p. 151, wrote that in May 1981, 75 of the 99 boats believed to have left Vietnam during that month were attacked a total of 210 times. St Cartmail relates that 77 percent of the boats arriving in two camps in Thailand during 1981 were attacked by pirates an average of 3.3 times each, with 590 females raped and 355 persons killed. In response, UNHCR and governments in Southeast Asia, along with countries of resettlement, have funded two programs designed to encourage rescues at sea by merchant ships. These programs are called Rescue at Sea Resettlement Offers (RASRO) and Disembarkation Resettlement Offers (DISERO). See *Refugees* 33 (September 1986), p. 5.

42. Though some refugees report that survivors have consumed the flesh of dead companions, there are no official estimates and little public discussion of the issue. One rare example is "Passing Ships Ignore Doomed Vessel," *Refugees* 21 (September 1985), p. 34. Estimates of the number of refugee vessels that have sunk in the South China Sea vary widely, as there is no way to accurately assess the total number of boats that fail to reach shore.

43. "Long-Stayers Battle to Fend off Despair," *Refugees* 32 (August 1986), pp. 9–10.

44. Refugee interview in *The Camp on Lantau Island*, documentary film (Oxford: Oxford Ethnographic Films, England, produced for UNHCR, 1984).

45. Brende and Parson, *Vietnam Veterans*, p. 47. Also see Arthur Egendorf, *Healing from the War: Trauma and Transformation after Vietnam* (Boston: Shambhala, 1986), pp. 54–61.

46. Terrence Des Pres, *The Survivor: An Anatomy of Life in the Death Camps* (New York: Washington Square Press, 1976), p. 103.

47. This description of the transformation of personality that occurred in most

soldiers in Vietnam, as well as in other wars, draws heavily upon Brende and Parson, *Vietnam Veterans*, pp. 47–49, and Egendorf, *Healing from the War*, pp. 65–67.

48. This analysis of psychological stresses among refugees draws from several sources. Matthew Suh, M.D., "Psychiatric Problems of Immigrants and Refugees," in *Southeast Asian Exodus: From Tradition to Resettlement*, edited by Elliot L. Tepper (Ottawa: Canadian Asian Studies Association, 1980), pp. 207–20; J. Donald Cohon, "Psychological Adaptation and Dysfunction among Refugees," *International Migration Review* 15 (1981), pp. 255–75; Elizabeth Hiok-Boon Lin, "An Exploration of Somatization among Southeast Asian Refugees and Immigrants in Primary Care," master's thesis, Seattle, University of Washington School of Public Health and Community Medicine, 1984; Keh-Ming Lin and Minoru Masuda, "Impact of the Refugee Experience: Mental Health Issues of Southeast Asian Refugees," in *Bridging Cultures—Southeast Asian Refugees in America: Social Work with Southeast Asian Refugees* (Los Angeles: Asian American Community Mental Health Training Center, 1983), pp. 35–52; *Refugee Mental Health in Resettlement Countries*, edited by Carolyn L. Williams and Joseph Westermeyer (Washington, D.C.: Hemisphere Publishing, 1986.)

49. See Robert Jay Lifton, "The Survivors of the Hiroshima Disaster and the Survivors of the Nazi Persecution," in *Massive Psychic Trauma*, edited by H. Krystal (New York: International Universities Press, 1968), pp. 168–89. Also Robert Jay Lifton, *Death in Life: Survivors of Hiroshima* (New York: Basic Books, 1967).

50. The Asian Sudden Death Information Center opened in March 1986 at the St. Paul Ramsey Medical Center in St. Paul, Minnesota. The center promotes communication and research about this unexplained syndrome. See *Southeast Asian Refugee Studies Newsletter* 6, nos. 3–4 (Minneapolis: University of Minnesota Southeast Asian Refugee Studies Project, Center for Urban and Regional Affairs, 1986).

51. See *Diagnostic and Statistical Manual of Mental Disorders*, 3rd ed. (Washington, D.C.: American Psychiatric Association, 1980).

52. See *Refugee Mental Health in Resettlement Countries*.

53. See Joseph Westermeyer, "Migration and Psychopathology"; Keh-Ming Lin, "Psychopathology and Social Disruption in Refugees"; and Jean E. Carlin, "Child and Adolescent Refugees: Psychiatric Assessment and Treatment," all in *Refugee Mental Health in Resettlement Countries*. Westermeyer estimates that some 20–25 percent of all refugees are at risk of suffering disabling mental illness. The incidence of paranoia and schizophrenia among immigrants generally is as much as double that of the overall U.S. population. See J. Donald Cohon et al., *Primary Preventive Mental Health in the ESL Classroom: A Handbook for Teachers* (New York: American Council for Nationalities Service, 1986), p. iv.

54. See Brende and Parson, *Vietnam Veterans*, p. 126.

55. See R. Taylor and D. Nathan, "Resettlement Casework: The Role of the Professional," paper presented at the Annual Meeting of the Conference of Jewish Community Service, Denver, Colo., 1980.

56. In Joan Morrison and Charlotte Fox Zabusky, *American Mosaic: The Immigrant Experience in the Words of Those Who Lived It* (New York: Dutton, 1980), p. 433.

57. This description of the breakdown of traditional family life draws upon Julia Menard-Warwick, "Addressing the Resettlement Needs of S.E. Asians: Three Seattle Programs," unpublished paper, Seattle: University of Washington, Department of English, 1987.

58. American high school students often claim that Southeast Asians who speak their own languages are "talking about us" or "talking behind our backs," and thus they may pressure Indochinese to speak only English. See interviews with high school students in "Children of Change," a documentary film (Seattle: University of Washington, Instructional Media Services, 1983).

59. Brende and Parson, in *Vietnam Veterans*, discuss this phenomenon among children of veterans, pp. 148–51.

60. Lin, *An Exploration of Somatization*. Also see "Caring for Refugees," *View* (Seattle: Group Health Cooperative Magazine), September 1985, pp. 8–11. Other studies suggest that moderate to disabling depression is the most common emotional problem of refugees. See Cohon et al., *Primary Preventive Mental Health*, p. iv.

61. Two of the best discussions of the meaning of community are Robert N. Bellah, *Habits of the Heart: Individualism and Commitment in American Life* (New York: Harper and Row, 1985), and M. Scott Peck, *The Different Drum: Community Making and Peace* (New York: Simon and Schuster, 1987).

62. Ngo Thi Bich Le, "Homesickness," *Refugees* 17 (May 1985), p. 8.

CHAPTER 3: BECOMING AMERICAN

1. Robert A. Carlson, *The Quest for Conformity: Americanization through Education* (New York: Wiley, 1975), p. 4.

2. Linda Schneider, "Back Again," *Passage: A Journal of Refugee Education* (Washington: Department of State), special Galang issue, undated, pp. 41–42.

3. Gil Loescher and John A. Scanlan, *Calculated Kindness: Refugees and America's Half-Open Door, 1945–Present* (New York: Free Press, 1986), p. xiii.

4. For an account of this period of migration, see Willi Paul Adams, "A Dubious Host," *Wilson Quarterly* (New Year's issue, 1983), pp. 101–113.

5. Statistics on yearly immigration between 1820 and 1910 are taken from the summary of official statistical sources prepared by the U.S. Immigration Commission and published in *Report of the Immigration Commission, vol. 3, Statistical Review of Immigration, 1820–1910* (Washington, D.C.: Government Printing Office, 1911). See especially pp. 9–13.

6. *Report of the Immigration Commission*, Vol. 3, p. 10.

7. Adams, "Dubious Host," p. 107.

8. Ibid., p. 103.

9. Ibid., pp. 104–5.

10. Richard Ruiz, "Foreign Language Study and Bilingual Education in the United States," paper presented at the annual meeting of the American Educational Research Association, Washington, D.C., April 20, 1987.

11. For instance, see the *Annual Report of the Board of Directors of the St. Louis Public Schools for the Year Ending August 1, 1875*, cited in ibid., p. 3.

12. James Bryce, *The American Commonwealth*, vol. 2 (New York: Macmillan, 1888), p. 710.

13. For a discussion of the role of labor and industry in the Americanization movement, see Kay Landolt, "The Americanization Movement and its Programs to Educate the Immigrant," unpublished paper, Seattle: University of Washington, Department of English, 1987.

14. See J. F. McClymer, "The Americanization Movement and the Education of

the Foreign-born Adult," *American Education and the European Immigrant: 1840–1940*, edited by B. J. Weiss (Urbana: University of Illinois Press, 1982), pp. 110–11.

15. Edward George Hartmann, *The Movement to Americanize the Immigrant* (New York: Columbia University Press, 1948), p. 197.

16. See Paul McBride, *Culture Clash: Immigrants and Reformers 1880–1920* (San Francisco: R and E Associates, 1975).

17. Carlson, *Quest for Conformity*, p. 122.

18. Ibid., pp. 121–31.

19. These factors are discussed in Ruiz, "Foreign Language Study and Bilingual Education," pp. 9–10.

20. See Charles A. Ferguson and Shirley Brice Heath, *Language in the USA* (New York: Cambridge University Press, 1981), p. xxxiv. Also see Heinz Kloss, *The American Bilingual Tradition* (Rowley, Mass.: Newbury House, 1977), p. 90, and Ruiz, "Foreign Language Study and Bilingual Education," pp. 10–11.

21. See Ruiz, "Foreign Language Study and Bilingual Education," pp. 27–28.

22. *Report of the Immigration Commission*, 42 vols. For a summary, see vols. 1–2, *Abstracts of Reports*.

23. Ibid., vol. 1, p. 44.

24. The full list of members of the Dillingham Commission was as follows: Senators William Dillingham, Henry Cabot Lodge, Asbury Latimer, Anselm McLaurin, and Le Roy Percy; representatives Benjamin Howell, William Bennett, and John Burnett; and Charles Neill, Jeremiah Jenks, and William Wheeler. (McLaurin was appointed to succeed Latimer, who died in 1908. Percy was appointed to succeed McLaurin, who died in 1910). The commission was established by an act of Congress on February 20, 1907, and completed its work on December 5, 1910.

25. Adams, "A Dubious Host," p. 110.

26. *Report of the Immigration Commission*, vol. 1, p. 42.

27. Ibid., p. 43.

28. In a series of interviews with ESL students in Seattle-area schools, Connie So found widespread concern that enrollment in ESL courses would limit rather than facilitate future educational opportunities. Connie So, "The Effectiveness of English as a Second Language: the ESL Students' Story," unpublished paper, Seattle, University of Washington, Department of English, 1987.

29. See McBride, *Culture Clash*, pp. 42–43.

30. See Peter Roberts's teaching manual, *English for Coming Americans, Teacher's Aids* (New York: Association Press, 1912).

31. Quoted in McBride, *Culture Clash*, p. 86. Also see Peter Roberts, "The Roberts Method of Teaching English to Foreigners," Illinois Miners and Mechanics Institute Bulletin No. 3 (Urbana: University of Illinois Press, 1914), pp. 37–40; and Peter Roberts, "The YMCA among the Immigrants," *Survey* 29 (February 15, 1913), pp. 697–700.

32. Quoted in McBride, *Culture Clash*, p. 121.

33. Roberts, "The Roberts Method of Teaching English to Foreigners."

34. U.S. Steel Corp., "Lessons for Teaching Foreigners English by the Roberts Method in Use by the YMCA Teachers in our Mill Districts," *Bulletin No. 4* (November 1913), p. 6.

35. A good example of the enthusiasm among industrial owners and managers

for Roberts's lessons is G. W. Tupper, "The Efficiency of Mill Operatives," pamphlet of the U.S. Steel Corp., cited in McBride, *Culture Clash*, p. 89. Similarly, T. J. Jackson Lears, *No Place of Grace: Antimodernism and the Transformation of American Culture 1880–1920* (New York: Pantheon, 1981), p. 81, argues that schooling "sought to train the lower classes for a subordinate role." Lears cites Clarence Osgood, "Raising the Standard of Efficiency in Work: Practical Training Given by the Manhattan School for Girls," *Craftsman* 12 (September 1907), pp. 634–40, who claimed that schools must train individuals for their proper role in society, because "too many parents educate their children out of their proper sphere of usefulness."

36. Bureau of Naturalization, *Federal Citizenship Textbook*, Part 1, "English for American Citizenship" (Washington, D.C.: Government Printing Office, 1922), Lesson 14A.

37. Ibid., Lesson 19A.

38. *Course of Study: Americanization* (Denver: Public Schools, 1926), pp. 50–51.

39. Ibid., p. 51.

40. *Report of the Immigration Commission*, vol. 1, p. 42.

41. The Dillingham Commission had noted in its general conclusions that "among the non-English-speaking races a much greater proportion are retarded of children in homes where English is not spoken than of children in homes where English has been adopted as the language commonly used by the family." Ibid., p. 43.

42. The Denver Public Schools Americanization materials included the claim that a majority of industrial accidents in New York State were due to workers' ignorance of English. See *Course of Study: Americanization*, p. 5.

43. Lears, *No Place of Grace*, p. 78. Also see pp. 74–83.

44. Ellen Gates Starr, "Art and Labor," in *Hull House Maps and Papers* (New York: Crowell, 1895).

45. Jane Addams, *Twenty Years at Hull House* (New York: Macmillan, 1932).

46. Jane Addams, *The Spirit of Youth and the City Streets* (New York: Macmillan, 1909), p. 122. Also cited by Lears, *No Place of Grace*, pp. 79–80.

47. *Course of Study: Americanization*, pp. 51–52.

48. Addams, *Spirit of Youth*, p. 135.

49. This discussion of the transformation in the cultural perception of time relies upon Lears, *No Place of Grace*, pp. 10–20; E. P. Thompson, "Time, Work-Discipline and Industrial Capitalism," *Past and Present* 38 (1967); and Anthony Giddens, *Social Theory and Modern Sociology* (Stanford, CA: Stanford University Press, 1987), pp. 140–65.

50. Lears, *No Place of Grace*, p. 13.

51. See T. Walch, *Catholic Education in Chicago and Milwaukee, 1840–1890*, Ph.D. diss., Evanston, Ill.: Northwestern University, 1975. Also see Ruiz, "Foreign Language Study and Bilingual Education," p. 6.

52. Mary McGroarty, "Images of the Learner in English Language Texts for Adults: From Citizen to Consumer," *Issues in Education* 3 (summer 1985), pp. 13–30.

53. Daniel Freeman, *Speaking of Survival* (New York: Oxford University Press, 1982), p. 101.

54. Robert E. Walsh, *Basic Adult Survival English with Orientation to American Life*, (Englewood Cliffs, N.J.: Prentice-Hall, 1984), Part 2, p. 66.

55. These and other examples of the extremes of the Americanization movement, which characterized its final days in the period immediately after World War I, are discussed in Carlson, *Quest for Conformity*, pp. 121–31.

56. Quoted in Carlson, *Quest for Conformity*, p. 127.

57. For instance, see Kathleen M. Corey, "ESL Curriculum Development in the Overseas Refugee Training Program: A Personal Account," *Passage* 2 (spring 1986), pp. 5–11.

58. For instance, in a speech given at the 25th anniversary of the Peace Corps in Washington, D.C., in September 1986, Kathleen M. Corey, an official at the Refugee Service Center in Manila, equated "adjustment" to U.S. society with "cultural assimilation." The speech was published in the State Department journal about the overseas education program. See Kathleen M. Corey, "The Cultural Assimilation of Indochinese Refugees," *Passage* 2 (winter 1986), pp. 41–43.

CHAPTER 4: COUNTERFEIT UNIVERSE

1. Robert Jay Lifton, *Home from the War: Vietnam Veterans, Neither Victims nor Executioners* (New York: Basic Books, 1973), pp. 187–88.

2. The teacher's words are taken from a description of the sewing assembly-line simulation in Privan Maew Limpanboon, "On-the-Job Training: An Approach for Advanced Students in Work Orientation," *Passage: A Journal of Refugee Education* 3 (Washington, D.C.: Department of State, spring 1987), pp. 6–10, and from the author's observations.

3. Limpanboon, "On-the-Job-Training," p. 9.

4. Ibid., p. 9.

5. J. T. Parker and P. B. Taylor, *The Delphi Survey: CBAE through the Eyes of Leading Educators* (Belmont, Calif.: Fearon Pitman, 1980), pp. 12–13.

6. Alene Grognet and Jodie Crandall, "Competency-based Curricula in Adult ESL," *ERIC/CLL News Bulletin* 6 (1982), pp. 3–4.

7. See Elsa Roberts Auerbach, "Competency-based ESL: One Step Forward or Two Steps Back?" *TESOL Quarterly* 20 (September 1986), pp. 411–29.

8. Terrell H. Bell, U.S. Commissioner for Education, press release, October 29, 1975.

9. Virginia H. Knauer, "The President's Commitment to Consumer Education," speech presented to the Consumer Education Catch-Up Conference, Washington, D.C., November 21, 1975, cited in William S. Griffith and Ronald M. Cervero, "The Adult Performance Level Program: A Serious and Deliberate Examination," *Adult Education* 27 (1977), p. 219.

10. *From the Classroom to the Workplace: Teaching ESL to Adults* (Washington, D.C.: Center for Applied Linguistics, 1983), p. 1.

11. Charles A. Findley and Lynn A. Nathan, "Functional Language Objectives in a Competency Based ESL Curriculum" *TESOL Quarterly* 14 (1980), p. 222.

12. Kathleen M. Corey, "ESL Curriculum Development in the Overseas Refugee Training Program: A Personal Account," *Passage* 2 (spring 1986), p. 6.

13. Herbert Spencer, *Education: Intellectual, Moral, Physical* (London: Williams and Norgate, 1861).

14. Franklin Bobbitt, *How to Make a Curriculum* (Boston: Houghton-Mifflin, 1926).

15. Griffith and Cervero, "Adult Performance Level Project," pp. 211–12.

16. For a survey of the criticisms of competency-based ESL, see Auerbach, "Competency-Based ESL," pp. 411–29.

17. See Henry A. Giroux, "Theories of Reproduction and Resistance in the New Sociology of Education: A Critical Analysis," *Harvard Educational Review* 53 (August 1983), pp. 257–93.

18. Paul Willis, "Cultural Production and Theories of Reproduction," in *Race, Class and Education*, edited by Len Barton and Stephen Walker (London: Croom-Helm, 1983), p. 110.

19. Grognet and Crandall, "Competency-based Curricula in Adult ESL," p. 3.

20. *English as a Second Language Resource Manual*, vol. 3 (Manila: Center for Applied Linguistics and Refugee Service Center of the Bureau for Refugee Programs, U.S. Department of State, 1983), p. 5.

21. Ibid., pp. 5–6.

22. John Latkiewicz and Colette Anderson, "Industries' Reactions to the Indochinese Refugees as Employees," *Migration Today* 11, nos. 2–3 (1983), pp. 14–20.

23. *ABE-in-Industry Handbook*, prepared for the Travis County Adult Basic Education Co-op Special Project by the Austin, Texas, Community College (June 1984).

24. Aliza Becker, Lisa Karimer, and Linda Mrowicki, "An Employer Needs Assessment," *Passage* 2 (summer 1986), p. 56.

25. Margaret Ammons, *Objectives and Outcomes: Encyclopedia of Educational Research* (London: Macmillan, 1969), p. 911.

26. J. MacDonald and D. Clark, "Critical Value Questions and the Analysis of Objectives and Curricula," *Second Handbook of Research in Teaching*, edited by R. M. W Travers (Chicago: Rand McNally, 1973), p. 408.

27. Loring Waggoner, interviewed in "Hope for the Future: An Orientation to PET," videotape, Bataan, Philippines, ICMC, 1984.

28. *Pre-Employment Training Resource Manual*, vol. 1 (Manila: Center for Applied Linguistics, CAL, and the Refugee Service Center of the Bureau for Refugee Programs, Department of State, 1984), p. 8.

29. "PRPC: A Profile," prepared for the brochure "Manila Jaycees for Indochinese Refugees: Operation Brotherhood," Manila, Jaycees, 1985.

30. J. Patrick Redding, "Cultural Orientation at Bataan," *Passage* 1 (summer 1985), pp. 22–26.

31. In the Philippine center, staff disputes, resulting in resignations, have broken out over curriculum development.

32. *English as a Second Language Resource Manual*, p. 33.

33. Christopher Blass, "Understanding Attitudes toward Public Assistance in the U.S.," *Passage* 2 (spring 1986), pp. 20–23.

34. Ibid., p. 21.

35. Ibid., p. 21.

36. This lesson is described in ibid., p. 22.

37. Ibid., p. 20.

38. This lesson is described by Carrie Wilson, cultural orientation program officer in the Philippines, and Barbara Garner, a curriculum developer at the Phanat Nikhom center, in "The Free Money Game," *Passage* 2 (spring 1986), pp. 58–64.

39. Ibid.

40. *Pre-Employment Training Resource Manual*, pp. 265–66.

41. *Cultural Orientation Curriculum* (Bataan: ICMC, 1985), Day 22.

42. Ibid., Unit 11, p. 1.

43. *Pre-Employment Training Resource Manual*, p. 266.

44. For instance, *English as a Second Language Resource Manual*, pp. 31–32.

45. *Pre-Employment Training Resource Manual*, pp. 358–59.

46. A major survey found that refugees' employment benefits vary considerably from one city to another. Fewer than half of employed refugees in Boston and Seattle report any benefits, while as many as three-fourths report benefits in Chicago; Houston; and Orange County, California. Refugees employed part time report few benefits, and those in jobs "peripheral" to the economy report fewer benefits than those in "core" industries. See *Southeast Asian Refugee Self-Sufficiency Study: Final Report* (Ann Arbor: Institute for Social Research, University of Michigan, report prepared for the Office of Refugee Resettlement, 1985), pp. 134–39.

47. *Cultural Orientation Resource Manual*, vol. 2 (Manila: Center for Applied Linguistics and Refugee Service Center of the Bureau for Refugee Programs, Department of State, 1982), pp. 373–74.

48. *Cultural Orientation Curriculum*, Day 29.

49. Ibid., Day 29.

50. *Pre-Employment Training Resource Manual*, p. 425.

51. *Cultural Orientation Curriculum*, Day 22.

52. Ibid., Day 66.

53. *Integrated Curriculum, Level One* (Bataan, Philippines: ICMC, 1983), p. 46.

54. Stanley Knee, *A Research Project to Determine the Law Enforcement Needs of the Southeast Asian Refugees in the Year 1995: To Develop Strategies to Meet those Needs* (Garden Grove, Calif.: Garden Grove Police Department Command College, undated), pp. 35–36.

55. For instance, a front-page story in the *Seattle Times* described the "nightmare" of violent attacks against Southeast Asians living in the Seattle area. "Not Always a Land of Opportunity," *Seattle Times*, August 9, 1987.

56. *Cultural Orientation Curriculum*, Day 11.

57. Ibid., Day 11.

58. Richard Lambrecht, "Developing a Survey Course in Indochinese Culture for PASS Students," *Passage* 3 (spring 1987), p. 23.

59. In one report, 57 percent of the refugees surveyed claim that they have been victims of racial prejudice. See Knee, *Research Project*, p. 35.

60. *Cultural Orientation Curriculum*, Day 11.

61. *Pre-Employment Training Resource Manual*, pp. 473–75.

62. Ibid., p. 270.

63. *English as a Second Language Resource Manual*, pp. 31–32.

64. Ibid., pp. 31–34.

65. Ibid., p. 29.

66. Ibid., pp. 34, 46–47.

67. This lesson is contained in the *Cultural Orientation Content Standards*, prepared for the Manila Conference on Cultural Orientation (Manila: ICMC cultural orientation staff, July 1983).

68. For an analysis of the role of preemployment training in the loss of cultural

identity, see Monica Avis Hughes, "The Role of Values and Attitudes in the Pre-Employment Training Curriculum Used in the U.S. Refugee Processing Centers in Southeast Asia," unpublished paper, Seattle: University of Washington, Department of English, 1987.

69. *Cultural Orientation Curriculum*, Day 13.

70. Ibid., Day 13, includes the objective "to have students understand that every American or resident of the U.S. (except perhaps the Native Americans) has his ethnic and racial roots outside the U.S. and that many ethnic and racial groups in the U.S. overcame adversity to set down roots in America."

71. Ibid., Day 13.

72. Ibid., Day 49.

73. Ibid., Day 56.

74. The suggestion that refugees form bonds outside their own communities is repeated in the ESL, cultural orientation, and preemployment curricula. For instance, the refugees are told that "relationships with co-workers will improve if refugees make an effort to make [American] friends." *Pre-Employment Training Resource Manual*, p. 445.

75. *Cultural Orientation Curriculum*, Day 45.

76. Ibid., Day 48.

77. Ibid., Day 49.

78. See Deborah McGlauflin, "Mainstreaming Refugee Women's Economic Development," in *Immigrants and Refugees in a Changing Nation: Research and Training*, edited by Lucy M. Cohen and Mary Ann Grossnickle (Washington: Catholic University of America, 1983), pp. 111–15. Also see Christine Robinson Finnan, "Occupational Assimilation of Refugees," *International Migration Review* 15 (1981), pp. 292–309.

79. Linda Schneider, "Back Again," *Passage* (special Galang issue, undated), pp. 41–42.

80. *Pre-Employment Training Resource Manual*, p. 8.

81. *Cultural Orientation Curriculum*, Days 11–12.

82. Ibid., Day 38.

83. Ibid., Day 47.

84. Ibid., Day 56.

85. Ibid., Day 9.

86. For instance, *Cultural Orientation Curriculum* includes the objective, "help students see how one's sense of cultural heritage can both help and hinder adjustment to life in the U.S." (Day 14). In general, lessons purported to be about the refugees' cultural traditions contain little about those traditions. Perhaps the best example is the Survey Course in Indochinese Culture for secondary students in the PASS program. The problems begin with the title of the course; there is no unified "Indochinese culture." Vietnamese, Khmer, lowland Lao, highland Hmong, and others differ widely from each other. Designed by American staff members without assistance from the Southeast Asians themselves, the course contains little about the rich historical traditions of Southeast Asia and a great deal about recent political conflict. For instance, one of the first activities "dramatize[s] the struggle between two political forces as evidenced in contemporary history." Discussion questions in this lesson focus entirely on how political leaders should be chosen, with the primary emphasis on "democratic" processes that have little relationship with the

traditional systems of leadership in Indochina. The purpose of these activities seems to be to teach the students to oppose the Communist governments in Vietnam, Laos, and Cambodia. For a description, see Lambrecht, "Developing a Survey Course," pp. 23–26.

87. For instance, the preemployment curriculum includes the objective that students will be able to state "why it will probably be necessary to take an entry level job" in the United States. *Pre-employment Training Resource Manual*, p. 265.

88. The Galang PET Program regularly conducted surveys of its students' work experience, education, language training, and job skills. The surveys were conducted for each entering group of refugees, called a cycle. In Cycles 34 and 35 in 1985, for instance, only 2.5 percent of 121 refugees had been farmers before 1975. The greatest number (26.4 percent) had been students. Although many people who had been soldiers or students had returned to their villages and become farmers after 1975, the surveys indicate that, in most cycles, fewer than 20 percent of the refugees had been farmers at any time. These surveys have not been published, but were presented in "Galang Student Surveys" at the regional PET meeting in Singapore in 1985. One survey is mentioned in Chuck Schumacher, "Work Orientation," *Passage* (special Galang issue, undated), p. 30.

89. See *Making It on Their Own: From Refugee Sponsorship to Self-Sufficiency* (New York: Church World Service, 1983), p. 88.

90. The assumption that employment is an effective means of improving language skills is widespread among officials in the refugee program. See John Williamson, *Refugee Resettlement: A Survey of Training Priorities* (Bangkok: Committee for Coordination of Services to Displaced Persons in Thailand and UNHCR branch office in Thailand, 1982), p. 10.

91. *Cultural Orientation Curriculum*, Day 54.

92. *Pre-Employment Training Resource Manual*, p. 275.

93. Ibid., p. 331.

94. No studies suggest that a job is a good way to learn English. One major study found that working and studying English seem to be mutually exclusive for most people. See Judith Arter, William Hadley, and Stephen Reder, *A Study of English Language Training for Refugees in the United States—Phase Three: The Influence of Language Training and Employment on Adult Refugees' Acquisition of English* (Portland, Oreg.: Northwest Regional Educational Laboratory, report prepared for ORR, June 1984), p. 11. Also see Finnan, "Occupational Assimilation of Refugees," pp. 292–309; David Cox, "Refugee Settlement in Australia: Review of an Era," *International Migration* 21 (1983), pp. 332–44; and Paul J. Strand, "Employment Predictors among Indochinese Refugees," *International Migration Review* 18 (1984), pp. 50–64.

95. See Robert L. Bach, *Labor Force Participation and Employment of Southeast Asian Refugees in the United States*, prepared for ORR under a grant to the Institute for Research on Poverty, University of Wisconsin, August 1984, p. 10.

96. *Pre-Employment Training Resource Manual*, p. 273.

97. *Cultural Orientation Curriculum*, Day 11, p. 1.

98. Ibid., Day 21.

99. In cultural orientation classes, teachers claim that refugee admissions depend upon the behavior and the employability of the resettled refugees. This message is repeated after arrival in the United States. For instance, a letter given to new arrivals in Connecticut states, "The United States has agreed to bring in more refugees

because the first group that came in 1975 did very well. . . . Most of you have left family members behind. . . . We will bring them if you show us that you are a responsible person willing to work, willing to learn, and willing to help themselves [sic]." Letter by Myra M. Oliver, Executive Director, International Institute of Connecticut, Bridgeport, March 5, 1979. Similarly, articles in the State Department publication *Passage* argue that welfare rates affect admission levels. See Blass, "Understanding Attitudes toward Public Assistance in the U.S.," p. 20.

100. Flordeliza T. Torrejos, "Starting Over," in *Life in the New Land* (Bataan, Philippines: ICMC, 1982).

101. *Pre-Employment Training Resource Manual*, p. 14.

102. Ibid., pp. 29, 39, 342.

103. Ibid., p. 12.

104. *English as a Second Language Resource Manual*, p. 29.

105. *Cultural Orientation Curriculum*, Day 66.

106. For example, one lesson depicts an American coworker who "always tries to be friendly with new people on the job" and invites a Vietnamese to eat lunch with him. *Pre-Employment Training Resource Manual*, p. 334.

107. Robert E. Walsh, *Basic Adult Survival English,* Part 2 (Englewood Cliffs, N.J.: Prentice-Hall, 1984), p. 66.

108. Torrejos, *Life in the New Land.*

109. This summary of PETCO is taken from materials prepared by Galang program staff for the regional PET meeting in Singapore, 1985.

110. Amy Johnston, "PETCO—An American Workplace Simulation," briefing paper prepared for the regional PET meeting in Singapore, 1985, p. 9.

111. Ibid.

112. Ibid., p. 7.

113. Ibid., p. 5.

114. See the history of PETCO in Schumacher, "Work Orientation," pp. 29–34.

115. In their survey of contemporary America, Robert N. Bellah and his colleagues describe the weakening of American success ideology in *Habits of the Heart: Individualism and Commitment in American Life* (New York: Harper and Row, 1985), pp. 275–96.

CHAPTER 5: KEEPERS OF THE CAMPS

1. Loren Baritz, *Backfire: American Culture and the Vietnam War* (New York: Ballantine Books, 1985).

2. "ICMC Program Management Plan for FY 1986," draft (Manila: ICMC, 1985), p. 1.

3. ICMC also operates the U.S. educational program for refugees in the Sudan.

4. This list is included in the *ICMC Management Plan, for April–October, 1983* (Manila: ICMC, February 2, 1983), Appendix A.

5. The most important intergovernmental agency with which ICMC must interact is the office of the United Nations High Commissioner for Refugees (UNHCR), established by the United Nations in 1951. Funded by donations from individual governments, UNHCR has three main purposes: offering protection to refugees, assisting them in camps, and seeking permanent solutions to refugee prob-

lems. To attain these ends, UNHCR has become the major recipient and disburser of governmental funds for refugees. Its budget grew rapidly during the crisis in Southeast Asia in the late 1970s, from less than $100 million in 1976 to approximately $500 million in 1980. More recently, its budget has come under severe constraints, with a 20 percent reduction in general programs from 1984 to 1985. See "UNHCR's Executive Committee—the 36th Session," *Refugees* 24 (Geneva: UNHCR, December 1985), pp. 17–18.

6. Although it lacks legally binding sanctions, UNHCR has worked to discourage forcible repatriation of Laotian and Cambodian refugees from Thailand and to ensure that boat refugees from Vietnam are offered the material asssistance they require by ships in the region and by first-asylum countries. In addition, it offers protection in UNHCR camps, including food, shelter, health and education, counseling, legal aid, transport, rural resettlement and assistance, and infrastructure (construction, roads, machinery, and supplies). UNHCR promotes three "durable solutions" to refugee situations: voluntary repatriation, local integration in asylum countries, and resettlement. The first is officially considered the most desirable, though the other solutions are supported, as in Southeast Asia, when voluntary repatriation is not feasible. Because asylum countries (Thailand, Malaysia, the Philippines, Hong Kong, and Singapore) have refused to permit refugees to permanently settle, resettlement in other countries is the only durable solution available for most Indochinese refugees. See Shelly Pitterman, "International Responses to Refugee Situations," in *Refugees and World Politics*, edited by Elizabeth G. Ferris (New York: Praeger, 1985), pp. 43–81.

7. The other major intergovernmental agency in the processing centers is the Intergovernmental Commission on Migration (ICM), which handles transportation for all refugees. A complex, highly efficient organization, ICM transports several hundred thousand refugees each year throughout the world, on ICM charters and commercial flights.

8. "The Refugees and ICMC," videotape, Bataan, Philippines, ICMC, 1985.

9. Daniel Parker, administrator, AID, in hearings on appropriations, House Appropriations Committee, Subcommittee on Foreign Operations and Related Agencies, 1976, part 2, 94th cong., 1st sess. (Washington, D.C.: Government Printing Office, 1975), pp. 131–32.

10. Robert F. Gorman, "Private Voluntary Organizations in Refugee Relief," in *Refugees and World Politics*, pp. 82–104.

11. The JVA officer is responsible for coordinating the paperwork for refugee movements and resettlement. As the largest voluntary agency, ICMC dominates JVA.

12. For an analysis of the limitations on the actions of PVOs, see Gorman, "Private Voluntary Organizations," pp. 97–102.

13. Federal officials emphasize that PVOs are useful for this reason. For instance, see the statement of Alex Shakow, Acting Assistant Administrator, Bureau for Programs and Policy Coordination, in hearings on appropriations, House Appropriations Committee, Subcommittee on Foreign Operations and Related Agencies, 1978, part 2, 95th cong., 1st sess. (Washington, D.C.: Government Printing Office, 1977), p. 631.

14. For a discussion of the impact of these changes on American PVOs in the Philippines, see Peter B. Payoyo, *The Role of Private and Voluntary Organizations in*

U.S. Foreign Policy, Research Report no. 2 (Quezon City, Philippines: International Studies Institute of the Philippines, University of the Philippines, 1985).

15. See Frances Moore Lappe, Joseph Collins, and David Kinley, *Aid as Obstacle* (San Francisco: Institute for Food and Development Policy, 1980), pp. 170–71.

16. The decision to locate the largest U.S. processing center in the Philippines was made possible by the close relationship between Ferdinand Marcos and the U.S. government. The center provided a major source of income for the local community, as well as for officers of the Philippine Constabulary, the branch of the military given control of the center. The agreement between the United States and the Philippines also ensured that the government of the Philippines would gain a fully developed, military-style camp upon closure of the refugee center. Under Marcos, the Philippines was one of the largest recipients of U.S. aid. During the first five years after Marcos declared martial law in 1972, AID loans and grants multiplied fivefold, while the nation's per-capita caloric intake dropped to the lowest in Asia except for war-torn Cambodia. See Lappe, Collins, and Kinley, *Aid as Obstacle*, pp. 21–22.

17. See the congressional debate about PVOs that depend solely upon the federal government for funding, in hearings on H.R. 14260, Senate Appropriations Committee, Foreign Assistance and Related Programs Appropriations, fiscal 1977, 94th cong., 2nd sess. (Washington, D.C.: Government Printing Office, 1976), p. 830.

18. Statement of Edward Coy, Acting Assistant Administrator for Latin America and the Caribbean, AID, before the Subcommittee on Inter-American Affairs of the House Foreign Affairs Committee, on Foreign Assistance Legislation for fiscal 1981: Economic Assistance in the Western Hemisphere, part 6, 96th cong., 2nd sess. (Washington, D.C.: Government Printing Office, 1980), p. 69.

19. For an analysis of the political difficulties experienced by PVOs in Thailand, see William Shawcross, *The Quality of Mercy: Cambodia, Holocaust, and Modern Conscience* (New York: Simon and Schuster, 1984).

20. These issues are discussed in Robert L. Bach and Jennifer B. Bach, "Employment Patterns of Southeast Asian Refugees," *Monthly Labor Review* 103 (1980), pp. 31–38; Austin T. Fragomen, "The Final Report and Recommendations of the Select Commission on Immigration and Refugee Policy: A Summary," *International Migration Review* 15 (1981), pp. 758–68; John Latkiewicz and Colette Anderson, "Industries' Reactions to the Indochinese Refugees as Employees," *Migration Today* 11, nos. 2–3 (1983), pp. 14–20; and James W. Tollefson, "Covert Policy in the U.S. Refugee Program in Southeast Asia," *Language Problems and Language Planning* 12 (spring 1988), pp. 30–43.

21. State programs are required to "strictly apply . . . sanctions in cases where recipients refuse to register and/or accept appropriate employment, including entry-level and minimum wage jobs." See "Statement of Program Goals, Priorities and Standards for State Administered Refugee Resettlement Programs, Fiscal Year 1984," Kansas City, Mo., ORR, 1984, p. A–4.

22. See James N. Purcell, Jr., "Refugee Assistance: Overseas and Domestic," address before the Subcommittee on Immigration, Refugees, and International Law of the House Judiciary Committee, April 17, 1983, *Current Policy* 693 (Washington, D.C.: Department of State, 1985). A proposal to make voluntary agencies legally responsible for financially assisting refugees was designed to make refugees ineligible for general public assistance. The proposal, contained in Section 4 of H.R. 1452,

known as the Lungren Amendment, met with fierce resistance from voluntary agencies. See *Federal Register* 52, no. 102 (October 19, 1987), and *Refugee Reports* (Washington, D.C. American Council for Nationalities Service, November 13, 1987), pp. 7–8.

23. Administrators justify the difference on the grounds that many Filipinos stay with family members or in Filipino-style pensions, charging much less per night than the international hotels frequented by Americans.

24. "ICMC Management Plan, April–October, 1983," p. 25.

25. The tension between U.S. and Filipino staff members is also based on other issues. Americans fill most high-level positions, but often stay for only one year, while Filipinos view their jobs as permanent. Many Americans view themselves as experts hired to teach the Philippine staff. Arriving from the United States with little knowledge of the Philippines or its language, they often have much less experience than their Philippine counterparts, who naturally resent the Americans' attitude of superiority.

26. The refugees are required to sign promissory notes for their plane tickets.

27. Corruption is one result of this system. For instance, concrete-block dormitories were constructed in 1984 for about $24,000. At a management meeting in 1985, an ICMC official estimated that half of this amount went to administrators and other individuals involved in construction. Among some suppliers in Manila, the camp is reportedly seen as a place that pays inflated prices without question.

28. For a discussion of the psychological dimensions of pseudocommunity, see M. Scott Peck, *The Different Drum: Community Making and Peace* (New York: Simon and Schuster, 1987), pp. 86–90.

29. In 1983, a cross-cultural workshop was offered to break down the divisions that plagued the ICMC staff. Most of the American staff members who were present at the workshop felt that it helped them understand how common American behavior might be offensive to Filipinos, and how they might develop better working relationships. Yet the benefits of the workshop were short lived. Fewer than two dozen employees completed the workshop, and later, when staff members suggested that the consultants offer it to a broader audience, the ICMC deputy director opposed the proposal. A possible explanation for ICMC's refusal to permit additional cross-cultural workshops is that the divisions between Americans and Filipinos serve the interests of ICMC management by precluding a unified employee organization.

30. The project director and deputy directors (Job Levels 1–3) are assigned private, air-conditioned cars with drivers. These cars are available for their use at any time, including weekends. Program officers (Level 4) are transported in an air-conditioned van that makes the trip three times each week. Trainers and curriculum staff (Level 5) and supervisors (Level 6) may use the van if space is available, with seating priority assigned by job level. Teachers use the ICMC buses, which are non-air-conditioned and overcrowded and make the trip only once each week, on Sundays.

31. On special occasions such as United Nations Day or visits by officials from the Geneva office of ICMC, staff dinners are prepared with separate menus for different job levels. The availability and quality of treatment in the camp clinic also varies according to job level, with program officers assured immediate attention, while refugees experience the longest delays. Until the Philippine nuclear power plant closed in 1986, program officers made evening trips to the plant to shop in

the commissary, swim in the company pool, and bowl in the small bowling alley. The program officers' dorm has a valley view and rattan furniture, while Level Five dorms are surrounded by other buildings and have simple wooden furnishings. The book by the curriculum officer that was used in camp is Robert E. Walsh, *Basic Adult Survival English with Orientation to American Life* (Englewood Cliffs, N.J.: Prentice-Hall, 1984). For a critical review of this book, see Elsa Roberts Auerbach and Denise Burgess, "The Hidden Curriculum of Survival ESL," *TESOL Quarterly* 19 (1985), pp. 475–95. The previous curriculum officer also adopted his own text, one that has been widely praised, Steven J. Molinsky and Bill Bliss, *Side by Side: English Grammar through Guided Conversation* (Englewood Cliffs, N.J.: Prentice Hall, 1983).

32. Kathy Opel, a Level 5 trainer, spent much of the latter half of 1983 developing and implementing the supervision system, and was promoted in 1984 to deputy director for instruction, in effect the head of the educational program.

33. In his analysis of the Vietnam War, Loren Baritz pointed out that the greatest tactical error of lower- or middle-level bureaucrats was to make accurate predictions that were viewed by superiors as not helpful to pursuit of policy. See Baritz, *Backfire*, pp. 331–32.

34. A third survey assessed the role of the supervisors. Because upper managers wished to reduce the authority of supervisors, a study was conducted to show that their job descriptions were not reasonable. The study concluded that it was not feasible for one individual working full time to supervise between six and eight teachers, because the skills to do so required a "Renaissance man." This survey is summarized in a report by the ICMC evaluation officer, Ben McDonald, *A Study of the Role of Supervisors in the ICMC ESL/CO Program* (Bataan, Philippines: ICMC, 1985).

35. The survey appeared in the ICMC document by Kathy Opel, *Survey Report on Supervision and Teacher Evaluation* (Bataan, Philippines: ICMC, 1984).

36. The results of this survey appear in Gaylord Barr, *Student Survey* (Bataan, Philippines: ICMC, 1985).

37. The required practices consisted of pattern drills and other techniques developed for the "audiolingual method," considered outdated and ineffective by most ESL professionals.

38. Ted Gochenour, "Memorandum to all Program Officers and staff regarding the *Survey Report on Supervision and Teacher Evaluation* by Kathy Opel," August 21, 1984.

39. No individuals responsible for the major models of second-language learning/teaching that have dominated the field during the 1980s have had involvement in the program, with the exception of Michael Long of the University of Hawaii, who was a consultant for two weeks at the Philippine center during 1985.

40. For instance, the curriculum officer in the Philippine center during 1985 supported a view of language learning that has been widely discredited since the 1960s. In this view, language "structures" must be practiced and memorized before communication can begin. The goal of curriculum development is to prepare lists of grammar points for students to practice. Only after several hundred hours of such practice are students allowed to use language to communicate messages. See Bob Walsh, ICMC Curriculum Officer, "Memorandum to Kathy Opel and everyone involved in ESL," May 4, 1985.

41. One result of the poor training of the program staff in the United States is the Mainstream English Language Training (MELT) project, a curriculum and assessment program that established nationwide curricular standards for domestic refugee classes. In the MELT project, a survey of teachers' opinions about the relative difficulty of various grammatical structures was the only basis for grammar sequencing in the curriculum. An additional problem was that the list of structures was linguistically unsophisticated, reflecting a school-grammar theory of language that linguists no longer consider to be an accurate description of English. The MELT sequence also contradicted significant new research, of which the MELT staff apparently was unaware, that may provide a basis for scientific sequencing of structures. See Jurgen Meisel, Harald Clahsen, and Manfred Pienemann, "On Determining Developmental Stages in Natural Language Acquisition," *Studies in Second Language Acquisition* 3 (1981), pp. 109–135; see also Manfred Pienemann, "Psychological Constraints on the Teachability of Language," paper presented at the Second European–North American Cross-Linguistic Second Language Acquisition Workshop, Gohrde, West Germany, 1982. For information on MELT, see *Mainstream English Language Training Project, Resource Package* (Washington, D.C.: Office of Refugee Resettlement, 1985).

42. See Mark A. Clarke, "On Bandwagons, Tyranny, and Common Sense," *TESOL Quarterly* 16 (December 1982), pp. 437–48.

43. See Richard Drinnon, *Keeper of Concentration Camps: Dillon S. Myer and American Racism* (Berkeley: University of California Press, 1987).

44. The official made what she considered to be the striking observation that Eastern European immigrants experience adjustment problems, even though they "look like Americans." Nevertheless, the expected difference in resettlement difficulties is reflected in the amount of time the State Department allots to classes before resettlement. Indochinese refugees are required to attend classes in processing centers for five months, while Eastern European refugees attend for only three days.

CHAPTER 6: KEEPING THE CHARTS

1. *Making It on Their Own: From Refugee Sponsorship to Self-Sufficiency* (New York: Church World Service, 1983), p. 92.

2. David Halberstam, *The Best and the Brightest* (Greenwich, Conn.: Fawcett, 1969), p. 774.

3. *The Pentagon Papers* (New York: Times Books, 1971), p. 146.

4. Loren Baritz, *Backfire: American Culture and the Vietnam War* (New York: Ballantine, 1985), p. 262. See also General Bruce Palmer, Jr., *The 25-Year War: America's Military Role in Vietnam* (New York: Simon and Schuster, 1984), p. 13.

5. Baritz, *Backfire,* p. 241.

6. Eliot Cohen, "Systems Paralysis," *American Spectator* (November 1980), pp. 26–27.

7. James N. Purcell, Jr., "Refugee Assistance: Overseas and Domestic," address before the Subcommittee on Immigration, Refugees, and International Law of the House Judiciary Committee, April 17, 1985, *Current Policy* 693 (Washington, D.C.: Department of State, 1985).

8. Ann Morgan, memorandum to all ESL/cultural-orientation implementing

agencies and refugee coordinators regarding changes in program design in fiscal 1986, Washington, D.C., Department of State, August 7, 1985, p. 3.

9. See Ann Morgan and Roger Harmon, memorandum to ESL/cultural-orientation implementors, Washington, D.C., Department of State, October 5, 1984, p. 1.

10. Report cited in ibid., p. 1.

11. Interview with Loring Waggoner, U.S. Embassy, Manila, "Hope for the Future: An Orientation to PET," videotape, Bataan, Philippines, ICMC, 1984.

12. *Cultural Orientation Curriculum* (Bataan, Philippines: ICMC, 1985), Day 27.

13. *Pre-employment Training Resource Manual*, vol. 1 (Manila: CAL and the Refugee Service Center of the Bureau for Refugee Programs, Department of State, 1984), p. 5.

14. Among the earliest studies on refugee employment and public assistance are Jacqueline S. Aames, Ronald L. Aames, and Edward Karabenick, *Indochinese Refugee Self-Sufficiency in California: A Survey and Analysis of the Vietnamese, Cambodians, and Lao and the Agencies That Serve Them*, report submitted to the Department of Health, State of California, September 30, 1977; Robert L. Bach, *Labor Force Participation and Employment of Southeast Asian Refugees in the United States*, prepared for ORR under a grant to the Institute for Research on Poverty, University of Wisconsin, 1984; Robert L. Bach and Jennifer B. Bach, "Employment Patterns of Southeast Asian Refugees," *Monthly Labor Review* 103 (1980), pp. 31–38; Reginald P. Baker and David S. North, *The 1975 Refugees: Their First Five Years in America* (Washington, D.C.: New TransCentury Foundation, 1984); Bruce B. Dunning and Joshua Greenbaum, *A Systematic Survey of the Social, Psychological, and Economic Adaptation of Vietnamese Refugees Representing Five Entry Cohorts, 1975–79* (Washington, D.C.: Bureau of Social Science Research, 1982); Young Yun Kim and Perry M. Nicassio, *Survey of Agencies and Organizations Serving Indochinese Refugees*, vol. 5 of the Research Project on Indochinese Refugees in the State of Illinois (Chicago: Travelers Aid Society of Metropolitan Chicago, February 1980); W. H. Meredith, S. L. Cramer, and H. Kohn, *Nebraska Indochinese Refugee Needs Assessment* (Lincoln: University of Nebraska, 1981); Darrel Montero, *Vietnamese-Americans: Patterns of Resettlement and Socioeconomic Adaptation in the United States*, (Boulder, Colo.: Westview, 1979); David S. North, *Refugee Earnings and Utilization of Financial Assistance Programs*, prepared for the Refugee Policy Forum at Wingspread Conference Center, Racine, Wisc., February 6–8, 1984, sponsored by ORR, the Refugee Policy Group, and the Johnson Foundation; Barry N. Stein, "Occupational Adjustment of Refugees: The Vietnamese in the United States," *International Migration Review* 13 (1979), pp. 25–45; and J. K. Whitmore, "Indochinese Resettlement in Michigan," unpublished, 1981.

15. RMC Research Corporation, *The Effects of Pre-Entry Training on the Resettlement of Indochinese Refugees, Final Report* (Hampton, N.H.: RMC, prepared under contract with the Bureau for Refugee Programs, Department of State, October 1984).

16. James N. Purcell, Jr., testimony before the Subcommittee on Immigration, Refugees, and International Law of the House Judiciary Committee, April 17, 1985, in "Refugee Assistance Extension Act of 1985," (Washington, D.C.: Government Printing Office, 1985), p. 49.

17. For instance, see Morgan and Harmon, memorandum, October 5, 1984, p. 2.

18. RMC, *Effects of Pre-Entry Training*, p. 14.

19. Ibid., p. 142.

20. Ibid., p. 75. The RMC study did not follow the trained and untrained groups beyond six months after their arrival in the United States. It is possible that differences in unemployment and public assistance rates show up at a later time, though the sources of such differences would be difficult to ascertain.

21. See Bach, *Labor Force Participation*, p. 1. Also see North, *Refugee Earnings and Utilization of Financial Assistance Programs*, pp. 28, 33.

22. RMC, *Effects of Pre-Entry Training*, p. 47.

23. Ibid., p. 143.

24. For example, see Elizabeth Tannenbaum, "Review of *The Effects of Pre-Entry Training on the Resettlement of Indochinese Refugees*," *Passage: A Journal of Refugee Education* 1 (Washington, D.C.: Department of State, summer 1985), p. 81. An additional problem with the RMC study is the way it uses the BEST test. The BEST test has no "total" score, but the RMC study obtained one by summing the scores of the five subtests: listening, communication, pronunciation, fluency, and reading/writing. The RMC report declares that "this total score must therefore be interpreted as a measure of total test performance and not as a measure of overall English proficiency." RMC, *Effects of Pre-Entry Training*, p. 28. The report emphasizes that this total score was developed to aid analysis, not to assess language proficiency. Yet throughout the report, the BEST score is assumed to be a measure of English proficiency, and conclusions are drawn as if the score reflected overall proficiency. If the distinction between English proficiency and test performance is as important as the investigators apparently believed, then conclusions about the refugees' overall English proficiency cannot be based upon a sum of the BEST subtests.

25. RMC, *Effects of Pre-Entry Training*, p. 30.

26. Ibid., p. 11.

27. Ibid., p. 91. The RMC study admits an additional problem with its opinion survey. "Since most case workers rated several refugees at the same site, it is possible that the ratings of a single caseworker or the ratings of a group of caseworkers at a single agency could significantly affect the results obtained from a particular site." Ibid., p. 89.

28. RMC, *Effects of Pre-Entry Training*, pp. 65, 91.

29. Ibid., p. 11.

30. Bach, *Labor Force Participation*, p. 14.

31. Ibid., p. 22.

32. Ibid., p. 29.

33. For a survey of research on refugee employment using regression analysis, see David W. Haines, "Patterns in Southeast Asian Refugee Employment: A Reappraisal of the Existing Research," *Ethnic Groups* 7 (1987), pp. 39–63.

34. James N. Purcell, Jr., testimony before the Subcommittee on Immigration, Refugees, and International Law, pp. 49, 278.

35. Rebecca Oxford-Carpenter, *Southeast Asia Refugee Testing Report* (Washington, D.C.: CAL, 1985), p. A1.

36. The decision to combine listening and speaking into a single category, and to do the same for reading and writing, is unusual in ESL testing. Most specialists

consider these to be quite different, as in the case of an individual who can understand a language but not speak it, or who can read a language but not write it.

37. Oxford-Carpenter, *Southeast Asia Refugee Testing Report*, p. A1.

38. This analysis of the CAL tests first appeared in James W. Tollefson, "Functional Competencies in the U.S. Refugee Program: Theoretical and Practical Problems," *TESOL Quarterly* 20 (December 1986), pp. 649–64.

39. Oxford-Carpenter, *Southeast Asia Refugee Testing Report*, p. A3.

40. Purcell, "Refugee Assistance: Overseas and Domestic," p. 3.

41. Ibid., p. 4.

42. H. Eugene Douglas, "Proposed Refugee Admissions for FY 1984," testimony before the Senate Judiciary Committee, September 25, 1983, *Department of State Bulletin* (Washington, D.C.: Department of State, December, 1983), p. 64.

43. H. Eugene Douglas, prepared statement for the House Judiciary Committee in hearings on the Refugee Admissions Program, fiscal 1986, September 19, 1985 (Washington, D.C.: Government Printing Office, 1986), p. 15.

44. Report of the Senate Judiciary Committee on the Refugee Assistance Extension Act of 1984 (Washington, D.C.: Government Printing Office, 1985), pp. 7–9.

45. H. Eugene Douglas, "Proposed Refugee Admissions for FY 1983," testimony before the Senate Judiciary Committee, September 29, 1982, *Department of State Bulletin* (December 1982), p. 62.

46. Report of the House Judiciary Committee on the Refugee Assistance Extension Act of 1985 (Washington, D.C.: Government Printing Office, 1985), p. 15.

47. Tannenbaum, "Review of *The Effects of Pre-Entry Training*," p. 81.

48. "Statement of Program Goals, Priorities and Standards for State Administered Refugee Resettlement Programs, Fiscal Year 1984," Kansas City, Mo.: ORR: 1984, Section 1.

49. Ibid., Section 2(1).

50. The regulations are published in the *Federal Register* 52, no. 102 (October 19, 1987). They are also outlined in *Refugee Reports* (Washington, D.C.: American Council for Nationalities Service, November 13, 1987), pp. 7–8.

51. "Statement of Program Goals, Priorities, and Standards for State Administered Refugee Resettlement Programs, Fiscal Year 1984," Section 3, B, (5), (7).

52. Santa Rose Community College, for example, has helped many refugee nurses prepare for state examinations. See *Refugee Reports* (January 22, 1988), p. 3.

53. Billie F. Gee, Director, ORR, "ORR Regional Letter: Program Monitoring and Operations—Information/External," Transmittal no. 87–16 (Washington, D.C.: Department of Health and Human Services, November 20, 1986).

54. See Myra M. Oliver, Executive Director, International Institute of Connecticut, letter to arriving refugees, Bridgeport, March 5, 1979.

55. Lance Clark, "Dependency Syndrome: Another Look," interview in *Refugees* 29 (Geneva: UNHCR, May 1986), p. 35.

56. *Southeast Asian Refugee Self-Sufficiency Study: Final Report*. (Ann Arbor: Institute for Social Research, University of Michigan, report prepared for ORR, 1985).

57. *Making It on Their Own*.

58. In the CWS study, 29 percent of the women not seeking employment were at home with young children. Another 20 percent were women in families with young children and at least one adult already working. Although these women did

not declare in the survey that they had to stay home to care for the children, the survey staff believed that many of them did so. See ibid., pp. 19–21.

59. See *Southeast Asian Refugee Self-Sufficiency Study*, pp. 118–19. Recent ORR regulations make it increasingly difficult for refugees to attend school. These regulations are designed to pressure the refugees to accept minimum-wage jobs even if they must drop out of school to do so. See "Statement of Program Goals, Priorities, and Standards," section 3, B,(5)-(7).

60. *Southeast Asian Refugee Self-Sufficiency Study*, pp. 244–45.

61. *Making It on Their Own*, p. 7.

62. Ibid., p. 93.

63. Bach, *Labor Force Participation*, p. 36.

64. *Making It on Their Own*, p. 85.

65. Ibid., p. 92.

66. Ibid., p. 84.

67. Morgan, memorandum of August 7, 1985, p. 3.

68. Bach, *Labor Force Participation*, p. 5.

69. *Southeast Asian Refugee Self-Sufficiency Study*, p. 141.

70. The ORR study adopted the standard definition of "poverty level" set forth by Mollie Orshansky, "How Poverty is Measured," *Monthly Labor Review* 92 (1969), pp. 37–41. The actual dollar amount is calculated monthly. At the time the ORR study was published, the level was $800 per month for a family of four. See *Southeast Asian Refugee Self-Sufficiency Study*, p. 179.

71. *Southeast Asian Refugee Self-Sufficiency Study*, p. 180.

72. Of the working refugees, about 17 percent were janitors or maids; 12 percent worked in restaurants; 21 percent worked in factories such as electronics assembly; and 4 percent worked as machine operators or mechanics. See ibid., p. 121.

73. Ibid., pp. 121–23.

74. Ibid., p. 129.

75. Ibid., pp. 131–32.

76. The average hourly wage for employed refugees at the time of the study was $4.90, with most earning between $3.07 and $6.77. In order to overcome the effects of such a low wage, refugees often live together, sharing their meager resources. For instance, 10 percent of all households had four or more jobs; only a third of employed households had only a single job. See ibid., p. 146.

77. The ORR study used standard measures for defining "peripheral" and "core" sectors of the job market as outlined by David L. Featherman, Michael Sobel, and David Dickens, *A Manual for Coding Occupations and Industries into Detailed 1970-Basis Duncan Socioeconomic and NORC Prestige Scores* (Madison, Wisc.: Center for Demography and Ecology, 1980). For a summary of these terms, see *Southeast Asian Refugee Self-Sufficiency Study*, pp. 132–33.

78. *Southeast Asian Refugee Self-Sufficiency Study*, pp. 133, 139.

79. Ibid., p. 184.

80. John Latkiewicz and Colette Anderson, "Industries' Reactions to the Indochinese Refugees as Employees," *Migration Today* 11, nos. 2–3 (1983), pp. 14–20. Preemployment training managers circulated this study at regional curriculum meetings held in Singapore and Thailand in 1984 and 1985.

81. *ABE-in-Industry Handbook*, prepared for the Travis County Adult Basic Ed-

ucation Co-op Special Project by the Austin, Texas, Community College (June 1984), p. 29.

82. Stephen Reder, et al., *A Study of English Language Training for Refugees: Public Report* (Portland Oreg.: Northwest Regional Education Laboratory, report prepared for ORR, June 1984).

83. Aliza Becker, Lisa Karimer, and Linda Mrowicki, "An Employer Needs Assessment," *Passage* 2 (summer 1986), p. 56.

84. Latkiewicz and Anderson, "Industries' Reactions to the Indochinese Refugees as Employees," pp. 17, 19.

CHAPTER 7: HUMILIATION AND DANGER

1. John Chr. Knudsen, *Boat People in Transit* (Bergen, Norway: Department of Social Anthropology, University of Bergen, 1983), p. 12.

2. "The Philippine Refugee Processing Center, Morong, Bataan," briefing paper by PRPC administration (1981), p. 11. Also appears as "Complementation of: Agency Programs and PRPC-Initiated Programs and Structures," permanent organizational charts and statement of purpose at the PRPC administration building, prepared by Community Action and Social Services Development Group (CASSDEG), Bataan, Philippines.

3. "Philippine Refugee Processing Center," p. 4.

4. CASSDEG organizational charts, PRPC administration building.

5. "Philippine Refugee Processing Center," p. 5.

6. See for example, ibid., and "ICMC Policies," mimeo distributed to arriving refugees by ICMC (1984).

7. Knudsen, *Boat People in Transit*, p. 62. Knudsen found that most refugees "feel the object [of the work credit system] is to keep the camp clean."

8. "Philippine Refugee Processing Center," p. 4. Also "ICMC Policies," p. 2.

9. "The Vietnamese Refugee Camp in Palawan, Philippines and the Vietnamese Refugee Problem," camp newspaper (1982), p. 4, also cited in Knudsen, *Boat People in Transit*, p. 61.

10. "ICMC Policies," p. 1, states, "Problems in an ICMC classroom are reported to ICMC only. Three or more absences are reported to the ICMC Registration Office. The problem is referred to the Refcoord [Refugee Coordinator from the U.S. Embassy] who decides if the student will be 'recycled' to make up the lessons that were missed. This is not a punishment."

11. This case is discussed in some detail in John Chr. Knudsen, "Health Problems in the Refugee Career: From Vietnam via Transit Camps to Norway," in *Health and International Life Courses: Labour Migrants and Refugees in Northern Europe*, edited by Karin Ask, et al. (Bergen, Norway: Bergen Studies in Social Anthropology, 1986).

12. This case was brought to the attention of camp authorities in 1985 by neighbors in the camp who had a long-simmering feud with the man.

13. "ICM [Intergovernmental Committee on Migration] PRPC Summary of Operational Activities," mimeo, Bataan, Philippines, 1983, p. 3.

14. This case is discussed in Knudsen, "Health Problems in the Refugee Career," p. 13.

15. The Community Mental Health and Family Services unit, initiated under the

capable direction of Steve Muncy, labors with inadequate staff. The need to use refugee translators also seriously limits program effectiveness, as clients are reluctant to reveal personal problems to peers who lack medical and psychiatric backgrounds.

16. Knudsen, *Boat People in Transit*, p. 169.

17. See ibid., p. 160.

18. For further discussion of this problem, see Knudsen, "Health Problems in the Refugee Career," p. 10.

19. ICM procedures state that "any medical conditions that require follow-up in the resettlement country (i.e.: mental conditions, VD, progressive diseases) will be telexed to the sponsor by ICM/JVA." "ICM PRPC Summary of Operational Activities," p. 4.

20. For a discussion of this case, see Knudsen, *Boat People in Transit*, p. 12.

21. Ibid., p. 12.

22. "ICMC Policies," p. 1.

23. It is impossible to know the extent to which these gifts are insurance against harmful attendance reports, or merely expressions of gratitude. Because gifts are given in most classes, any teacher not receiving one is likely to feel insulted. Given the teachers' authority to delay resettlement, refugees may be unwilling to risk the consequences of not offering gifts.

24. Knudsen, *Boat People in Transit*, p. 164.

25. Chloroquine phosphate is the prescribed antimalaria prophylactic. Fansidar is occasionally used to treat malaria, but it is generally not dispensed to refugees.

26. Knudsen, *Boat People in Transit*, p. 7.

27. "Summary of Food Calories per Person per Day," PRPC chart maintained in the central administration building, Bataan, Philippines, 1985.

28. "Water should not be collected from drainage off the roof and used for drinking or cooking purposes; only potable water provided by the processing centre should be used." "Final Results of the Environmental Survey and Evaluation of Refugee Processing Centres in Bataan Peninsula, Philippines and Phanat Nikhom, Chonburi, Province, Thailand, 8–16 February 1984," report prepared by Richard A. Lemen, John T. Jankovic, and Kenneth M. Wallingford (Atlanta: Centers for Disease Control, National Institute for Occupational Safety and Health [NIOSH], April 10, 1984), p. 18.

29. "Final Results of the Environmental Survey," p. 1.

30. The petition was addressed to Bob Dira, who was the acting director while Conrad Spohnholz was out of town.

31. Memorandum to Joseph E. Gettier, U.S. Refugee Coordinator, from Conrad S. Spohnholz, ICMC Director, October 12, 1982.

32. The letter quoted the program management plan, which listed the goal of improving the physical environment. Letter to Conrad Spohnholz, ICMC Director, from "The Supervisory Body," May 25, 1983.

33. While this was taking place, Steve DeBonis wrote to Irving Selikoff, the foremost researcher on asbestos diseases, who had first established a link between asbestos fibers and lung cancer in 1964. Selikoff explained that the crucial health issue is whether fibers are released in the air, and he warned that "significant erosion" of the material can be expected "when it is used for roofs, with fibers then brought to the ground by heavy rains, etc." Letter from Irvin J. Selikoff to Steve DeBonis, July 6, 1983.

34. Memorandum to Matt Henrickson from author, November 28, 1983. This memo was followed by a meeting in Manila.

35. Memorandum to Robert Knouss from Richard A. Lemen, regarding "Refugee Center Asbestos Analysis, Risk Estimate and Preliminary Recommendations," January 30, 1984, p. 4.

36. Knouss's question is cited in ibid., p. 5: "whether the facilities should be closed completely or if a phased renovation of the structures could be conducted as the quarters are vacated."

37. Ibid., p. 2.

38. "I write this memo to advise you of the potential for publicity and to request particular scrutiny of the report which I am currently preparing." Memorandum to Frank Hearl and Bob Glenn from John Jankovic, January 26, 1984.

39. "Final Results of the Environmental Survey," pp. 1–2.

40. Ibid., p. 7.

41. Memorandum to Donald J. Dunsmore from John T. Jankovic, team leader for refugee center asbestos analysis, regarding risk estimate and preliminary recommendations, January 30, 1984, p. 3.

42. "Final Results of the Environmental Survey," p. 19.

43. Lemen's estimate was a minimum of 1.1 cancer deaths per 100,000, a maximum of 58.2, and a "most reasonable" estimate of 9.3. My estimates are derived by multiplying Lemen's estimates by a factor of 2.25, assuming 225,000 refugees to have lived in the processing centers by the end of fiscal year 1987. Lemen's estimates are contained in his memorandum to Robert Knouss, "Refugee Center Asbestos Analysis, Risk Estimates and Preliminary Recommendations," p. 4.

44. For instance, a memo to teacher trainers from their program officer expressed the "good news" that the issue of asbestos was finally over. That officer is now the ICMC director. Memo to trainers from Ann Wederspahn, training officer, undated.

45. Memorandum from ICMC Manila director to author, April 25, 1984.

46. Letter to James N. Purcell, Jr., from Robert F. Knouss, May 1, 1984, p. 2. "In Phanat Nikhom, the general practice is to use refugee labor in the repair and construction of buildings. For these refugees, the risk of subsequent cancer development will be greater than for the refugees not so employed."

47. Statement for distribution in processing centers sent to James N. Purcell, Jr., by Robert F. Knouss, with accompanying letter, May 9, 1984.

48. Handwritten note to Gregg Beyer, UNHCR representative, from Steve DeBonis, undated.

49. Note to Gregg Beyer from Steve DeBonis, August 18, 1984.

50. For a while during 1983 and 1984, Gochenour served as site director, while Spohnholz and later Henrikson directed the Manila operation. The system was soon abandoned, however, and Gochenour became director for the entire ICMC operation in the Philippines. In 1985 he was replaced by Jon Darrah, who was later succeeded by Steve Cook.

51. Letter to Ted Gochenour from Gregg Beyer "Re: Attached letter from Steven DeBonis," August 31, 1984.

52. Memorandum to Steve DeBonis from Ted Gochenour, regarding "your letter to UNHCR," September 7, 1984.

53. Note to Steve DeBonis from Ted Gochenour, undated.

54. Don Ronk, cultural orientation curriculum developer, "Notes on Asbestos for C.O. Instructors," August 1984.

55. The Puget Sound Air Pollution Control Agency and the Washington State Department of Ecology are authorized to fine companies up to $1,000 per day if their workers handle asbestos without protective clothing or if asbestos escapes into the environment during demolition. See "Firms Could Face Fines for Careless Work with Asbestos," *Seattle Post–Intelligencer*, March 31, 1987, p. D1.

56. "Results of Air Monitoring during Removal of Asbestos Roofs," report prepared by Melchor D. Morales, Subic Bay, Philippines, Public Works Center Safety Engineer, June 3–4, 1986, pp. 2–3.

57. "Results of Air Monitoring," written by Melchor D. Morales, Subic Bay, Philippines, Public Works Center safety engineer, July 7–8, 1986, p. 2.

58. Memorandum to Denis Nihill from Bill Twyford, July 16, 1986.

59. "Final Results of the Environmental Survey," p. 8.

60. While the renovation took place, a sealant was sprayed on exposed asbestos in other dorms, offices, and classroom buildings. In some cases, the spraying reportedly took place while the buildings were occupied.

CHAPTER 8: THE FUTURE AND THE PAST

1. Loren Baritz, *Backfire: American Culture and the Vietnam War* (New York: Ballantine, 1985), p. 346.

2. This discussion of community memory relies heavily upon Robert N. Bellah, *Habits of the Heart: Individualism and Commitment in American Life* (New York: Harper and Row, 1985), pp. 153–55.

3. For instance, Henry Kissinger asked in his memoirs, "What has inspired people to such flights of heroism and monomania . . . that not only thwarted the foreigner's exertions but hazarded his own internal balance?" Henry Kissinger, *White House Years* (Boston: Little, Brown, 1979), p. 226.

4. For example, Richard Nixon claims that "excessive idealism in the American character" led to defeat. Richard Nixon, *No More Vietnams* (New York: Avon, 1985), p. 22.

5. Ted Koppel, "ABC News Nightline," December 10, 1987.

6. Among the many published discussions of the lessons of Vietnam, perhaps the best is *Vietnam Reconsidered: Lessons from a War*, edited by Harrison E. Salisbury (New York: Harper and Row, 1984).

7. Secretary of State George Shultz, statement before the Subcommittee on Immigration and Refugee Policy of the Senate Judiciary Committee, September 17, 1985, printed in *Department of State Bulletin* (Washington, D.C.: Department of State, November 1985), p. 21.

8. "Vietnam under Two Regimes," *Department of State Bulletin* (September 1985), p. 55.

9. Ibid., pp. 51, 53, 55.

10. Arthur Egendorf, *Healing from the War: Trauma and Transformation after Vietnam* (Boston: Shambhala, 1986), p. 29.

11. See Joel Osler Brende and Erwin Randolph Parson, *Vietnam Veterans: The Road to Recovery* (New York: New American Library, 1985); Egendorf, *Healing from the War*; Ellen Frey-Wouters and Robert S. Laufer, *Legacy of a War: The American*

Soldier in Vietnam (Armonk, N.Y.: M. E. Sharpe, 1986); Robert Jay Lifton, *Home from the War: Vietnam Veterans, Neither Victims nor Executioners* (New York: Basic Books, 1973).

12. Erwin R. Parson, "The Vietnam Vet: The Inner Battle Rages On," *Jamaica Times Magazine* 2 (1981), pp. 6–9.

13. Brende and Parson, *Vietnam Veterans*, p. 42.

14. See ibid., p. 47, and Egendorf, *Healing from the War*, pp. 54–61.

15. See Mark Baker, *Nam: The Vietnam War in the Words of the Men and Women Who Fought There* (New York: Quill, 1982), p. 278.

16. See *Diagnostic and Statistical Manual of Mental Disorders*, 3rd ed. (Washington, D.C.: American Psychiatric Association, 1980).

17. See Brende and Parson, *Vietnam Veterans*, pp. 148–51.

18. See Lifton, *Home from the War*, pp. 191–216.

19. See Brende and Parson, *Vietnam Veterans*, p. 83.

20. For example, see Baker, *Nam*, and the film *Platoon*.

21. For discussions of veterans' groups, see Egendorf, *Healing from the War*, and Lifton, *Home from the War*.

22. Mark Hatfield, "U.S. Refugee Policy and Southeast Asia: Time for a Renewed Commitment," *World Refugee Survey, 1984* (Washington, D.C.: U.S. Committee for Refugees, 1985), p. 28.

23. Much of what is called "delayed stress" may be due to the concrete problems (employment, housing, health care, etc.) that refugees and veterans experience. Indeed, many veterans from poor and working-class families confront economic problems like those facing refugees. Huddleston argues that posttraumatic stress disorder is an "outdated concept popularized . . . to promote martyrdom and feelings of . . . guilt. . . . It was then extended to encompass all reactions and depressions due to currently unreasonable conditions by ascribing them to events located in the past." Art Huddleston, "Delayed Stress," unpublished paper, Seattle, 1988.

24. For a discussion of common assumptions about the economic circumstances of immigrants' lives, see Rita Simon, *Public Opinion and the Immigrant* (Lexington, Mass.: Lexington Books, 1985). Also see Julian L. Simon, *How do Immigrants Affect us Economically?* (Washington, D.C.: Georgetown University Center for Immigration Policy and Refugee Assistance, 1985).

25. There is a vast literature on such pedagogies. See for example Paulo Freire, *Pedagogy of the Oppressed* (New York: Seabury, 1970), and Elsa Roberts Auerbach and Nina Wallerstein, *ESL for Action: Problem Posing at Work* (Reading, Mass.: Addison-Wesley, 1987).

26. See Norman L. Zucker and Naomi Flink Zucker, *The Guarded Gate: The Reality of American Refugee Policy* (San Diego, Calif.: Harcourt Brace Jovanovich, 1987), pp. 282–83.

27. See *Future Directions in the U.S. Refugee Resettlement Program: Final Report*, prepared by the Refugee Policy Group, Lewin and Associates, and Berkeley Planning Associates for ORR, August 1987, p. 3.20.

28. See Zucker and Zucker, *The Guarded Gate*, p. 283.

29. See *Future Directions in the U.S. Refugee Resettlement Program*, pp. 3.31–33.

30. The importance of community support can be clearly seen in a study of the needs of older refugees. *Older Refugees in the United States: From Dignity to Despair* (Washington, D.C.: Refugee Policy Group, 1988), pp. 34–36.

31. See "Hurdles Bar Path to Continuing Medical Practice for Refugee Physicians," *Refugee Reports* 9 (Washington, D.C.: American Council for Nationalities Service, January 22, 1988), pp. 1–7.

32. Most analysts agree that Southeast Asian communities in the United States are overwhelmingly Republican. For example, in 1984, 67 percent of the Asian population in California voted for Ronald Reagan. In some places, Southeast Asian community leaders are beginning to run for political office. In 1986, Nil S. Hul, a Cambodian businessman, lost in his bid for a seat on the Long Beach City Council. See *Refugee Reports*, November 14, 1986, pp. 1–7.

33. This is a key recommendation of a major study of immigrant children in American schools. *New Voices: Immigrant Students in U.S. Public Schools* (Boston: National Coalition of Advocates for Students, 1988), p. 56.

34. For an example of the effective involvement of Southeast Asians in county and city services, see *Refugee Reports*, April 17, 1987, pp. 1–5.

35. See *New Voices*, p. 49.

36. For information on the Gose camp and on collective decision-making in refugee camps generally, see John Chr. Knudsen, *Boat People in Transit* (Bergen, Norway: Department of Social Anthropology, University of Bergen, 1983), pp. 83–94.

37. *Older Refugees in the United States: From Dignity to Despair.*

CHAPTER 9: EPILOGUE, THINKING OF HUNG

1. John Wheeler, *Touched with Fire: The Future of the Vietnam Generation* (New York: Avon Books, 1985), p. 5.

2. Helen Aguilar, et al., "The ESL-A/B Book Project," in *Passage: A Journal of Refugee Education* 4 (Washington, D.C.: Department of State, spring–summer 1988), p. 69.

Selected Bibliography

BOOKS AND MONOGRAPHS

American Refugee Policy: Ethical and Religious Reflections. Edited by Joseph M. Kitagawa. Minneapolis: Winston, 1984.

Baker, Reginald P., and North, David S. *The 1975 Refugees: Their First Five Years in America.* Washington, D.C.: New TransCentury Foundation, 1984.

Becker, Elizabeth. *When the War Was Over.* New York: Simon and Schuster, 1986.

Bentley, Judith. *Refugees: Search for a Haven.* New York: Julian Messner, 1986.

The Boat People: An AGE Investigation. New York: Penguin, 1979.

Bridging Cultures—Southeast Asian Refugees in America: Social Work with Southeast Asian Refugees. Los Angeles: Asian American Community Mental Health Training Center, 1983.

Cambodians in Thailand: People on the Edge. Issue paper prepared by the U.S. Committee for Refugees. Washington, D.C.: American Council for Nationalities Service, 1985.

Cohon, J. Donald; Lucey, Moira; Paul, Michael; and Penning, Joan LeMarbre. *Primary Preventive Mental Health in the ESL Classroom: A Handbook for Teachers.* New York: American Council for Nationalities Service, 1986.

From the Classroom to the Workplace: Teaching ESL to Adults. Washington, D.C.: Center for Applied Linguistics, 1983.

Immigrants and Refugees in a Changing Nation. Edited by Lucy M. Cohen and Mary Ann Grossnickle. Washington, D.C.: Catholic University of America, 1983.

Involuntary Migration and Resettlement: The Problems and Responses of Dislocated People. Edited by Art Hansen and Anthony Oliver-Smith. Boulder, Colo.: Westview, 1982.

Kampuchea: Decade of the Genocide—Report of the Finnish Inquiry Commission. Edited by Kimmo Kiljunen. London: Zed, 1984.

Knudsen, John Chr. *Boat People in Transit.* Bergen, Norway: Department of Social Anthropology, University of Bergen, 1983.

Loescher, Gil, and Scanlan, John A. *Calculated Kindness: Refugees and America's Half-Open Door, 1945–Present.* New York: Free Press, 1986.

Making It on Their Own: From Refugee Sponsorship to Self-Sufficiency. New York: Church World Service, 1983.

Muller, Thomas, and Espenshade, Thomas J. *The Fourth Wave: California's Newest Immigrants.* Washington, D.C.: Urban Institute Press, 1985.

New Voices: Immigrant Students in U.S. Public Schools. Boston: National Coalition of Advocates for Students, 1988.

Older Refugees in the United States: From Dignity to Despair. Washington, D.C.: Refugee Policy Group, 1988.

The Orderly Departure Program: The Need for Reassessment. Prepared by the Migration and Refugee Affairs Committee of InterAction. Washington, D.C.: U.S. Catholic Conference, Migration and Refugee Services, 1986.

Refugee Mental Health in Resettlement Countries. Edited by Carolyn L. Williams and Joseph Westermeyer. Washington, D.C.: Hemisphere Publishing, 1986.

Refugees: Dynamics of Displacement. A report for the Independent Commission on International Humanitarian Issues. London: Zed, 1986.

Refugees and World Politics. Edited by Elizabeth G. Ferris. New York: Praeger, 1985.

Refugees from Laos: In Harm's Way. Issue paper prepared by the U.S. Committee for Refugees. Washington, D.C.: American Council for Nationalities Service, 1986.

Reimers, David M. *Still the Golden Door: The Third World Comes to America.* New York: Columbia University Press, 1985.

Seeking Shelter: Cambodians in Thailand. New York: Lawyers Committee for Human Rights, 1987.

Shawcross, William. *The Quality of Mercy: Cambodia, Holocaust, and Modern Conscience.* New York: Simon and Schuster, 1984.

Southeast Asian Exodus: From Tradition to Resettlement. Edited by Elliot L. Tepper. Ottawa: Canadian Asian Studies Association, 1980.

St. Cartmail, Keith. *Exodus Indochina.* Auckland, New Zealand: Heinemann, 1983.

Stein, Colman Brez. *Sink or Swim: The Politics of Bilingual Education.* New York: Praeger, 1986.

U.S. Immigration and Refugee Policy: Global and Domestic Issues. Edited by Mary M. Kritz. Lexington, Mass.: Lexington Books, 1983.

Uncertain Harbors: The Plight of Vietnamese Boat People. Issue paper prepared by the U.S. Committee for Refugees. Washington: American Council for Nationalities Service, 1987.

Vickery, Michael. *Cambodia: 1975–1982.* Boston: South End Press, 1984.

Wain, Barry. *The Refused: The Agony of the Indochina Refugees.* New York: Simon and Schuster, 1981.

Zucker, Norman L., and Zucker, Naomi Flink. *The Guarded Gate: The Reality of American Refugee Policy.* San Diego, Calif.: Harcourt Brace Jovanovich, 1987.

SERIAL PUBLICATIONS

Adult Education.
Amnesty International Report.
Asiaweek.
Christian Science Monitor.
Cultural Survival Quarterly.

CURA Reporter. Minneapolis, Minn.: Center for Urban and Regional Affairs, University of Minnesota.

ERIC/CLL News Bulletin.

Ethnic Groups.

Far Eastern Economic Review.

Forum. Washington, D.C.: National Clearinghouse for Bilingual Education.

Harvard Educational Review.

International Migration.

International Migration Review.

Language Problems and Language Planning.

Migration Today.

Monday. New York: National Council of Churches.

Monthly Labor Review.

Refugee Reports. Washington, D.C.: American Council for Nationalities Services.

Refugees. 1984–88. Geneva: UNHCR.

Southeast Asian Refugee Studies Newsletter. Minneapolis, Minn.: Southeast Asian Refugee Studies Project, Center for Urban and Regional Affairs, University of Minnesota.

Studies in Second Language Acquisition.

TESOL Quarterly.

Update. Washington, D.C.: U.S. Catholic Conference.

Volunteer Voice. Tacoma, Wash.: Tacoma Community House.

Walk with a Refugee. Seattle, Wash.: Archdiocese of Seattle.

World Refugee Survey. Washington, D.C.: American Council for Nationalities Service.

PUBLIC AND PRIVATE AGENCIES: DOCUMENTS AND PUBLICATIONS

Federal Register. 1983–87.

U.S. Congress

Congressional Record. 1983–87.

House Appropriations Committee, Subcommittee on Foreign Operations and Related Agencies. Hearings on foreign assistance and related appropriations, 1976, 1978.

House Foreign Affairs Committee, Subcommittee on Asian and Pacific Affairs. Hearings and staff reports, "Overview of Refugee Situation in Southeast Asia," 1984–86.

House Foreign Affairs Committee, Subcommittee on Inter-American Affairs. Hearings on Foreign Assistance Legislation, 1980, 1981.

House Judiciary Committee. Hearings on the Refugee Admissions Program, 1984–87.

House Judiciary Committee. Reports on the Refugee Assistance Extension Act of 1984 and 1985.

House Judiciary Committee, Subcommittee on Immigration, Refugees, and International Law. Hearings and staff reports on refugee assistance, overseas and domestic, 1983–86.

House Judiciary Committee, Subcommittee on Immigration, Refugees, and International Law. Hearings on the Refugee Assistance Extension Act of 1985.

Senate Appropriations Committee. Hearings on foreign assistance and related programs appropriations, 1977.

Senate Judiciary Committee. Hearings on proposed refugee admissions, 1983, 1984, 1986.

Senate Judiciary Committee. Report on the Refugee Assistance Extension Act of 1984.

Senate Judiciary Committee, Subcommittee on Immigration and Refugee Policy. Hearings and staff reports on refugee and migration problems in Southeast Asia, 1984–86.

U.S. Department of State

Cultural Orientation Resource Manual. Vol. 2. Manila: Center for Applied Linguistics and Refugee Service Center of the Bureau for Refugee Programs, 1982.

Department of State Bulletin.

The Effects of Pre-Entry Training on the Resettlement of Indochinese Refugees. Hampton, N.H.: RMC Research Corporation, 1984.

English as a Second Language Resource Manual. Vol. 3. Manila: Center for Applied Linguistics and Refugee Service Center of the Bureau for Refugee Programs, 1983.

Passage: A Journal of Refugee Education.

Pre-Employment Training Resource Manual. Vol. 1. Manila: Center for Applied Linguistics and Refugee Service Center of the Bureau for Refugee Programs, 1984.

Oxford-Carpenter, Rebecca. Southeast Asia Refugee Testing Report. Washington: Center for Applied Linguistics, 1985.

U.S. Office of Refugee Resettlement

Arter, Judith; Hadley, William; and Reder, Stephen. A Study of English Language Training for Refugees in the United States. Portland, Oreg.: Northwest Regional Education Laboratory, 1984.

Bach, Robert L. Labor Force Participation and Employment of Southeast Asian Refugees in the United States. Prepared under a grant to the Institute for Research on Poverty, University of Wisconsin, 1984.

Direct Mail Survey of State Refugee Coordinators, 1985.

Evaluation Compilations of the MELT Project, 1985.

Future Directions of the U.S. Refugee Resettlement Program. Prepared by the Refugee Policy Group, Lewin and Associates, and Berkeley Planning Associates, August 1987.

Mainstream English Language Training Project, Resource Package, 1985.

North, David S. Refugee Earnings and Utilization of Financial Assistance Programs. Prepared for the Refugee Policy Forum, Racine, Wisc., 1984.

The Refugee Family: Region V Consultation. Arlington Heights, Ill.: Northwest Educational Cooperative, 1987.

Southeast Asian Refugee Self-Sufficiency Study: Final Report. Ann Arbor: Institute for Social Research, University of Michigan, 1985.

"Statement of Program Goals, Priorities and Standards for State Administered Refugee Resettlement Programs, Fiscal Year 1984."

U.S. Centers for Disease Control

"Final Results of the Environmental Survey and Evaluation of Refugee Processing Centers, 1984," and related files.

U.S. Immigration Commission

Report of the Immigration Commission. 42 vols. Washington, D.C.: Government Printing Office, 1911.

U.S. General Accounting Office

Report to the Refugee Subcommittee of the Senate Judiciary Committee, "Problems in the Khmer Republic (Cambodia) concerning War Victims, Civilian Health and War-related Casualties," February 2, 1972.

United Nations High Commissioner for Refugees

The Camp on Lantau Island. Documentary film. Oxford: Oxford Ethnographic Films, 1984.

International Bibliography of Refugee Literature. Geneva: International Refugee Integration Resource Center, 1985.

Williamson, John. *Refugee Resettlement: A Survey of Training Priorities.* Bangkok: Committee for Coordination of Services to Displaced Persons in Thailand and UNHCR branch office in Thailand, 1982.

Intergovernmental Committee on Migration

"ICM PRPC Summary of Operational Activities." Mimeo. Bataan, 1983.

Philippine Refugee Processing Center Administration

Community Action and Social Services Development Group. "Complementation of: Agency Programs and PRPC-Initiated Programs and Structures." Bataan, 1981.

"The Philippine Refugee Processing Center, Morong, Bataan." Briefing paper, 1981.

International Catholic Migration Commission

Annual Reports. 1982–87.
Cultural Orientation Content Standards. 1983.
Cultural Orientation Curriculum. Bataan, 1985.
"Hope for the Future: An Orientation to PET." Videotape. 1984.
Integrated Curriculum, Level One. Bataan, 1983.
ICMC Management Plan. 1984, 1985.
ICMC Newsletter. 1980–87.
"ICMC Policies." Mimeo. Philippine Refugee Processing Center, 1983–86.
Life in the New Land. 1982.
Migration News.
PV Curriculum. 1982–83.
Student Survey. 1985.
A Study of the Role of the Supervisor in the ICMC/ESL Program. 1985.
Survey Report on Supervision and Teacher Evaluation. 1984.

Index

ABOUT THE AUTHOR

JAMES W. TOLLEFSON received his Ph.D. in linguistics from Stanford University in 1978 and is currently Associate Professor of English and Director of the Master's Program in teaching English as a second language at the University of Washington in Seattle. He has published a book on the social and political aspects of language in Yugoslavia, as well as numerous articles on language acquisition and language policy in *TESOL Quarterly*, *Word, Language Problems and Language Planning, Studies in Second Language Acquisition, Language Sciences,* and elsewhere. He is a former President of the Washington Association for the Education of Speakers of Other Languages.